1001 Flying Facts and Firsts

Joe Christy

TAB BOOKS Inc.
Blue Ridge Summit, PA

REF
TL
553
.C46
1989

FIRST EDITION
FIRST PRINTING

Copyright © 1989 by TAB BOOKS Inc.
Printed in the United States of America

Reproduction or publication of the content in any manner, without express permission of the publisher, is prohibited. No liability is assumed with respect to the use of the information herein.

Library of Congress Cataloging in Publication Data

Christy, Joe.
   1001 flying facts and firsts / by Joe Christy.
      p.   cm.
   ISBN 0-8306-9428-5 (pbk.)
   1. Aeronautics—Miscellanea. I. Title. II. Title: One thousand and one flying facts and firsts.
   TL553.C46 1988
629.13—dc19   88-24990
                  CIP

TAB BOOKS Inc. offers software for sale. For information and a catalog, please contact TAB Software Department, Blue Ridge Summit, PA 17294-0850.

Questions regarding the content of this book should be addressed to:

Reader Inquiry Branch
TAB BOOKS Inc.
Blue Ridge Summit, PA 17294-0214

Edited by Steven H. Mesner

Contents

	Introduction	iv
I	**Significant Events in Aviation**	1
II	**Quiz of "Firsts"**	88
III	**Record Flights**	91
IV	**Significant U.S. Military Aircraft**	104
V	**Significant U.S. Civil Aircraft**	139
VI	**U.S. Manned Space Flights**	185
VII	**U.S. Aircraft Company Geneologies**	189
VIII	**Aerobatics**	203
IX	**American Aces**	212
X	**Medal of Honor Recipients**	217

Introduction

This book is for reference—and for fun. It is an argument-settler and a memory-jogger, and it can provide the basis for discussions about most aeronautical subjects since 400 B.C.—well, anyway, since 1903.

Once, when I happened to be paying attention in class, I heard a history professor say that there are two kinds of knowledge: that which is stored in your mind for instant recall, and that which is stored elsewhere, if you know where to instantly find it. (He was quick to add that he tested only for the former kind.) So this is your in-depth knowledge of aviation facts and trivia "stored elsewhere" for your convenience—and for the amazement of your fellow aeronauts.

I

Significant Events in Aviation

400 B.C.

The Chinese and Koreans employed large kites as a means of sending messages during warfare.

1505 A.D.

Leonardo da Vinci made sketches of a man-powered flapping wing device, and demonstrated the principle of the parachute.

1783

June 5—Etienne and Joseph Montgolfier, having observed that smoke rises, concluded that smoke contained a mysterious gas that was lighter than air. The brothers constructed a 35-foot balloon (*balon*) of linen-reinforced paper under which they built a fire fueled by damp straw and sheep's wool. Their unmanned balloon filled with the dense smoke and rose to an estimated height of 6,000 feet over Annonay, France.

September 19—The Montgolfiers sent aloft a duck, a sheep, and a rooster to establish that the "upper atmosphere" was safe to breathe.

November 2—French scientist Pilatre de Rozier and the Marquis d'Arlandes rose to more than 3,000 feet in a Montgolfier hot-air balloon, and sailed 5 miles over Paris in a 20-minute flight. This was the world's first manned flight. (De Rozier had ascended to 84 feet in a tethered balloon the month before.)

1001 Flying Facts and Firsts

December 1—Prof. Jacques A.C. Charles, a physicist, built a balloon of rubber-impregnated taffeta, filled it with hydrogen (discovered in 1776) and, with a man by the name of Roberts aboard, remained aloft for two hours, landing some 27 miles from Paris. This was the first hydrogen-filled balloon.

1785

January 7—Jean-Pierre Blanchard, a Frenchman, accompanied by Dr. John J. Jefferies, an American, crossed the English Channel from Dover to Calais in a balloon. These aeronauts, who were apparently out of ballast to control their hydrogen-filled craft, jettisoned everything—including their clothing.

June 25—Englishwoman Mrs. L.A. Sage became the first female aeronaut. She was taken aloft in a balloon on this date by French balloonist Vincent Lundari.

1793

January 9—The first balloon ascension in the United States was made by Jean-Pierre Blanchard, from Philadelphia to Gloucester County, New Jersey, a flight that lasted 45 minutes. Blanchard carried a "passport" from President George Washington to ensure friendly treatment upon landing. In Europe, "monsters from the sky" had been attacked with pitchforks by peasants.

1794

June 26—First use of a military balloon apparently occurred on this date when two French soldiers soared above enemy territory at the Battle of Fleurus in Belgium to direct artillery fire with the use of signal flags. A conflicting account of this event states that the French used a captive balloon (tethered), and the pilot was given as "Capt. Coutelle."

1797

October 22—The world's first parachute jump was accomplished from 3,000 feet above Paris by Andre J. Garnerin on this date. The parachute was of silk and was held partially open with a center pole.

1804

During this year, England's Sir George Cayley built a hand-launched glider with a stick fuselage, monoplane wing, and adjustable, cruciform tail, which he sailed from a hill near his home at Brompton Hall, Yorkshire. Cayley thus defined the logical shape of the heavier-than-air flying machine. He also described the stabilizing effect of wing dihedral, and recognized that the upper wing surface should be curved upward in cross section to create lift. His triple paper "On Aerial Navigation" was published in Nicholson's *Journal of Natural Philosophy, Chemistry and the Arts* for November 1809, February 1810, and March 1810, and was the basis for almost all serious aerial experimenters for nearly a century. Although there were many attempts at manned, heavier-than-air flight during the next 90 years, almost nothing of value was added to man's meager store of knowledge on the subject until Germany's Otto Lilienthal published *Bird Flight as the Basis for Aviation* in 1889, and followed with the gliding experiments that attracted the Wrights.

Significant Events in Aviation

1852

September 24—The first flight of a steerable airship was made by Henri Giffard from Paris to Trappes, about 17 miles. The airship, filled with coal gas and propelled by a steam engine, flew at a speed of four to five mph.

1859

August 17—The world's first official air mail flight was made by John Wise (who would make 446 balloon flights in 20 years before disappearing over Lake Michigan at age 71) in the balloon *Jupiter*. The flight went from Lafayette, Indiana, to the vicinity of Crawfordsville, Indiana, approximately 30 miles in four and a half hours. Wise carried 123 letters and 23 circulars, and was designated an official carrier by the Lafayette postmaster.

1861

July 21—Early in the American Civil War, during the Battle of Bull Run, America's first "Chief of Aeronautics," Prof. Thaddeus S.C. Lowe, ascended over the battle lines in a tethered Federal balloon and attempted to signal Gen. Irvin McDowell with a heliograph.

1862

May 30—Lowe made important intelligence reports to the Union forces from his balloon, the *Intrepid*, during the battle of Fair Oaks and in subsequent actions.

The Confederates' balloon, made of silk dresses donated by Southern ladies, fell into Union hands during its initial ascent.

1870–1871

September '70 to January '71—The great Parisian Airlift was accomplished by 67 balloons carrying passengers, mail, and carrier pigeons (which returned with messages) out of the surrounded city of Paris during the Franco-Prussian War. More than 2,000,000 letters were carried; seven balloons were lost.

The first air combat took place above Paris during the siege when French and German balloon crews exchanged small arms fire.

1876

The first four-stroke internal combustion engine was marketed by the German firm of Otto and Langen. This engine was based on Otto's 1867 engine, a three-cylinder affair that operated on coal gas. Gottlieb Daimler employed the four-stroke principle to produce a one-cylinder petrol engine in 1887.

1887

American balloonist Capt. Thomas Scott Baldwin made the first parachute jump in the United States above San Francisco's Golden Gate Park.

1896

August 9—Otto Lilienthal, German glider pioneer, crashed while gliding over the Rhinower Hills near Stollen. He died the following day. Lilienthal built and flew his first fixed-wing glider in 1891.

4 1001 FLYING FACTS AND FIRSTS

A famous German air pioneer who died in the crash of one of his gliders. (August 9, 1896.)

1899

August—The Wright brothers built their first aircraft, a biplane kite with a wingspan of 5 feet. It was used to test the brothers' flight control system of wing warping for roll control.

1900

July 2—The first rigid dirigible left her floating hangar on Lake Constance near Manzell with designer-builder Count Ferdinand von Zeppelin at the controls. This first Zeppelin, LZ-1, was 420 feet in length, and contained 17 internal "baloonets" filled with hydrogen. Power was provided by two 14-hp water-cooled Daimler engines fitted with four-bladed propellers.

1903

October 7; December 8—Prof. S.P. Langley's tandem-wing "Aerodrome," launched from a spring-loaded catapult atop a houseboat in the Potomac River, failed to fly in two attempts, suffering structural failure each time. Pilot and builder of the machine and its engine was C.M. Manly.

December 14–December 17—The world's first successful flight by a controllable, self-propelled heavier-than-air flying machine was accomplished on December 17th, with Orville Wright at the controls. The Wright Flyer, designed and built by Orville and brother Wilbur, was airborne for 12 seconds, covering a distance of 120 feet. Three additional flights that morning, with the brothers alternating at the controls, ended after Wilbur flew 852 feet in 59 seconds.

SIGNIFICANT EVENTS IN AVIATION

The Wrights almost achieved success three days before the actual first flight. Who was flying this day? (December 14-17, 1903.)

Earlier, on December 14th, Wilbur had stalled the Flyer and mushed into the sand at Kill Devil Hill, North Carolina, almost immediately after takeoff, and the brothers chose not to count that effort as a true flight.

1904

May 23–December 9—The Wrights made approximately 80 short flights in the second Flyer (the longest of which covered 2¾ miles in five minutes, four seconds) from the world's first airport, Huffman Prairie, a 90-acre pasture at Sims Station, located about eight miles east of Dayton, Ohio, the Wrights' home town.

1905

March 16; April 29; July 18—Professional parachutist D. Maloney descended in a balloon-launched tandem-winged glider on these dates, crashing to his death at the end of the third flight. These gliders were designed by Californian John J. Montgomery, who was himself killed in one of his machines in 1911.

Montgomery, along with several other early experimenters (including Russian Alexander F. Mozhaisky), claimed to have successfully flown a powered, heavier-than-air machine prior to the Wrights' success, but no such claim has withstood careful investigation.

1905

June 8—Gabriel Voisin was towed aloft in his float-equipped biplane glider from the River Seine by motorboat for a flight of 150 meters. This glider, designed by Voisin and Ernest Archdeacon, appears to have made the first use of floats on a flying machine.

1905

June 23–October 16—The Wrights made some 40 flights from Huffman Prairie in the Flyer III, the longest of which was more than 24 miles in 38 minutes, 3 seconds, on October 5. Satisfied that they had perfected their invention, the brothers did not fly again for two and a half years, while they tried to sell their secrets to the American and British governments.

1906

October 23; November 12—Alberto Santos-Dumont, the son of a wealthy Brazilian landowner, made the first heavier-than-air flights in Europe. Flying a "cellular" biplane of his own design, the culmination of five years' experimenting, Santos-Dumont was aloft near Paris on these dates for 197 and 722 feet, respectively.

A Brazilian air pioneer living in Paris circled the Eiffel Tower in October 1901 in an elongated gas bag fitted with a small gasoline engine. Pitch control was achieved by the pilot moving forward and aft along the tubular frame suspended from beneath the airship. This pilot later built a series of flying machines. Who was he? (October 23, 1906.)

1907

August 1—An Aeronautical Division was established in the Office of the Chief Signal Officer, U.S. Army, in anticipation of the delivery of a Baldwin dirigible, an elongated gas bag fitted with a Curtiss air-cooled engine. The Division comprised one officer, Capt. Charles Chandler, and two enlisted men.

1908

January 13—Henri Farman made the first official circle and was airborne for 90 seconds. In July, Farman flew just over 12 miles in 20 minutes. He was an Englishman working in France.

August 8–December 31—Wilbur Wright made numerous flights near Le Mans, France, one of them lasting 2 hours, 20 minutes, 27 seconds. On October 7, Mrs. Hart O. Berg became the first American female airplane passenger when she flew with Wilbur near Le Mans. (The Wrights' mechanic, Charles Furnas, was the world's first airplane passenger, flying with Wilbur at Kitty Hawk, May 14, 1908. The world's first female passenger was Theresa Peltier, who flew with Delagrange July 8 at Turin, Italy.)

July 4—Glen Curtiss flew 5,090 feet in his *June Bug*, one of four machines financed by Alexander Graham Bell's "Aerial Experiment Association" (actually, Mrs. Bell's money). The Curtiss machine and Casey Baldwin's *White Wing* (which flew almost 300 feet on May 8, 1908), were fitted with ailerons set between the wings for roll control. Curtiss knew (via a letter from the Wrights) that the Wright patents specified wing warping as a means of roll control.

Actually, the first "ailerons"—perhaps more properly, "elevons"—were on a machine built by French aviation pioneer Robert Esnault-Pelterie in 1904, but that craft did not fly, and when Farman made his 360 early in 1908, he did so with rudder alone, skidding precariously. He had no means of roll control.

September 3–September 17—Orville Wright flew almost six hours in 10 demonstration flights for the U.S. Army at Ft. Myer, Virginia, until propeller failure resulted in a crash that killed his passenger, Lt. T.E. Selfridge—the world's first aeroplane fatality (the word "airplane" first appeared in an American aviation publication in 1916).

October 8—Leon Levavasseur's *Antoinette IV*, a 50-hp tractor monoplane that flew at Issy, France, also possessed ailerons; these hinged to the trailing edges of the wings. Both Farman and Bleriot were using ailerons hinged to the trailing edges of their wings—Farman on his Voisin-built biplane, and Bleriot on his Bleriot VIII monoplane—late in 1908.

October 5—American S.F. Cody, working in Great Britain, flew his biplane for 496 yards at a height of about 50 feet at Laffan's Plain, Aldershot, Hampshire. This was the first aeroplane flight in Britain.

October 28—Hans Grade, the first native German pilot, flew a triplane of his design at Magdeburg.

1909

February 23—The first aeroplane flight by a British subject anywhere in the British Empire was made by J.A.D. McCurdy when he flew his 35-hp *Silver Dart* (one of the "Aerial Experiment Assoc." machines) for half a mile at a height of about 40 feet over the frozen surface of Bras d'Or Lake at Baddeck Bay, Nova Scotia.

8 1001 FLYING FACTS AND FIRSTS

July 25—Louis Bleriot made the first aeroplane crossing of the English Channel from Barraques, near Calais, to Dover in a Bleriot monoplane fitted with a 25-hp Anzani engine. His speed was approximately 45 mph.

August 2—The United States Army bought its first aeroplane from the Wright brothers. The price was $25,000 plus a $5,000 bonus for a speed of 2.5 mph over the Army's 40 mph specification. The Army's first pilot was Lt. Frank P. Lahm. The Baldwin dirigible, delivered a year earlier, cost the Army $6,700.

August 22-August 29—The first International Air Meet, held on the Plain of Betheny near Reims, France, attracted 38 flying machines and 22 pilots, plus all the crowned heads of Europe, and records were broken daily. Curtiss attained a speed of 48 mph; Hubert Latham reached an altitude of 508 feet, and Farman flew more than 111 miles nonstop.

1910

March 28—The first seaplane flight in the world was accomplished by Capt. F. Ferber, a French artilleryman. (Glenn Curtiss would make the first hydroplane takeoff in the U.S. on January 26, 1911).

November 14—Curtiss pilot Eugene Ely became the first to fly off the deck of a ship. The U.S. Navy cruiser *Birmingham*, anchored at Hampton Roads, was fitted with a 28 × 83 foot platform for this trial.

What is going on here? (November 14, 1910.)

The world's first jet aeroplane, designed by Rumanian Henri Coanda, was exhibited at the 1910 Paris Air Show. A petrol engine powered its nose-mounted compressor. Of biplane configuration, the wings were full cantilever. Coanda wrecked this machine attempting to take off on its first test flight (which was also Coanda's first flight).

John Moisant, a Chicago architect, designed, built, and flew an all-metal tractor monoplane. Moisant learned to fly in France, and made the first English Channel flight with a passenger. His aerial exhibition team, including his sister, Mathilda (second American woman pilot), toured the United States prior to WWI.

Meanwhile, in England, Geoffrey deHavilland flew his first airplane, while Igor Sikorsky built another unsuccessful helicopter in Russia.

In Germany, Count von Zeppelin formed DLAG (Deutsche Luftschiffarts-Aktien-Gesellschaft) and, with four dirigibles—*Schwaben*, *Viktoria-Luise*, *Hansa*, and *Sachsen*—operated a passenger service between Berlin and major German cities, including Dresden, Frankfurt, Hamburg, and others. For five years, 1910-1914, this service operated without a fatality to a passenger, flying about 100,000 miles in 1,600 flights. Schedules depended upon weather.

America's first woman pilot was Dr. Bessica Raiche, who learned to fly in an aeroplane built by her husband.

1911

January—Glenn Curtiss established a flying school on barren North Island in San Diego Bay. The Wrights also trained pilots, beginning early in 1910 at Huffman Prairie and Montgomery, Alabama, at a site now known as Maxwell AFB.

January 18—Eugene Ely took off from shore at San Francisco, landed on the cruiser *Pennsylvania*, then flew back to shore. On February 17, Glenn Curtiss landed in the water beside the *Pennsylvania*, and was hoisted aboard by ship's crane.

July 1—The U.S. Navy's first aeroplane, the Curtiss Triad amphibian, was delivered, following demonstration flights on Lake Keuka, Hammondsport, New York.

July 3—The first Navy pilot, Lt. Theodore Ellyson, made the first night flight operating from Lake Keuka without lights.

August 14—The first air-sea rescue was accomplished by Hugh Robinson, flying a Curtiss hydroplane, when he landed on Lake Michigan to save Rene Simon following the crash of Simon's monoplane.

September 17-December 10—Calbreath P. Rodgers flew from New York to Long Beach, California in his Wright biplane, *Vin Fiz* (named for his sponsor, a popular soft drink). He crashed 15 times along the way.

1912

January 10—Curtiss demonstrates the first successful flying boat.

April 16; May 19—Women pilots Harriet Quimby (the "Dresden China Aviatrice" flying with the Moisant exhibition team) and Julia Clark die in crashes at Boston and Springfield, Illinois, respectively.

Auto magnate Henry Ford (R) with the designer/pilot of the first flying boat. Ford was an admirer of this air pioneer and sent his top patent attorney, W.B. Crisp, to aid this man in his court battles with the Wrights over patent disputes. Who is the man on the left? (January 10, 1912.)

April—Britain's Royal Flying Corps was authorized by a Royal Warrant. It included a Naval Wing, Military Wing, Flying School at Upavon, Wilts, and an aircraft factory at Farnborough, Hants.

May 22—Three U.S. Marines, led by Lt. Alfred A. Cunningham (Naval Aviator Number 5), formed the nucleus of the Marine Corps' Aviation Branch after Cunningham learned to fly at the Burgess school. The Marines possessed no aeroplanes of their own until after America went to war in April 1917.

May 30—Wilbur Wright died of typhoid at age 45.

June 7—Capt. Charles DeF. Chandler fired a Lewis machine gun from a Wright Model B aeroplane. Although a "first," the gun could not be aimed except at a fixed, downward angle.

July—Katherine Stinson, perhaps the most famous of U.S. female exhibition pilots prior to WWI, was taught to fly by Anthony Jannus at Max Lillie's school on Chicago's Cicero Field. Sister Marjorie would follow in 1914, and brother Eddie would learn to fly at the Wrights' school in 1915.

July 26—The first plane-to-ground wireless experiments were conducted by the Navy at Annapolis, followed by the Army's wireless tests on November 2 at Ft. Riley, Kansas.

SIGNIFICANT EVENTS IN AVIATION 11

Big sister takes younger brother Jack for a ride in her flying machine. Who is this famous woman pilot? (July 1912.)

November 12—The Navy's first successful launching of an aeroplane by catapult was made at the Washington Navy Yard by Lt. Ellyson. The following month, a Curtiss flying boat was launched from this catapult.

1913

January—Lt. Harold E. Geiger establishes the U.S. Army's flying school at North Island. About 15 Army pilots had been trained at College Park, Maryland (in warm weather), and in Augusta, Georgia (during the winter months).

May 13—In Russia, Igor Sikorsky designed and flew the largest aeroplane the world had seen up to that time, a four-engine biplane with a span of 93 feet. It seated eight in an enclosed cabin.

June 21—Georgia Thompson "Tiny" Broadwick became the first women to parachute from an aeroplane, at Los Angeles, California. Tiny—she was five feet tall and weighted 80 pounds—was 20 years old at the time. She had made her first parachute jump from a hot air balloon in 1908. She would eventually make 1,100 jumps during a 14-year barnstorming career.

French pilot Adolphe Pegoud performed the first inside loop.

September 29—French pilot Maurice Prevost flew 126.59 mph in a Deperdussin monoplane to win the Gordon Bennet Cup.

1914

January 20—The aviation unit from Annapolis, consisting of nine officers, 23 men, and seven aircraft, under Lt. John H. Towers, arrived at Pensacola, Florida aboard the USS *Mississippi* and *Orion* to establish a flying school.

January 1—P.E. Fansler started the world's first scheduled airline with Anthony Jannus as pilot, flying Benoist flying boats two round trips daily between Tampa and St. Petersburg, Florida. The operation ceased for lack of customers within a few months.

June 2—Glenn Curtiss flew a redesigned version of the Langley Aerodrome on several short hops at Hammondsport in a fraudulent effort to establish that Langley should be recognized as the inventor of the aeroplane. Curtiss was facing a losing court battle with the Wrights.

July 18—The U.S. Congress authorized formation of the Aviation Section of the Signal Corps. Lt. Col. Samuel Reber, head of the former Aeronautical Division, was to command 60 officers and 260 enlisted men.

July 28—WWI began. Nine declarations of war among the nations of Europe (plus Japan, who exploited the madness to grab strategic Pacific islands belonging to Germany) were made from July 28 to August 23, following the assassination of the Archduke Franz Ferdinand at Serajevo on June 28.

September 16—Formation of the Canadian Aviation Corps was approved. It possessed two officers and one aircraft, a Burgess-Dunne.

October 5—The first air combat between aeroplanes occurred. French pilot Sgt. Joseph Franz of the 24th Escadrille, and his mechanic, Cpl. Quenault, flying a Voisin pusher, shot down a German Aviatik two-seater near the Fort of Brimont. This was one of the first aeroplanes on either side armed with a machine gun (an infantry Hotchkiss).

1915

January 19—The world's first strategic bombers, two German Zeppelins, dropped bombs at King's Lynn, Norfolk, England. During the war, about 56 tons of bombs were dropped on London, and 214 tons on other parts of the country. Of the 120 Zeppelin-type airships built by Germany from 1914-1918 (inclusive), only six remained at war's end.

March 3—The National Advisory Committee for Aeronautics (NACA) was established by act of Congress. The NACA was the forerunner of NASA and provided many advances in aviation, including a wide range of wing airfoils, the NACA cowling for radial engines, etc.

April 1—The first fighter airplane; French pilot Roland Garros was the first to enter air combat with a fixed machine gun firing forward through the propeller disk of a single-seat aeroplane. Steel deflectors on the rear of each blade protected the prop from those rounds that did not pass between the blades. Later that year, Tony Fokker perfected an engine-driven interrupter system for the fixed guns on German fighters.

July 15—The U.S. 1st Aero Squadron was formed from the personnel of the Army's aviation school at North Island. On July 26 it was posted to its first duty station, Ft. Sill, Oklahoma.

August 12—The first ship sunk by an aerial torpedo went down after being attacked by a British seaplane during the Dardanelles operation.

November—First cross-country "mass" flight was accomplished by the 1st Aero Squadron, flying from Ft. Sill, Oklahoma, to San Antonio, Texas. Capt. Benjamin Foulois was in command of the 1st Aero, which comprised 15 officers, 85 enlisted men, and 8 Curtiss JN-2 aeroplanes.

1916

March 19–April 22—The 1st Aero Squadron accompanied Gen. John "Blackjack" Pershing's 5,000-man army into Mexico in an unsuccessful attempt to capture the Mexican bandit Pancho Villa after Villa raided the U.S. border town of Columbus, New Mexico, on March 9, killing nine civilians and seven U.S. Army troopers.

March 30—The first Coast Guard pilots, 2nd. Lt. C.E. Sugden and 3rd. Lt. E.F. Stone, were assigned to the Navy's flying school at Pensacola.

April 15—First insignia for U.S. Navy aeroplanes was an anchor and two-digit numeral, both dark blue on a white background; this was painted outboard on upper and lower wing surfaces. The anchor was generally placed on the vertical tail surfaces, and the numeral fore-and-aft on both sides of the fuselage.

April 20—The Lafayette Escadrille (French squadron N-124) was organized, entering combat the following month during the Battle of Verdun. It was composed of young Americans and soldiers of fortune, and had the financial backing of an American committee headed by William K. Vanderbuilt. It was absorbed into the U.S. Air Service as the 103rd Squadron on February 18, 1918.

July 15—Boeing Airplane Company was formed in Seattle. Originally a partnership between lumberman William E. Boeing and U.S. Navy officer Conrad Westervelt and called "Pacific Aero Products," the name was changed when the U.S. entered WWI. Boeing is the oldest aircraft company in the U.S. in continuous operation.

1917

April 6—The United States declared war on Germany. The U.S. Army had 35 pilots on active duty, along with 55 aeroplanes; the Navy had 48 pilots and 54 seaplanes and flying boats, as well as two captive balloons and one dirigible.

June 13—The first heavy daylight aeroplane raid on London was carried out by 14 Gotha two-engine bombers, killing 162 people.

August 13—The U.S. 1st Aero Squadron sailed for Europe, commanded by Maj. Ralph Royce (Maj. Foulois was head of the Signal Corps Airplane Division).

1918

March 19—First U.S. Navy aviation intelligence officer was authorized.

March 19—First American naval aviator to shoot down an enemy airplane was Ens. Stephan Potter, while on a reconnaissance flight over the German coast.

March 19—The first operational flights across the lines in France by American aircraft were made by the 94th Squadron of the 1st Pursuit Group.

The deHavilland D.H.4 was the only U.S.-built combat aircraft type to reach the fighting front in WWI; the type was later modified for air mail service by the U.S. Post Office Dept.

March 25—The first attack on an enemy submarine by a U.S. Naval Aviator was carried out by Ens. John F. McNamara, flying out of RNAS, Portland, England. Adm. Sims described the attack as "apparently successful."

April 1—England's Royal Air Force (RAF) was formed by the merger of the Royal Flying Corps and the Royal Naval Air Service. The Women's Royal Air Force was also formed this date.

April 15—The 1st Marine Aviation Force was formed at Miami NAS under Capt. A.A. Cunningham.

April 21—Baron Manfred von Richthofen, fatally wounded by a single bullet, crashed in his red Fokker triplane near Corbie in the Somme Valley. Canadian Camel pilot Capt. Roy Brown claimed the victory, as did four Australian machine gunners and an Australian rifleman on the ground.

May 15—The true beginning of regularly scheduled U.S. Air Mail; on this date, mail flights were begun between Washington, D.C. and New York City, with U.S. Air Service planes flying under the direction of the U.S. Post Office. Post Office civilian pilots took over on August 12.

May 20—U.S. Army aviation was separated from the Signal Corps with the two new departments established, the Bureau of Military Aeronautics, and the Bureau of Aircraft Production. The latter was due to the blatant boondoggle in U.S. aircraft production by the automobile interests which controlled it, while the term "Bureau of Military Aeronautics" was

SIGNIFICANT EVENTS IN AVIATION 15

Tethered observation balloons, known as "sausages" or "rubber elephants," were hydrogen-filled and normally took a two-man crew aloft who directed artillery fire via telephone and observed enemy troop movements. Used by both sides, this one is a British unit. The tail was wind-inflated by way of a cloth tunnel under the nose.

never used. From early 1917, most people used the term "U.S. Air Service," which became official in 1920.

May 31—The first U.S. Air Service ace was Lt. Douglas Campbell, who first scored on April 14, and became an ace on May 31. Other Americans scored earlier and became aces sooner than did Campbell, but they did so wearing French or British uniforms. Campbell was American-trained, in an American uniform, and posted to an American air unit (94th).

July 25—The U.S. Navy was selected by the Secretary of War as the U.S. military service to operate Zeppelin-type airships. The Navy had no Zeppelins and no desire for any, but feared encroachment on Navy defense responsibilities if the Army got them.

September 24—The first U.S. Navy ace was Lt. (jg) David S. Ingalls, who scored five air victories while flying with RAF Squadron 213. A number of American Air Service and Navy pilots were temporarily assigned to RAF units while awaiting delivery of airplanes (purchased from France and Britain) and establishment of their own aerodromes in France.

16 1001 FLYING FACTS AND FIRSTS

Along with the SE-5a, the Sopwith Camel was the principal British single-seat fighter of WWI.

October 1—The first deck landing on the world's first aircraft carrier, the British ship HMS *Argus* (known to her crew as the "Flatiron"), was accomplished. Britain had previously fitted landing platforms aft, and takeoff platforms forward, on a pair of cruisers, but without much success.

November 11—World War I ended. Hostilities ceased at 11 A.M. At war's end, the RAF was the largest air force in the world, with 27,333 officers, 263,410 men, and 22,647 airplanes. There were 45 American combat squadrons in action with a strength of 740 airplanes, approximately 800 pilots, and 500 observers.

Altogether, the U.S. Air Service accepted 11,754 American and Canadian-built airplanes between April 6, 1917, and November 11, 1918. Prior to war's end, the Air Service purchased 4,881 French, 258 British, and 19 Italian airplanes. Therefore, the Air Service received a total of 16,912 airplanes during the war, the Navy and Marines 2,156, for a total of 19,068. U.S. Naval aviation could count 6,716 officers and 30,693 men, plus 282 Marine officers and 2,180 men. Of these numbers, 18,000 Navy and Marine officers and men, along with 570 aircraft, were sent overseas.

December 12—In a test to determine the feasibility of carrying fighter aircraft on dirigibles, the Navy's C-1 airship, flown by Lt. George Crompton, lifted an Army Jenny (JN-4) piloted by Lt. A.W. Redfield to 2,500 feet over Ft. Tilden, New York, and released the airplane for a free flight back to its base.

SIGNIFICANT EVENTS IN AVIATION   17

The barnstormers of the 1920s employed wingwalkers to attract crowds from which paying passengers could be solicited. The war surplus Curtiss JN-4 Jenny trainer was widely used by the pasture pilots.

1919

May 16–May 17—First Atlantic flight. The U.S. Navy flying boat Curtiss NC-4, commanded by Lt. Cmdr. Albert C. Read, flew from Newfoundland to Horta in the Azores, and then on to Plymouth, England (May 31) via Lisbon, Portugal.

June 14–15—First nonstop Atlantic flight. A British Vickers Vimy bomber, crewed by pilot Capt. John Alcock and navigator Lt. Arthur Whitten Brown, flew from St. John, Newfoundland, to Clifden, Ireland, nonstop in 16½ hours.

July 2–6 and 9–13—First Atlantic flight by dirigible, first round trip across the Atlantic, and first airborne stowaway on Atlantic flight. The British airship R.34, commanded by RAF Maj. G.H. Scott, with a crew of 30, flew from East Fortune, Scotland, to New York—3,600 miles in 108 hours. The return trip reached Pulham in Norfolk, 3,800 miles away, in 75 hours. The stowaway, carried on the outward journey, was airship rigger W.W. Ballantyne.

18 **1001 Flying Facts and Firsts**

U.S. aircraft designers were building transport airplanes before there was a civilian market for them. This 1923 Burnelli, with airfoil fuselage and nose-mounted twin engines, is an example.

July 11—The U.S. Navy's first aircraft carrier and first dirigible were authorized in the Naval Appropriations Act for 1920. The carrier was the *Langley*, converted from the collier *Jupiter*, commissioned in 1922, with first flight operations on October 17th that year. The dirigible was the ZR-1 *Shenandoah*, commissioned September 4, 1923. A second dirigible, the ZR-2, purchased from Britain as the R.38, crashed in England during a test flight.

1920

March 27—First autopilot; a successful test of the Sperry gyrostabilized automatic pilot system in a Navy F5L flying boat was completed at Hampton Roads, Virginia.

Significant Events in Aviation

June 4—The U.S. Army Air Service was officially established with U.S. Congress approval of the Army Reorganization Bill. Air Service authorized strength was 1,516 officers and 16,000 men, serving as "a separate and coordinate branch of the Army."

1921

February 22-23—First coast-to-coast air mail flight, San Francisco to New York, 33 hours 20 minutes. It was flown by Jack Knight and E.M. Allison.

March 31—Australian Air Force established by proclamation pending passage of the Air Defense Act.

July 12—U.S. Navy Bureau of Aeronautics was created by act of Congress. Rear Adm. William A. Moffett was first chief of "BuAer."

July 21—Army bombers sink a battleship. The WWI German battleship *Ostfriesland*, a war prize, was sunk by eleven 1,000 and 2,000-pound bombs dropped by Air Service Martin bombers commanded by Brig. Gen. William Mitchell.

1922

October 14—The Air Service Verville-Sperry R-3 entered in the Pulitzer Race featured retractable landing gear, rubber-spool engine shock mounts, and a full-cantilever low wing. The Navy's Booth and Thurston racer was similarly configured, and had wing-skin radiators for its water-cooled Hispano-Suiza V-8 engine.

October 20—The first American to be saved by use of a free-fall parachute was Air Service Lt. Harold R. Harris, who bailed out of an experimental Loening monoplane fighter over McCook Field, Ohio, following structural failure.

1923

January 9—The first successful autogiro—designed, built, and flown by Spain's Juan de la Cierva—accomplished a 3-mile circle at an altitude of approximately 1,000 feet.

May 2-3—The first nonstop crossing of the United States was made by Lts. O.G. Kelly and J.A. Macready. Flying a Fokker T-2, the Air Service pilots covered the 2,520 miles from New York to San Diego in 26 hours, 50 min.

June 27—The first pipeline refuelling between two aircraft in flight was accomplished by Lts. Lowell H. Smith and J.P. Richter. Later that year (27-28 August), they remained airborne for 37 hours and 15 minutes while fuel was transferred to their DH-4B via pipeline at regular intervals.

September 4—The rigid dirigible USS *Shenandoah* (ZR-1) made its first flight at Naval Air Station Lakehurst, Capt. F.R. McCrary commanding.

1924

April 1—The Royal Canadian Air Force was established on a permanent basis as part of Canada's defense forces.

20 1001 FLYING FACTS AND FIRSTS

Juan de la Cierva produced the first successful autogiro. He is shown here (center) discussing a later version of his invention with Harold Pitcairn (right). Which appeared first, autogiro or helicopter? (January 9, 1923 and July 5, 1937.)

April 6–September 28—First round-the-world flight, first trans-Pacific flight, and the first westbound airplane crossing of the North Atlantic. Two of four hefty Douglas biplanes completed the journey from Seattle to Seattle in 15 days, 11 hours, and 7 minutes flying time, a distance of 26,350 miles. The Air Service machines, Liberty-powered, were flown by Lts. Lowell Smith and Eric Nelson.

July 1—Regular round-the-clock air mail service was begun on the New York-Chicago-San Francisco transcontinental route as the airway was lighted from Chicago to Cheyenne.

1925

February 2—Passage of the Kelly Bill, the first Air Mail Act, provided for the transfer of air mail operations from the Post Office Department to private contractors.

SIGNIFICANT EVENTS IN AVIATION

Douglas World Cruiser Chicago *over the South China Sea. How many World Cruisers completed this first world flight? How many began the flight? (April 6, 1924.)*

September 3—The U.S. Navy's dirigible *Shenandoah* ("Daughter of the Stars") broke up in a storm near Marietta, Ohio. Of the 43 crew members, 14 were killed, including Lt. Cmdr. Zachary Landsdowne, the commander.

December 17—Brig. Gen. William Mitchell, an outspoken critic of the government's aviation policies, was found guilty by a court martial of conduct prejudicial to good order and military discipline under the 96th Article of War, and was sentenced to suspension from duty for five years. He resigned his commission and retired to his farm in Vermont.

1926

February 15—Ford Air Transport Company became the first to fly the mail as a contract air mail operator, operating between Detroit and Cleveland.

May 9—The first flight over the North Pole was accomplished in a trimotor Fokker Monoplane piloted by Floyd Bennett and commanded by Lt. Cmdr. Richard E. Byrd. The *Josephine*

There's no question about the identity of this airplane and its engines and where it went—so who piloted this Fokker Trimotor over the North Pole? (May 9, 1926.)

Ford reached the pole at 9:03 GCT, then returned to base at Kings Bay, Spitzbergen, completing a round trip of 15½ hours.

May 11–14—The first dirigible flight over the North Pole was made from Spitzbergen to Alaska in the *Norge* by Lincoln Ellsworth and Col. Umberto Nobile with Raold Amundsen.

May 20—The Air Commerce Act, the first federal legislation in the United States regulating civil aviation, was signed by President Coolidge.

July 2—The U.S. Congress passed the Air Corps Act, which changed the name from "Air Service" to "U.S. Army Air Corps" and authorized an Assistant Secretary of War for Air, plus a "five-year plan" for upgrading the equipment. All of this was obviously designed to counter criticism following the Mitchell trial.

October 22—First fleet demonstration of dive-bombing. In a display of tactics developed by VF Squadron 2, Lt. Cmdr. F.D. Wagner led his Curtiss F6C-2 fighters in a simulated dive-bombing attack on heavy ships of the Pacific Fleet. Ship commanders agreed that they possessed no effective defense against such a tactic. On December 13, one Marine and two Navy squadrons repeated the demonstration.

On July 17 the following year, Marine Maj. Ross E. Rowell led five DH-4s in a dive-bombing and strafing attack against "bandit" forces surrounding a Marine garrison at Ocotal, Nicaragua. Actually, Marine pilots had used this tactic as early as 1919 in Haiti, although some historians credit its development to Germany's Ernst Udet during the early 1930s.

1927

May 20–21—First nonstop solo crossing of the Atlantic, New York to Paris, was made by air mail pilot and Air Corps Reserve Capt. Charles A. Lindbergh in a specially built Ryan

SIGNIFICANT EVENTS IN AVIATION 23

Charles A. Lindbergh's New York/Paris Ryan monoplane. An important ingredient of Lindbergh's successful flight was his engine. What was it? (May 20, 1927.)

monoplane fitted with a Wright Whirlwind engine of 225 hp. Time was 33 hours and 30 minutes for the 3,610 miles.

June 4—The first nonstop New York to Germany flight was made by Clarence Chamberlin in a Whirlwind-powered Bellanca with plane owner Charles Levine as a passenger.

June 28-29—The first flight from the U.S. to Hawaii was made by Lts. Albert F. Hegenberger and L.J. Maitland in a trimotor Fokker. They flew from Oakland, California, to Honolulu's Wheeler Field—2,407 miles—in 25 hours, 50 minutes. A low-frequency radio beacon at San Francisco and another on Maui aided navigation.

July 1—Cmdr. Richard Byrd, with pilots Bert Acosta and Bernt Balchen, plus navigator George Noville, flew the trimotor Fokker *America* across the Atlantic and crash-landed in the sea off Ver-su-Mer, Normandy.

During the year after Lindbergh's flight, either from Europe or from America, 31 crossings were attempted. Ten were successful; 20 men and women died in the failures.

July 15—The first civilians to fly to Hawaii were Ernest L. Smith and Emory Bronte, who reached Molokai in 25½ hours flying a Whirlwind-powered Travel Air 5000.

October 14—The first nonstop crossing of the South Atlantic by air was from St. Louis, Senegal, to Natal, Brazil, by Dieudonne Costes and Lt. Lebrix of France in a Breguet.

October 19—Pan American Airways began operation with a 90-mile route between Key West, Florida, and Havana, Cuba.

November 16—The USS *Saratoga*, the first carrier and fifth Navy ship to bear that name, was placed in commission at Camden, New Jersey, Capt. H.E. Yarnell commanding.

December 14—The USS *Lexington*, the first carrier and fourth Navy ship to bear that name, was commissioned at Quincy, Massachusetts, Capt. A.W. Marshall commanding.

1928

January 6—The Medal of Honor was awarded to Marine Lt. C.F. Schilt who, flying an O2U-1 Corsair, made 10 flights under fire to land in the streets of Quilali, Nicaragua, to evacuate 18 wounded Marines.

April 12–13—The first east-to-west crossing of the North Atlantic by airplane was accomplished by Germans Herman Koehl and Baron Guenther von Huenefeld, flying a Junkers all-metal monoplane from Baldonnel, Ireland, to a crash-landing on Greenly Island, Labrador. Time was 36½ hours.

May 31–June 10—The first flight from the U.S. to Australia was accomplished by Australia's Capt. Charles Kingsford-Smith with copilot Capt. C.T.P. Ulm, along with their American navigator, Lt. Harry W. Lyon, Jr. Their aircraft was a trimotor Fokker F-7, *Southern Cross*, and the route was from Oakland, via Hawaii and the Fiji Islands, to Brisbane.

1929

January 1–7—An endurance record was set by the crew of an Army Fokker trimotor, the *Question Mark*, flying approximately 11,000 miles during a 150-hour 40-minute mission around the Los Angeles area, employing air-to-air refuelling. The crew was Maj. Carl Spaatz, Capt. Ira Eaker, Lts. Harry Halverson and Elwood Quesada, plus Sgt. Roy Hooe.

August 8–29—The German rigid dirigible *Graf Zeppelin* flew around the world, commanded by Dr. Hugo Eckener.

August 23–November 1—The Russion seaplane *Land of the Soviets*, carrying a four-man crew, flew from Moscow to Seattle via Siberia and Alaska.

September 30—First flight by a rocket-propelled airplane. In Germany, Fritz von Opel flew for slightly over a mile, reaching a speed of 85 mph. The flight ended in a crash.

November 28–29—The first flight over the South Pole was made by Cmdr. Richard Byrd in the Ford trimotor *Floyd Bennett*; Bernt Balchen was the pilot, Harold June copilot, and Capt. A. McKinley photographer. The round trip from "Little America" on McMurdo Sound required almost 19 hours.

SIGNIFICANT EVENTS IN AVIATION

The German rigid airship Graf Zeppelin accomplished a notable flight soon after its launching. What was it? (August 8, 1929.)

1930

May 15—The first air stewardess was Miss Ellen Church, a registered nurse, who flew on United Air Lines' Boeing 80-A between Chicago and San Francisco. It was Miss Church's idea, not United's. She was so popular with passengers and flight crews that more "stews" were soon added.

July 23—Glenn Curtiss died of complications following an appendectomy.

October 4—Britain's new rigid airship, R-101, bound for Egypt and India, struck a hill and burned near Beauvais, France. Of the 54 passengers and crew, 48 died. This disaster ended Britain's airship program.

October 25—The first coast-to-coast through air service in the U.S. began simultaneously from New York and Los Angeles by Transcontinental and Western Air (TWA), an air carrier formed by the merger of Transcontinental Air Transport and Western Air Express.

1931

April 1—The Airline Pilots Association was organized by the American Federation of Labor and David L. Bencke, a former Northwest Airlines pilot.

June 23–July 1—Wiley Post and Harold Gatty flew around the world in a Lockheed Vega fitted with a Pratt & Whitney Wasp engine of 450 hp. The 15,474-mile journey was via Germany, Russia, Japan, Alaska, and back to New York. Time was 8 days, 15 hours, and 51 minutes. Post would repeat the trip solo two years later (see entry for July 15–22, 1933).

October 3–5—The first nonstop flight between Japan and the United States was made by Clyde Pangborn and Hugh Herndon in a Bellanca monoplane. They landed at Wenatchee, Washington.

26 1001 Flying Facts and Firsts

The burned-out hulk of Britain's rigid airship R-101 lies in a field near Beauvais, France, October 4, 1930; 48 died, six survived. Name three other of the great airships that would later crash. (April 4, 1933; February 12, 1935, and May 6, 1937.) (Photo courtesy British Air Ministry)

1932

January 26—Pioneer aviator and aircraft builder Eddie Stinson was killed during an emergency landing attempt near Detroit.

May 20–21—The first solo flight across the Atlantic by a woman. Amelia Earhart (Putnam) flew her red Lockheed Vega from Harbor Grace, Newfoundland, to Londonderry, Northern Ireland. Her time was 13 hours and 30 minutes.

November 14—A record coast-to-coast flight, east to west, was flown by Roscoe Turner in a Wedell-Williams racer. Turner flew from Floyd Bennett Field, New York, to Burbank, California, in 12 hours and 33 minutes, including two refuelling stops.

1933

January 30—Adolf Hitler became Chancellor of Germany.

April 4—The rigid airship USS *Akron* (ZRS-4) crashed in a storm off Farnegat Light, New Jersey. Among the 73 fatalities were Rear Adm. William A. Moffett, Chief, Bureau of Aeronautics; and Cmdr. Frank C. McCord, Commanding Officer of the *Akron*.

June 23—The U.S. Navy's dirigible USS *Macon* (ZRS-5), having made its first flight on April 21, was commissioned at Akron, Ohio, with Cmdr. Alger H. Dressel commanding.

July 1-15—A formation of 24 aircraft flown across the North Atlantic was led by Italian Gen. Italo Balbo, from Italy, via Iceland, to Chicago. This mass flight was made by Savoia-Marchett twin-engine (one pusher, one tractor), twin-hulled flying boats. Gen. Balbo had led a similar flight across the South Atlantic to Rio de Janeiro in January 1931.

July 15-22—First solo flight around the world. Wiley Post flew his Lockheed Vega *Winnie Mae*, over much the same route he had traversed with Gatty but cut the time to 7 days, 18 hours, 49 minutes.

1934

February 19—The U.S. Army Air Corps began flying domestic air mail following cancellation of civilian contracts by President Roosevelt, who charged fraud and collusion in the manner the contracts had been let.

May 8—The U.S. government began return of mail contracts to the airlines. On July 14, 1941, the U.S. Court of Claims held that the charges against the Postmaster General and the airlines were unfounded.

June 4—The USS *Ranger* (CV-4), America's fourth aircraft carrier, was placed in commission at Norfolk, Capt. A.L. Bristol commanding.

October 20—The MacRobertson Race, England to Australia, was won by C.W.A. Scott and T. Campbell Black, who flew their twin-engine deHavilland Comet from Mildenhall, Suffolk, to Melbourne in 71 hours, 18 seconds.

October 22-November 4—The first airplane flight from Australia to the United States was accomplished by Sir Charles Kingsford-Smith, flying a Lockheed Altair *Lady Southern Cross* from Brisbane to Oakland.

December 12—Wearing a specially made pressure suit, Wiley Post took his Lockheed Vega *Winnie Mae* to an estimated altitude near 50,000 feet (the official barograph aboard malfunctioned). His engine was a special supercharged Wasp SC. The two-stage supercharger provided 450 hp to 35,000 feet.

1935

January 11-12—Amelia Earhart flew solo in her Wasp-powered Vega from Honolulu to Oakland, California, in 18 hours, 16 minutes.

February 12—The U.S. Navy's dirigible USS *Macon* crashed off Point Sur, California, as a result of structural failure. There were two fatalities.

April 19-20—Amelia Earhart flew from Burbank, California, to Mexico City in 13 hours, 32 minutes, including one stop. Then on May 5 she made the first nonstop flight from Mexico City to Newark, New Jersey, in 14 hours, 19 minutes.

May 21—Adolf Hitler announced Germany's repudiation of the military clauses in the Versailles Treaty and introduced military conscription.

July 28—The prototype of the Boeing B-17 Flying Fortress (Boeing Model 299) made its first flight at Seattle, Washington.

August 15—Will Rogers and Wiley Post were killed near Point Barrow, Alaska, when their engine failed on takeoff. Their float-equipped airplane was a Lockheed hybrid Orion-Explorer operated on a restricted license; it was too nose-heavy to be properly controlled without power.

November 11—A world's altitude record was established by Air Corps Capt. O.A. Anderson and Capt. A.W. Stevens, who ascended in a balloon, the *Explorer II*, from Rapid City, South Dakota, reaching an altitude of 72,395 feet.

November 12—First scheduled flight across the Pacific. Capt. Edwin C. Musick took off from San Francisco in a Pan American World Airways Martin M-130 flying boat on the first scheduled air mail flight to Honolulu, and subsequently to the Philippines via Midway, Wake, and Guam. Passenger service was added October 21, 1936.

Despite the hard times, the 1930s were a great time for civilian air racing, much of it done on a shoestring. The Bellanca Flash was planned as a distance racer. Its designer, Al Mooney, also designed the Dart, Culver Cadet, and the M-20 series of well-known lightplanes, among others.

1935-1942

The major fighter aircraft of WWII were developed during the late 1930s and beginning of the 1940s. They are lumped together here in the order of prototype first flights:

April 15, 1935:	Curtiss P-36
September, 1935:	Messerschmitt Me 109
November 8, 1935:	Hawker Hurricane
March 5, 1936:	Vickers Supermarine Spitfire
September 2, 1937:	Grumman F4F Wildcat
December 10, 1937:	Brewster F2A Buffalo
October 14, 1938:	Curtiss P-40
January 9, 1939:	Lockheed P-38 Lightning
April 1, 1939:	Mitsubishi A6M Zero-sen
May, 1939:	Focke-Wulf FW 190
May 6, 1940:	Republic P-47 Thunderbolt
May 29, 1940:	Chance Vought F4U Corsair
October 26, 1940:	North American P-51 Mustang (originally, Apache)
July 20, 1942:	Grumman F6F Hellcat

1936

February 19—Brig. Gen. William Mitchell died in Doctor's Hospital, New York.

July 18—The civil war in Spain began.

September 15—The USS *Langley*, America's first aircraft carrier, was detached from Battle Force, then converted to a seaplane tender with the forward part of her flight deck removed.

1937

April 12—Britain's Frank Whittle tested his first gas turbine engine.

May 6—The world's largest airship, Germany's *Hindenburg*, was destroyed by fire just prior to landing at Lakehurst, New Jersey, after a flight from Frankfurt-am-Main, Germany. Of the 97 passengers and crew, 33 were killed.

July 2—Amelia Earhart and Capt. Fred Noonan, during an attempt to fly around the world, were lost in the pacific between British New Guinea and Howland Island. The aircraft was a twin-engine Lockheed Electra.

July 2—Army motorized balloons and other lighter-than-air elements were transferred to the Navy.

July 5—The world's first successful helicopter, the Focke-Achgelis Fa 61, flew at Bremen, Germany, remaining airborne one hour, 20 minutes, 49 seconds, attaining an altitude of 8,125 feet and a maximum speed of 81.7 mph.

July 9—Fraulein Feodora Schmidt of Germany remained aloft in a glider for 23 hours, 42 minutes above the North Frisian Islands.

The Douglas DC-2. The first of 191 built went to TWA, the airline that prompted the design in the first place. Powered by two 710-hp Wright Cyclones, the DC-2 could seat up to 18. The prototype, the DC-1, entered service with TWA on September 13, 1933. The famed DC-3 would follow in 1936.

July 12–14—Russian airmen Mikhail Gromoff (pilot), Yumasheff, and Danilin establish a nonstop distance record by flying from Moscow to a pasture near San Jacinto, California—6,262 miles in 62 hours, 17 minutes.

September 30—The USS *Yorktown* (CV-5) was placed in commission at Norfolk, Virginia, with Capt. E.D. McWhorter in command.

1938

January 11—The Pan Am Sikorsky flying boat *Samoa Clipper* crashed in the Samoan Islands during the second flight of the mail/freight service begun December 29, 1937. The crew of seven lost their lives.

May 12—The USS *Enterprise* (CV-6), America's sixth aircraft carrier, was commissioned at Newport News, Virginia, Capt. N.H. White commanding.

July 14—Howard Hughes and four companions returned to New York to complete a 15,432-mile around-the-world flight in three days, 19 hours, 17 minutes. They flew a Lockheed Model 14-N2 Super Electra via Paris, Moscow, Yakutsk, Fairbanks, and Minneapolis.

August 22—The Civil Aeronautics Act became law, ending four years of a politically inspired vendetta by the New Dealers against the United States.

September 14—A new German rigid dirigible, the LZ-130—the second to be named *Graf Zeppelin* and the last of the great sky giants—made its first flight at Friedrichshafen. It used hydrogen as a lifting agent because the U.S. refused to supply Nazi Germany with nonflammable helium (at the time, there was no other known source of helium in the world. It was later discovered in Russia). The *Graf Zeppelin II* would be dismantled on Goering's order in 1942. The LZ-131, a super zep larger than the *Hindenburg*, was started but never completed.

In the United States, the German-built *Los Angeles*, in storage at Lakehurst, was dismantled late in 1939.

September 22—Maj. Gen. Henry H. "Hap" Arnold was appointed chief of the U.S. Army Air Corps, succeeding Maj. Gen. Oscar Westover, who had been killed the day before in an air accident at Burbank, California.

September 30—Britain's Prime Minister Neville Chamberlain signed an agreement at Munich reneging on pledges to Czechoslovakia, agreeing to Hitler's occupation of the Czech Sudetenland with the French concurring. Chamberlain said that the act meant ". . . peace for our time," but it may have been a bid for time because the British and French were not prepared for a showdown with Hitler.

October 17—Trans-Canada Air Lines began mail and freight service between Montreal and Vancouver. Passenger service was added later.

1939

January 26—The Canadian Government authorized the Royal Canadian Air Force to increase its uniformed strength to a total of 269 officers and 2,043 men.

March 26—In Spain, Loyalist forces in Madrid surrendered to Gen. Franco's forces. Official end to the civil war was announced April 2nd.

April 26—In Germany, the experimental Messerschmitt Me 209V1 (identified to the world for propaganda purposes as the Me 109R) established an absolute world's speed record of 469.22 mph. Its pilot was Fritz Wendel.

May 20—The Pan Am flying boat *Yankee Clipper* (Boeing Model 314) left New York on the first flight of regularly scheduled mail service to Europe. On June 30 the *Dixie Clipper* arrived at Marseilles, France, with the first load of passengers. Round trip fare was $675. Then, on August 30 of that year the Pan Am flying boat *California Clipper* arrived at Auckland, New Zealand, initiating fortnightly service from San Francisco.

August 27—The first flight by a jet-propelled aircraft was made secretly in Germany. The aircraft was a Heinkel He 178, flown at Rostock by Capt. Warsitz. The first British jet was the Gloster E28/39, which flew at Cranwell May 15, 1941. The first American jet was the Bell XP-59A first flown by Robert Stanley at Muroc, California, on October 1, 1941. The Bell was fitted with engines built by GE and copied from the British Whittle.

September 1—Germany invaded Poland to start the Second World War.

September 3—Great Britain, France, Australia, and New Zealand declared war on Germany. Japan said it would remain neutral.

September 5—President F.D. Roosevelt proclaimed the neutrality of the United States in the European war and directed the Navy to organize a "neutrality patrol" of the sea approaches to the United States and the West Indies.

September 28—Warsaw surrendered; Germany and Russia divided up Poland.

November 30—Russia invaded Finland without warning.

1940

March 26—The airlines of the United States completed one year's operation without a fatality.

April 9—German forces overran Denmark and invaded Norway.

April 14—The first U.S. air unit arrived in Fairbanks, Alaska. This was the 28th Composite Group, equipped with 12 Douglas B-18 bombers and 20 Curtiss P-36A pursuits (fighters).

April 25—The USS *Wasp* (CV-7), America's seventh aircraft carrier, was commissioned at Boston with Capt. J.W. Reeves, Jr., commanding.

May 10—Winston Churchill became Britain's Prime Minister and Minister of Defense as Germany invaded Holland, Belgium, and Luxembourg.

May 13—Igor Sikorsky made the first free flight in his VS-300 helicopter at Stratford, Connecticut.

May 30–June 4—Dunkirk evacuation. The mechanized German Army's "Lightning Warfare" tactics (*blitzkrieg*) overwhelmed the French and British forces on the Continent and the British made a desperate evacuation at the Port of Dunkirk, saving four-fifths (338,226) of the British forces along with some French and Poles. Almost all of their equipment was left behind. The British also began evacuation of their troops in Norway at this time.

June 10—Italy declared war on the Allies.

June 14—The Germans entered Paris.

June 22—The French accepted German Armistice terms in the same railway coach in the Compiegne Forrest in which the 1919 Treaty of Versailles was signed following Germany's defeat in WWI. Hostilities ended at 1:35 A.M. on June 25.

August 13—The Battle of Britain began, according to the Germans. The British regard the start of the Battle of Britain as July 10, when the Luftwaffe began concentrated attacks on Channel shipping and southern British ports. September 15 saw the showdown air battles over England; the Luftwaffe was unable to defeat the Royal Air Force, and on September 17 Hitler "postponed" his planned invasion of the British Isles ("Operation Sea Lion"). The Battle of Britain was over by October 31.

August 20—Prime Minister Winston Churchill said in the House of Commons: "The gratitude of every home in our Island, in our Empire, and indeed throughout the world, except in the abodes of the guilty, goes out to the British airmen who, undaunted by odds, unwearied in their constant challenge and mortal danger, are turning the tide of world war by their prowess and devotion. Never in the field of human conflict was so much owed by so many to so few."

SIGNIFICANT EVENTS IN AVIATION

The Sikorsky VS-300 helicopter first flew, tethered, in September 1939. Pictured is the modified version, which flew in free flight in May 1940 with Igor Sikorsky at the controls. (Photo courtesy United Technologies)

September 2—The U.S. traded 50 overage destroyers to Great Britain for 99-year leases on naval and air bases in the Atlantic and Caribbean. To that date, the British had purchased 2,633 airplanes in the United States.

September 27—A Tripartite Pact between Germany, Italy, and Japan for mutual cooperation in the establishment of a "new world order" was signed in Berlin.

A 1940 Dart, flown by Charles Hellinger of Mansfield, Ohio, arrives at a 1966 antiquers' meet at Otumwa, Iowa. The Dart was an Al Mooney design that first appeared in 1936, while Mooney worked for Monocoupe. In 1938 the Dart design was purchased by the Culver Aircraft Company of Columbus, Ohio, and Mooney (who had, as a 19-year-old, started with Eaglerock in 1926) went with Culver to design the Cadet. He later formed the post-WWII Mooney Aircraft Company.

October 8—The first RAF squadron entirely manned by American volunteers was formed as the Eagle Squadron. It would later become the U.S. 4th Fighter Group.

November 5—Roosevelt was re-elected President of the United States. Churchill announced that 14,000 civilians had been killed during air raids on Britain, and 20,000 seriously wounded, about four-fifths of them in London.

November 25—The deHavilland Mosquito twin-engine fighter-bomber made its first flight as a prototype. Deliveries to the RAF began in July 1941.

1941

March 11—The "Lend-Lease" bill was signed by President Roosevelt. It allowed the U.S. to transfer, lease, or lend war material to any country whose defense was considered vital to the defense of the United States.

April 1—Mexico agreed to permit the United States to transport military supplies and troops across Mexico.

Significant Events in Aviation

The Beech Model 18 "Twin Beech" was modified for military use during WWII. Pictured is the Navy JRB-2. For the USAAF it was the AT-7 as a bombardier trainer, AT-11 as a navigational trainer, C-45 as a light transport, and F-2 for photoreconnaissance. (Beech photo)

May 27—Roosevelt proclaimed that an unlimited national emergency confronted the United States.

June 16—Roosevelt ordered the closing, by July 15, of all German consulates and other German organizations in the United States.

June 20—The U.S. Army Air Corps became the U.S. Army Air Force under Maj. Gen. H.H. Arnold.

July 1—The first U.S. overseas air transport services began with a flight of B-24 bombers led by Col. Caleb V. Haynes from Washington, D.C. to Scotland. The Army Air Forces Ferry Command would begin flights over the Himalayas in May 1942 as the Assam-Burma-China Ferry Command, and then as the Air Transport Command and Naval Air Transport Service, would expand to support the United States and Allied forces in all theaters of war. After WWII, it would become the Military Air Transport Service (MATS).

July 7—Occupation of Iceland by U.S. Marines was announced in Washington. Thirty P-40s of the 33rd Pursuit Squadron flew off the deck of the *Wasp* to Reykjavik a week later, and U.S. Navy Patrol Squadrons 73 and 74 began routine patrols from Iceland over North Atlantic ship convoy routes.

August 9–12—Churchill and Roosevelt met on warships in Placentia Bay, Newfoundland, and drafted the Atlantic Charter, a declaration of their war and peace positions.

October 20—The USS *Hornet* (CV-8) was commissioned at Norfolk, Capt. Marc A. Mitscher commanding.

November 26—Six Japanese carriers and their escorts sailed from the Kurile Islands to attack Pearl Harbor.

December 1—The Civil Air Patrol was formed in the U.S. under the office of Civilian Defense. These civilian pilots and observers carried out coastal, border, and forest patrols, courier flights, target towing, and other tasks. The CAP was transferred to the War Department in April 1943.

December 7—Japanese carrier aircraft launched a devastating surprise attack on U.S. Navy ships at Pearl Harbor and on the military and air installations in the area.

December 8—The U.S. Congress declared a state of war with Japan.

December 8—At midday, Japanese aircraft attacked Clark and Iba Fields on Luzon in the Philippines, destroying 16 of 17 B-17s and 31 of 38 P-40s.

December 11—Germany and Italy declared war on the United States.

December 22—Japanese forces captured Wake Island. Some 400 U.S. Marines, with a few airplanes, had held out for two weeks.

1942

February 27—The USS *Langley* was sunk by enemy aircraft 74 miles from her destination while transporting 32 AAF P-40s to Tjilatjap, Java.

April 18—First U.S. raid on Tokyo. From a position at sea 668 miles from Tokyo, the *Hornet* launched 16 B-25s led by Lt. Col. J.H. Doolittle for the first attack on the Japanese homeland.

May 4-8—Battle of the Coral Sea. In the first naval battle in history fought without opposing ships making contact, U.S. carrier forces foiled a Japanese attempt to land at Port Moresby (the staging point for an invasion of Australia). The U.S. Navy lost the *Lexington* and the *Yorktown* was damaged in exchange for the sinking of a small enemy carrier, the *Soho*, and most of the Japanese air groups. Although the score seemed to favor the Japanese, they were never able to threaten an invasion of Australia again, and Japan could ill afford the loss of so many of her most experienced navy pilots.

May 6—The Japanese captured Corregidor in Manila Bay and took 11,574 American and Filipino prisoners.

June 3-6—The Battle of Midway. Japan's Adm. Isoroku Yamamoto assembled a battle fleet of immense proportions for the invasion of Midway Island in the Central Pacific: eight aircraft carriers; 10 battleships, 24 battle cruisers, 70 destroyers, 15 submarines, plus eight tankers, 40 troop transports, and supporting vessels for a total of 185 ships and 450 aircraft. Opposing this armada, the U.S. Navy could muster but three carriers (*Enterprise*, *Hornet*, and the hastily-repaired *Yorktown*), no battleships, 13 cruisers, 24 destroyers, 25 submarines, three tankers, and supporting vessels for a total of 68 ships and 306 airplanes, including 73 based on Midway.

Significant Events in Aviation 37

Adm. Chester Nimitz was able to plan a successful ambush of this superior enemy force because U.S. Navy cryptographers had partially deciphered the Japanese naval code. Believing that it was they who possessed the advantage of surprise, the Japanese had lost all four carriers of their strike force before they knew they had been attacked by three U.S. carriers. The Japanese also lost 258 aircraft and most of their pilots. The United States lost the *Yorktown* (torpedoed by an enemy submarine as it was being towed, crewless, to port), and 92 carrier-based airplanes, plus 40 Midway-based airplanes.

August 7, 1942–February 9, 1943—Guadalcanal Campaign. Air support for the U.S. Marines' first amphibious landing of WWII was provided by three carriers and by Navy, Marine, and Army aircraft operating from bases in New Caledonia and the New Hebrides. On August 9th the carriers withdrew from direct support, but remained in the area with space to maneuver against the enemy, who made a maximum effort to repulse the Americans, and participated in several of the naval engagements fought over the island. *Saratoga* sank the Japanese light carrier *Ryujo* during the Battle of the Eastern Solomons (23-25 August); *Enterprise* was hit by carrier-based bombers (24 August) and forced to retire; *Saratoga* was damaged by a submarine torpedo on August 31 and forced to retire, and *Wasp* was sunk by a submarine on September 15 while escorting a troop convoy to Guadalcanal. *Hornet*'s air groups struck at targets in the Buin-Tonolei-Faisi area on October 5, attacked Japanese transports and supply dumps on Guadalcanal, destroyed a concentration of seaplanes at Rekata Bay on October 16 and, with *Enterprise*, fought in the Battle of Santa Cruz on October 26-27, in which she was sunk by air attack. In final carrier actions of the campaign, *Enterprise* took part in the last stages of the Naval Battle for Guadalcanal (12-15 November), assisting in sinking 89,000 tons of war and cargo ships, and in the Battle of Rennell Island (29-30 January), in which two escort carriers also participated.

Ashore, air support came from all U.S. services, Navy patrol squadrons operating from sheltered coves and harbors. Marine, Navy, and Air Force units flew from Henderson Field on Guadalcanal until the island was declared secured on February 9, 1943.

September 21—The prototype of the Boeing B-29 Superfortress first flew at Seattle.

November 4—After 12 days of intense fighting, the British 8th Army broke out of its defensive position at Al Alamein, Egypt, and began to pursue Field Marshal Rommel's Afrika Korps and its Italian allies into Libya.

November 8—Operation Torch, the invasion of French North Africa, began during the early morning hours as U.S. troops went ashore at numerous points, the main objectives being Casablanca, Oran, and Algiers. The landings were assisted by the British Navy and air forces. Lt. Gen. Dwight D. Eisenhower was Torch commander.

December 31—The USS *Essex* (CV-9), Capt. D.B. Duncan commanding, was commissioned at Norfolk, the first of 17 carriers of this class commissioned during WWII.

1943

January 9—The first Lockheed Constellation, Model 49, fitted with four Wright R-3350 piston engines of 2,000 hp each, and converted to a C-69 military transport, made its maiden flight at Burbank, California.

January 14-24—The Casablanca Conference: Roosevelt and Churchill mapped out their priorities, which included the unconditional surrender of Germany, high priority for antisubmarine operations, assembly of a powerful force for the invasion of Europe, etc.

38 1001 Flying Facts and Firsts

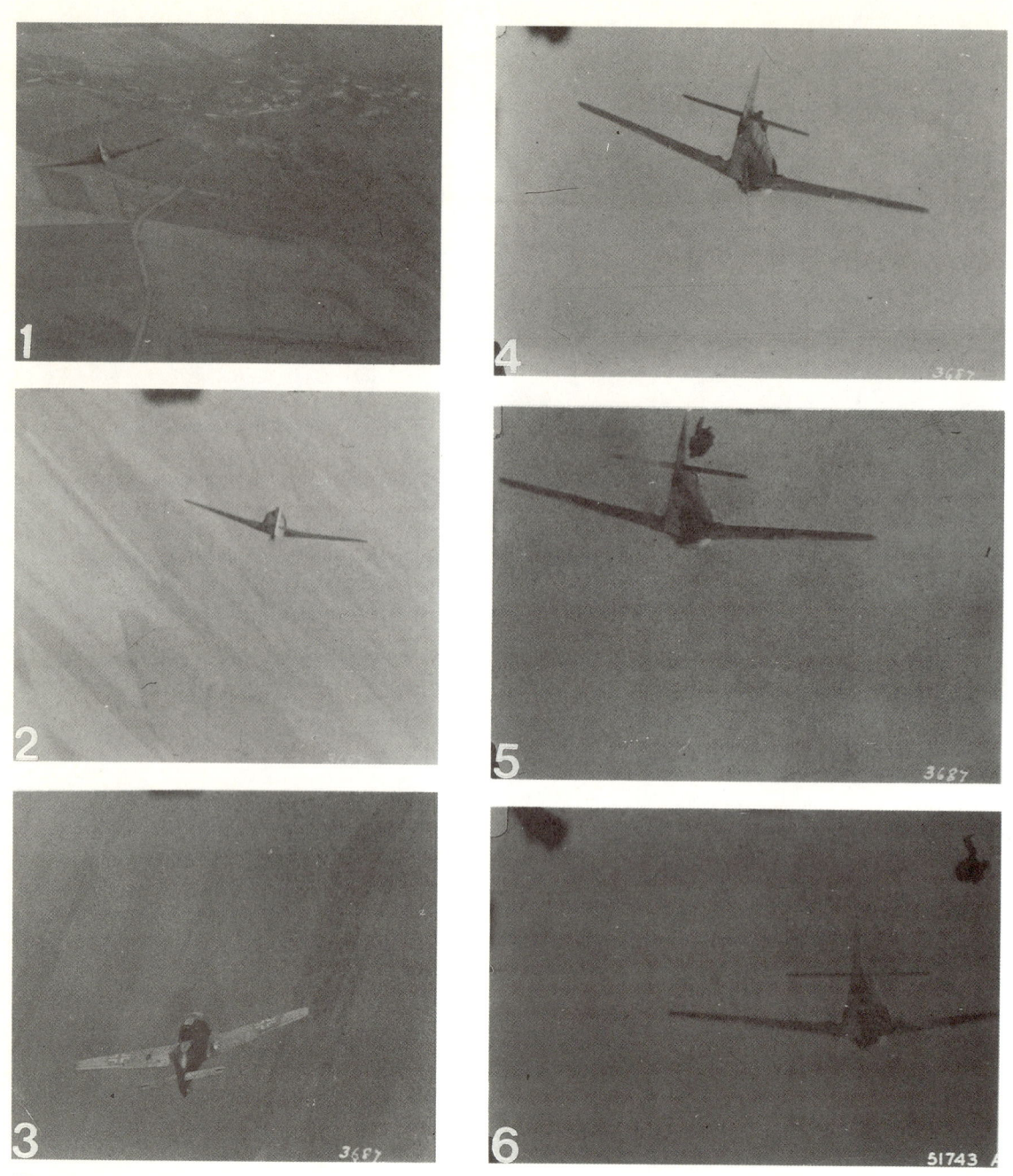

This is the film sequence from the camera gun as a U.S. fighter pilot shoots down a German FW 190 and enemy pilot bails out with flame showing beneath right wing root. Victorious American was Capt. Alvin Jucheim of Grenada, Mississippi. (USAF)

Significant Events in Aviation

Gen. Dwight Eisenhower congratulates Lt. Charles B. Hall on his three victories against German fighters (two FW 190s and an Me 109) and presents Hall with the Distinguished Flying Cross. Hall served with the 99th Fighter Squadron, an all-black unit that saw action in North Africa and Italy flying P-40s and P-51s. Later, as more black pilots were trained, the 332nd Fighter Group was activated under the command of Col. Benjamin O. Davis, Jr. Of the 992 pilot graduates of Tuskegee Institute, 450 went overseas during WWII. (USAF)

January 27—First American air raid on Germany during WWII; it was against Wilhelmshaven and other targets in northern Germany.

February 1–November 1—In a series of amphibious operations, supported by Army, Navy, and Marine aircraft, U.S. Central Pacific Forces moved from Guadalcanal up the Solomon Islands towards the Japanese naval base at Rabaul. Beginning with the unopposed landing in the Russells (February 21), these forces leapfrogged through the islands, establishing bases and airfields as they went, reaching Bougainville, where landings on Cape Torokina were additionally supported by carrier air strikes on November 1.

March 10—The U.S. 14th Air Force formed in China under Maj. Gen. Claire Chennault.

A B-26 Marauder plunges earthward after taking a hit from enemy flak, which blasted away the left engine. This machine is painted with "invasion stripes," a measure taken at the time of the invasion of Europe (largely in vain) to prevent friendly ground troops from firing on their own airplanes. (USAF)

Significant Events in Aviation

April 18—The Palm Sunday Massacre resulted when 46 P-40 Warhawks from the 57th and 324th Fighter Groups in North Africa, with 12 RAF Spitfires flying top cover, destroyed 58 German Ju 52 trimotor transports, 14 Me 109s, and two Me 110s (plus 29 enemy craft damaged) out of a force of 90 Ju 52s and 30 escorting fighters that were attempting to supply Rommel's forces from Sicily. The action took place off Cape Bon, Tunisia. Six Warhawks were lost.

May 3—Lt. Gen. Frank M. Andrews, commanding the European Theater of Operations, U.S. Army, was killed in an air crash in Iceland. Andrews' job would go to Eisenhower.

May 13—German and Italian forces in North Africa surrendered in Tunisia; 270,000 prisoners were taken after the 1,200-mile pincer is closed by Montgomery's 8th British Army advancing from the east, and Eisenhower's forces closing from the west. An ailing Rommel had earlier escaped to Italy.

June 28—Aerial photos of the German research facility at Peenemunde on the Baltic revealed large rockets which, it was feared, could have a range of up to 130 miles.

June 28—A change in the design of the U.S. national star insignia added white rectangles to the left and right sides of the blue circular field to form a horizontal bar, with a red border stripe around the entire design. The following September, Insignia Blue was substituted for the red.

July 10—Operation Husky, the occupation of Sicily, began as the U.S. 82nd Airborne Division was flown at night and in bad weather from North Africa. Of the 137 gliders released, 69 went down at sea.

July 18—The U.S. Navy blimp K-74, while on night patrol off the Florida coast, attacked a surfaced U-boat (U-134), and in the gun duel that followed was hit and brought down, the only Navy airship lost to enemy action in WWII. The damaged U-134 was later sunk by British bombers.

July 19—The first air raid on Rome was made by 158 B-17s flying from North Africa, along with 112 B-24s.

July 25—The Italians deposed their dictator, Benito Mussolini; the new Prime Minister, Marshal Badoglio, interned Mussolini on the Island of Ponza, west of Naples. The Germans rescued Mussolini on September 12 from the more secure internment at La Maddelena.

August 1—The U.S. 9th Air Force attacked the oil refineries at Ploesti, Rumania. Of 177 aircraft dispatched, 56 were lost. The craft were based at Benghazi.

August 17—Unescorted by fighters, 230 8th Air Force B-17s attacked the ball bearing factories at Schweinfurt, Germany, and 146 B-17s raided the fighter airplane factory complex at Regensburg. The Schweinfurt mission cost 36 Fortresses destroyed, 100 damaged, while the Regensburg strike cost 24 Fortresses. A return mission to Schweinfurt on October 14 by 291 Fortresses cost another 60 destroyed.

September 8—Italy's unconditional surrender was announced at 5:30 P.M. by Gen. Eisenhower in a broadcast over Algiers Radio. Italy, however, was occupied by 26 German divisions.

42 **1001 Flying Facts and Firsts**

An F4F Navy Wildcat fighter strikes the elevated barrels of twin 40mm Bofors cannon during wave-off from a landing on the escort carrier Altamaha, May 17, 1943. The Wildcat went into the sea, but its pilot was rescued.

October 16—The U.S. Navy accepted its first helicopter, a Sikorsky YR-4B (HNS-1), at Bridgeport, Connecticut.

November 18-26—Occupation of the Gilbert Islands began with the support of six heavy and five light aircraft carriers. Marines and Army troops went ashore on Tarawa and Makin Atolls on the 20th.

November 27—President Roosevelt and Prime Minister Churchill flew by different routes from Egypt to meet with Russia's dictator Stalin at Teheran.

December 13—The U.S. 8th and 9th Air Forces in Britain dispatched 1,462 aircraft, the largest force used by the Allies to that time, for attacks against Kiel, Bremen, Hamburg, and Schipol Airfield in Holland.

December 24-29—During this period, the following appointments were announced:

- Gen. Dwight D. Eisenhower, Supreme Allied Commander of the British and American forces for the liberation of France.
- Air Chief Marshall Sir Arthur Tedder, Deputy Supreme Commander.
- Adm. Sir Bertram Ramsay, Naval C-in-C under Eisenhower.
- Gen. Sir Bernard Montgomery, C-in-C British Armies under Eisenhower.
- Lt. Gen. Carl Spaatz, C-in-C U.S. strategic bombing force.
- Maj. Gen. James Doolittle, commanding general, 8th Air Force.
- Gen. Sir Harold Alexander, C-in-C Allied Armies, Italy.
- Lt. Gen. Ira Eaker, C-in-C Allied air forces, Mediterranean.
- Lt. Gen. Nathan F. Twining, commanding general, U.S. 15th Air Force.

1944

January 3—The first helicopter mercy mission occurred when Cmdr. Frank A. Erickson of the U.S. Coast Guard, flying an HNS-1 helicopter, made an emergency delivery of 40 units of blood plasma from lower Manhattan Island to Sandy Hook for the survivors of an explosion on the destroyer *Turner*. The flight was made through sleet and snow squalls that had grounded all other aircraft in the area.

January 9—First flight of the Lockheed P-80 Shooting Star, the first combat jet acquired by the U.S. Army Air Forces.

January 11—Eight hundred bombers of the U.S. 8th Air Force, escorted by Mustangs, attacked aircraft factories at Halberstadt, Brunswick, and Oschersleben at the cost of 55 bombers and five fighters.

January 22-February 17—Occupation of the Marshall Islands: Six heavy and six light carriers, in four groups of Task Force 58, commanded by Rear Adm. Marc Mitschner, opened the campaign for the Marshalls with attacks on Maloelap, Kwajalein, and Wotje, joined on the following day by eight escort carriers of the Joint Expeditionary Force. Kwajalein and Majuro Atolls were seized on the 31st, and Eniweto on February 17, along with the initial air strikes on Truk by three fast carrier groups under Vice Adm. Spruance.

January 22—About 50,000 troops of the U.S. 5th Army, with sea and air support, went ashore at Anzio, about 30 miles south of Rome. This force was pinned down by the Germans and avoided annihilation by the narrowest of margins. With good air support from Eaker's command, the 5th Army finally broke out, aided by British and Polish forces, and reached Rome on June 4th.

February 3—The U.S. 8th Air Force bombed Wilhelmshaven.

February 8—The 8th Air Force bombed Frankfurt.

February 22—8th and 9th Air Force bombers attacked aircraft plants in Halberstadt and Bernbur. 15th Air Force bombers struck Regensburg.

The above February bombing dates are representative. A complete list of the U.S. air strikes against European targets is much too long and too repetitive for inclusion here. Along with the U.S. strategic air offensive, carried out by day, the RAF was concurrently attacking the common enemy by night, while the tactical air units, both British and American, were taking out bridges, trains, troop concentrations, etc., in a more direct support of the ground armies.

April 4—The U.S. 20th Air Force was formed for the strategic bombing of Japan. Equipped with Boeing B-29 Superfortresses, based in India, later operating from bases in the Marianas with addition of the 21st AF, these units would be directed by the U.S. Chiefs of Staff in Washington, D.C. There would be no intermediate command.

May 29—The only carrier lost in the Atlantic, the USS *Block Island* (CVE-21), was torpedoed by a German U-boat while engaged in hunter-killer operations in the Azores area.

June 6—D-Day: More than 4,000 ships and countless smaller vessels took British and American troops and supplies across the English Channel for the invasion of Europe, the first landings achieved at 6:30 A.M.. The main forces landed at various points on the Normandy Coast, preceded and followed by American and British airborne units. Allied air supremacy was virtually complete, totalling 14,647 sorties.

June 10—Allied aircraft began operating from airstrips and airfields in Normandy built and captured since D-Day.

June 13—The first German flying bomb, the V-1, exploded in Britain at Swanscombe, near Gravesend, at 4:18 A.M.

June 10-August 10—Occupation of the Marianas included the Battle of the Philippine Sea (June 19-20), in which Mitschner's Task Force 58, encompassing seven heavy and eight light carriers, sank the Japanese carrier *Hiyo* and downed 402 enemy aircraft. U.S. troops landed on Guam July 21, and on Tinian July 24. When Guam was secured, August 10, U.S. carrier aircraft had accounted for 110,000 tons of enemy shipping sunk and 1,223 aircraft destroyed.

July 15—The U.S. 15th Air Force attacked the Ploesti oil complex in Rumania, the fourth such attack (July 2, '43; May 5, '44, and May 31, '44).

July 17—Napalm was used for the first time, dropped by P-38 Lightnings on a fuel depot at Coutances, near St. Lo.

August 14-15—Operation Dragoon, the Allied landings in the south of France, began with the dropping of parachutists, who secured areas for glider troops. More than 9,000 airborne troops participated. Opposition was light.

September 8—The first German V-2 rocket launched against London fell in Chiswick at 6:40 P.M. A few seconds later, another fell at Epping. The first one fired operationally had been directed at Paris earlier that day.

October 10–November 25—Occupation of Leyte and resulting sea battles: Vice Adm. Mitschner's Task Force 38, built around 17 aircraft carriers, launched air strikes that destroyed 438 enemy aircraft in the air and 366 on the ground in northern Luzon, Philippines, and on Formosa. Fast Carrier support of the ground operation for the retaking of the Philippines was also provided by 18 escort carriers in Rear Adm. T.L. Sprague's Task Group 77.4. Elements of the 7th Fleet, and the Fast Carrier Task Force of the 3rd Fleet, fought the Battle For Leyte Gulf in which the *Princeton* (CVL-23) was lost in exchange for the 63,000-ton Japanese battleship *Musashi* and an escorting destroyer (October 24). In the related Battle of Surigao Strait on October 25, the 7th Fleet surface elements sank two enemy battleships and three destroyers.

Also on the 25th of October, in a sea battle off Samar, Vice Adm. W.F. Halsey, then in command of TG 77.4, lost the *Gambier Bay* (CVE-73) and two destroyers while his carrier units sank three Japanese heavy cruisers.

At the same time, the Fast Carrier Force met the Northern Force in the Battle Off Cape Engano, sinking the heavy carrier *Zuikaku* and light carriers *Chiyoda*, *Zuiho*, and *Chitose*, the latter with the help of cruiser gunfire.

Off Leyte, kamikaze pilots, in the first planned suicide attacks of the war, struck at the escort carriers and sank the *St. Lo* (CVE-63) and damaged the *Sangamon*, *Suwannee*, *Santee*, *White Plains*, *Kalinin Bay*, and *Kitkun Bay*.

As remnant of the Japanese Fleet limped homeward through the Central Philippines on October 26–27, U.S. carrier aircraft sank a light cruiser and four destroyers to bring the enemy's battle losses to 26 major combatant ships totalling over 300,000 tons, plus 1,046 aircraft destroyed.

During November, TF 38, then under Vice Adm. J.S. McCain, struck at airfields on Luzon and Mindoro, plus ships in Manila Bay, sinking three cruisers, eight destroyers, 20 merchant ships, and a number of auxiliaries. They wound up the month with an aerial score of 770 enemy aircraft—but not without a price: Kamikaze attacks damaged the carriers *Intrepid* (twice), *Franklin*, *Belleau Wood*, the new *Lexington*, *Essex*, and *Cabot*.

Meanwhile, by October of this year, both the Americans and British were mounting 1,000-plane bombing raids on Germany while suffering minimal losses to the severely weakened Luftwaffe.

December 16—The German Army's last offensive of the war was launched by Field Marshal von Runstedt in the Ardennes, and became known as the "Battle of the Bulge."

1945

January 3–22—Invasion of Luzon: The 7th Fleet escort carriers of TG 77.4, with help from fast carriers in TF 38, covered landings in Lingayen Gulf and the troops' advance inland with a total of 29 heavy and escort carriers. Kamikazes sank the *Ommaney Bay* (CVE-79) and damaged seven other carriers. During the three-week operation, 600 enemy aircraft were destroyed, along with 325,000 tons of shipping.

February 2—President Roosevelt arrived by sea at Malta. That night, he and Prime Minister Churchill flew in separate aircraft to Saki Airfield in the Crimea to attend the Yalta Conference, where Roosevelt, sick and debilitated a couple of months before his death, made ruinous concessions to Stalin that haunt the Free World to this day.

February 16–March 16—Capture of Iwo Jima: The U.S. Marine assault on Iwo was supported by 11 heavy, five light, and one night carrier in Vice Adm. Mitschner's TG 58,

The aircraft carrier Franklin *lists to port as fires rage following a kamikaze attack, March 19, 1945. During the Okinawan Campaign, March 18 through June 21, the Japanese expended more than 2,000 aircraft and pilots in suicide attacks against American warships. The* Franklin *had been hit by kamikaze attack the previous November. She survived both.* (U.S. Navy)

with 11 escort carriers in Rear Adm. C.T. Durgin's TG 52.2, plus shore-based aircraft of TG 50.5, and Army and Marine aircraft from Saipan. A total of 648 enemy aircraft were destroyed, along with 30,000 tons of merchant shipping. Kamikazes sank the escort carrier *Bismark Sea*, and damaged *Lunga Point* and *Saratoga*.

March 21–June 21—The Okinawa Campaign: The last—and, for the U.S. Navy, the most violent—of the major amphibious campaigns of WWII was supported by three separately operating carrier forces, tender-based patrol squadrons, and by Marine and Army air units.

The fast carriers of Mitschner's TF 58 began the attack with 10 heavy and six light carriers, destroying 482 enemy aircraft by air attack, and 46 ships' gunfire. During these preliminaries, kamikazes and *baka* flying bombs (first observed on March 21) seriously damaged the carrier *Franklin* and scored hits on four others. For the next three months, the fast carrier force operated continuously in a 60-square-mile area northeast of Okinawa and within 250 miles of Japan.

On March 27, Durgin's TG 52.1, with 18 escort carriers, joined the action, along with British TF 57 (Vice Adm. H.B. Rawlings, RN) with four carriers (all four of which took kamikaze hits but remained operational).

On April 1, Army and Marine Corps troops landed on the western shores. Strong enemy opposition developed in the first of a series of mass suicide attacks involving some 400 aircraft. In seven mass raids interspersed by smaller, scattered ones, April 6 through May 28, the Japanese expended some 1,500 aircraft, mostly against supporting naval forces. Thus, the U.S. Navy took the heaviest punishment in its history (a story that was minimized via heavy censorship at the time). Although TF 58 lost no ship during the campaign, eight heavy and one light carriers were hit, along with three light carriers of TF 52.

A task force of one light cruiser, eight destroyers, and *Yamato*, the world's largest battleship, made what was to be the last sortie of the Japanese Navy and was soundly beaten by carrier aircraft in the Battle of the East China Sea on April 7. Only four Japanese destroyers survived.

Carrier aircraft had flown over 40,000 sorties and destroyed 2,516 enemy aircraft. Several records for continuous operations in an active combat area were marked up by the carriers during the campaign; the most outstanding was logged by the *Essex* with 79 consecutive days.

The newly developed helicopter saw limited service in WWII with both U.S. and German forces. This Sikorsky R-6 lands on a rice paddy levee in China, June 4, 1945. (USAF)

March 27—The last German rocket to fall in Britain came down at Orpington, Kent at 4:54 P.M. Between September 8, 1944, and March 27, 1945, 1,115 rockets arrived in England, and some 500 reach London. British casualties were 2,855 killed and 6,268 seriously injured. Over 1,500 V-2s were launched against Antwerp, Belgium.

The last flying bomb (V-1) to arrive over Britain was destroyed near Sittingbourne, Kent, on March 29, 1945. Between June 13, 1944, and March 29, 1945, at least 9,200 of these "vengeance" weapons were fired at England from launching sites in France, Belgium, and Holland, and by German aircraft. More than 1,000 fell near their launching sites and some fell into the sea after malfunctioning. Of those reaching Britain, 3,957 were destroyed—1,878 by ground fire, 1,847 by fighters, and 232 by balloon cables. The V-1s killed 6,139 Britons, and seriously injured 17,239. Nearly 12,000 flying bombs were aimed at cities in Belgium, two-thirds against Antwerp.

April 12—President Roosevelt died at Warm Springs, Georgia, of a cerebral hemorrhage at age 63. Vice President Harry Truman became President of the United States.

April 28—Mussolini and his mistress, Clara Petacci, were captured by Italian communists at Dongo, near Lake Como, and shot.

April 29—Hitler and Eva Braun, whom he had recently married, committed suicide in the air raid shelter under the Chancellery in Berlin. Their bodies were burned.

May 8—V-E Day: The President proclaimed an end of the war in Europe. The agreement for the unconditional surrender of the German armed forces was signed at Gen. Dwight D. Eisenhower's headquarters near Rheims, France, at 1:41 A.M., May 7.

German casualties totalled over five million: 3,200,000 killed or missing in action; 500,000 civilians killed in bombing raids, and about 200,000 disabled war veterans. These figures, provided by the Federal Bureau of Statistics in Bonn, are on the consecutive side, the Germans say.

The U.S. Strategic Bombing Survey, ordered by the President at the close of WWII, lists 18,000 American and 22,000 British airplanes lost or damaged beyond repair; 79,265 American and 79,281 British airmen lost in action. German aircraft losses were placed at 57,000, including those destroyed on the ground.

May 25—The U.S. Joint Chiefs of Staff promulgated a plan for the invasion of Japan. Target date was November 1, 1945.

May 25—An incendiary bomb raid on Tokyo by more than 500 B-29s of the 21st Bomber Command destroyed almost 17 square miles of the city. On this raid, and the five previous fire-bomb raids, over half of the city's built-up area was destroyed. On the 29th, a similar raid on Yokohama by 450 Superforts burned nearly seven square miles of that city.

May 31—The U.S. War Department announced that a woman and five children had been killed on March 5 near Lake View, Oregon, by a Japanese bomb-carrying balloon. An unknown number of these free balloons was released in Japan for the purpose of (hopefully) starting fires in the heavily forested areas of Canada and the northwestern United States.

June 28—Gen. MacArthur announced that Japanese resistance on Luzon, Philippines, had ceased.

July 28—A B-25 Mitchell medium bomber, in conditions of poor visibility, struck the 79th story of the Empire State Building in New York City. Its crew of six were killed, along with 13 people killed and 26 injured in the building and in the street below.

August 6—The first atom bomb was dropped on Hiroshima, Honshu, at 8:15 A.M. from the B-29 *Enola Gay*, flying 31,000 feet and commanded by Col. Paul W. Tibbets. The device was timed to detonate at 2,000 feet above the surface. Japanese estimates of casualties were 71,739 killed or missing, 68,023 injured. (The Japanese estimated that the fire-bomb raid on Tokyo, March 9-10, killed 83,739 and injured 40,918).

On August 9, the B-29 *Bock's Car*, flown by Maj. Charles Sweeney, loosed the second A-bomb on Nagasaki, Kyushu, Japan, killing an estimated 25,680 and injuring 23,345.

August 14-15—At midnight, President Truman announced Japan's unconditional surrender. The formal surrender, on board the battleship *Missouri* (inappropriately; it should have taken place aboard an aircraft carrier, the true symbol of victory in the Pacific), was on September 2, V-J Day. The event took place at 10:30 A.M. Tokyo time in Tokyo Bay.

Official Japanese records list 23,835 Japanese Army airplanes expended, of which 16,255 were lost in combat. Japanese Navy airplanes expended totaled 27,120, of which 10,370 were lost in combat. The total American claims, both Air Force and Navy, were 25,345 Japanese aircraft destroyed in combat, so the totals are remarkably close.

Throughout the war, Japanese aircraft production totaled 69,888 units, of which 52,242 were combat aircraft. So great were Japanese losses (50,955 altogether) that at no time did she have more than 8,000 aircraft committed to combat duty.

1946

January 21—The U.S. War Department announced that the Army Air Forces, which had attained a peak strength of almost 2,400,000 during WWII, had been reduced to 900,000 and would be further reduced to no more than 400,000.

Between July 1, 1940, and August 31, 1945, America produced almost 300,000 airplanes for ourselves and for our Allies, 174,768 of which were combat aircraft.

March 21—The U.S. Army Air Forces Strategic Air Command was formed at Bolling Field, Washington, D.C., with Gen. George C. Kenney commanding. (He had been boss of the 13th and Far East Air Forces in the Southwest Pacific during WWII.)

July 1—Operation Crossroads, tests to determine the effects of nuclear weapons on Navy ships, were conducted at Bikini Atoll in the Pacific.

July 21—The first U.S. test of a jet airplane on an aircraft carrier was flown by Lt. Cmdr. James Davidson in an FD-1 Phantom in landings and takeoffs on the USS *Franklin D. Roosevelt*.

August 8—The Consolidated Vultee XB-36, the world's largest bomber, made its maiden flight at Fort Worth, Texas.

September 27—Geoffrey deHavilland, son of Sir Geoffrey deHavilland, was killed when a DH-108 research aircraft broke up in the air over the Thames Estuary.

October 15-16—Ten of the Nazi leaders sentenced to death by the International Military Tribunal at Nuremburg were executed during the night. Reichs-Marshal Hermann Goering, boss of the Luftwaffe, dodged the execution by taking poison in his cell.

50 1001 Flying Facts and Firsts

A forerunner of today's jumbo air transports was the Lockheed Constitution, which made its first flight November 9, 1946 at Burbank, California. It had a span of 189 feet and weighed 92 tons loaded (the C-5A weighs 387 tons and spans 223 feet). Only two Constitutions were built for the Navy. (Lockheed-California Company)

1947

April 15—Trans-Canada Air Lines began scheduled service between Montreal and London flying Canadair DC-4M North Star airliners.

June 8—American Airlines began scheduled service between New York and Los Angeles with Douglas DC-6 airliners.

June 17—Pan AM began round-the-world service from New York.

SIGNIFICANT EVENTS IN AVIATION

The speed of sound was exceeded in level flight for the first time October 14, 1947. Left-to-right: Bell X-1 Project Officer Richard Frost, Capt. Keith Garrison USAF, and Chuck Whats-his-name entering the X-1. (Bell Aerosystems)

July 25—The National Security Act of 1947 was signed by President Truman. It would become effective on September 18th, and provided for separation of the Air Force from the Army, making the new United States Air Force (USAF) a co-equal arm of the U.S. military. This act also established a Secretary of Defense with cabinet rank, plus a Secretary of the Army, Secretary of the Navy, and Secretary of the Air Force, all civilians, without cabinet rank, and appointed by the President. The first Secretary of the Air Force was Mr. Stuart Symington. Maj. Gen. Carl A. Spaatz was appointed as the first Chief of Staff of the USAF. This act also created the Central Intelligence Agency (CIA), among other things.

October 1—The prototype of the North American F-86 jet fighter made its initial flight. This machine would go operational with the 1st FG in February 1949.

October 14—Speed of sound exceeded: USAF Capt. (later, Brig. Gen.) Charles Yeager was the first to exceed the speed of sound. Flying the Bell X-1 research craft *Glamorous Glennis*, dropped from a B-29 at 20,000 feet, Yeager achieved a speed of 697 mph over Muroc Air Force Base (renamed Edwards AFB in 1951 in honor of Capt. Glen W. Edwards, killed test-flying the XB-49 Flying Wing in 1948).

October 21—The Northrop XB-49 flying wing jet bomber made its initial flight at Hawthorne, California.

November 24—The Consolidated Vultee XC-9-9, a cargo version of the B-36 six-engine global bomber, made its first flight at San Diego. This behemoth was not put into production.

December 17—The prototype of the Boeing B-47 jet medium bomber made its first flight at Seattle.

December 31—The total number of passengers carried on the scheduled airlines during 1947 was 21 million, according to the International Civil Aviation Organization (ICAO).

1948

January 15—The Boeing 314 Flying boats operated by BOAC between New York and Bermuda were replaced by Lockheed Constellations. This was the last scheduled service for the American-built flying boats.

March 23—The world altitude record for airplanes was established by Group Capt. John Cunningham of Great Britain, when he flew a deHavilland Vampire jet to 59,446 feet at Hatfield, near London.

May 14—British control of Palestine was terminated, and the independent State of Israel was proclaimed. At midnight, Palestine was invaded by Egypt and other Arab forces, including Lebanese and Jordanians. On the 15th, Tel Aviv was raided by Egyptian Spitfires.

June 1—Idlewild International Airport on Long Island began operation on a limited basis. It would later be named Kennedy International Airport in honor of President John F. Kennedy.

June 18, 1948–May 12, 1949—Berlin Airlift: The Russians attempted to force the Allies out of Berlin, which was/is located 110 miles inside the Russian zone of occupation (at the end of WWII, occupation of Berlin was divided—temporarily, the Allies thought—among the Allies and Russians). Actually the Russians began the squeeze on April 1, 1948, when they stopped railroad passenger service across their zone of occupation to West Germany. Barge traffic on the Elbe River to West Germany was blocked two weeks later. All motor traffic on the autobahn linking Berlin with the Free World was halted on the 19th and, finally, on the 24th of June, 1948, the communists cut the last railroad line to the West. Berlin was isolated—well, almost.

June 26—Three air corridors into West Berlin—one each into the American, British, and French areas of West Germany—could not be closed short of shooting down Allied airplanes, and the Russians were apparently unwilling to risk the consequences of that. The new (June 1) Military Air Transport Service (MATS), born of the wartime ATC and Naval ATS, had an airlift in operation by this date, flying C-47s into Tempelof Aerodrome in Berlin with essential foods and medicines. Within a month, the Berlin Airlift could count more than 100 American C-54s, 82 C-47s, and 50 British heavy haulers such as Avro Tudors, Yorks, and Handley Page Hastings. Aircrews from Australia, New Zealand, and South Africa came to help. By the end of January 1949, Operation Vittles had marked up 60,000 lifegiving flights into West Berlin, and the number of transport aircraft involved had more than doubled. Cargos included a steamroller and candy for Berlin's children. During the 11 months of operation, more than 181,000 round trips were flown, carrying one and a half million tons—mostly food and fuel—to more than two million West Berliners.

The Russians, unable to think of a face-saving way out, ended their blockade at midnight, May 11, 1949. The Soviets' clumsy act gave a firm push to America's B-52 program, and greatly strengthened the NATO alliance.

SIGNIFICANT EVENTS IN AVIATION

December 31—The ICAO reported that the world's scheduled airlines carried 23,500,000 passengers in 1948, and that the average number of passengers per aircraft was 16.5.

1949

Israeli fighters shot down four Spitfires and one Tempest near the Egyptian border, killing two RAF pilots. The Israeli Air Force reportedly possessed about 114 aircraft, including 40 fighters obtained from Czechoslovakia.

January 26—Gen. Hoyt Vandenberg, USAF Chief of Staff, announced that the official color of future Air Force uniforms would be "shade 84 blue."

February 24—An armistice agreement between Egypt and Israel was signed at Rhodes.

March 2—The first nonstop flight around the world was accomplished by USAF Capt. James Gallagher and crew in the B-50 *Lucky Lady II* from Ft. Worth, Texas. Distance covered was 22,500 miles in 94 hours, one minute.

April 4—The North Atlantic Treaty was ratified by Belgium, Britain, Canada, Denmark, France, Holland, Iceland, Italy, Luxembourg, Norway, Portugal, and the United States.

April 26—A lightplane endurance record was established by Dick Reidel and Bill Harris in an Aeronca Sedan *Sunkist Lady* from Fullerton, California. They remained aloft 1,008 hours, one minute (six weeks and one minute). Fuel and food were passed to the fliers from a Jeep.

August 10—The "National Military Establishment," so named under the National Security Act of 1947, was renamed "Department of Defense."

September 23—President Truman announced that the Soviets had tested an A-bomb.

October 1—After defeating the Nationalist forces of China's Chiang Kai-shek in a 25-year guerilla war, the communist forces of Mao Tse-tung proclaimed the inauguration of the "Peoples' Republic of China" in Peking. Chiang Kai-shek took his followers to the former Japanese Island of Formosa, 100 miles off the coast of the China mainland (Formosa is now Taiwan).

1950

January 15—Gen. Henry H. Arnold died at Sonoma, California.

April 8—A PB4Y Privateer of U.S. Navy Patrol Squadron 26, with 10 aboard, was shot down by Soviet fighters over the Baltic Sea. It was not the first; just a week after WWII ended, the Russians shot down an unarmed B-29 that was dropping food to Allied prisoners in North Korea.

May 15—The Soviets announced that all German prisoners of war had been returned to Germany. More than 200,000 remained unaccounted for, having died in East German camps or Siberia.

June 25—The communist North Koreans invaded South Korea and occupied Kaesong. Russian-built Yak fighters attacked Kimpo Airfield at Seoul, capitol of South Korea. On the 27th, President Truman announced that he had ordered the USAF to aid South Korea.

June 27—The first enemy aircraft shot down in the Korean war was a Yak-9 blasted by USAF pilot Lt. William G. Hudson flying an F-82 Twin Mustang.

June 27-28—The United Nations Security Council voted to go to the aid of the South Koreans. The Soviets walked out prior to the vote and forfeited their chance at a veto.

June 30—President Truman announced that he had, in keeping with the UN Security Council request for support in repelling the communist invaders, authorized the USAF to attack targets in North Korea, the use of U.S. Army ground troops in action to support Republic of Korea (ROK) forces, and had directed a naval blockade of the Korean coast. He appointed Gen. MacArthur as Supreme Commander of all United Nations forces in Korea.

There were four major offensives and counteroffensives in the Korean War: 1) The initial thrust by the North Koreans, which carried all the way to the southern end of the country by September 15, 1950, with the South Korean and UN troops backed into a pocket around Pusan; 2) A UN counteroffensive with an amphibious landing by the U.S. Marines at Inchon, which trapped half of the invader's army and allowed the UN troops to drive the enemy all the way to the Yalu River, which separated North Korea from Manchuria; 3) On November 3, 1950, Communist China entered the war by sending 300,000 troops across the Yalu and pushed the UN forces back into South Korea again by late January 1951; 4) The UN forces counterattacked and once again advanced into North Korea, halting along a line that stabilized by November

This Vought F4U Corsair of the 1st Marine Air Wing returns to Seoul Airport after striking at communist forces 10 miles to the north. (U.S. Marine Corps)

SIGNIFICANT EVENTS IN AVIATION 55

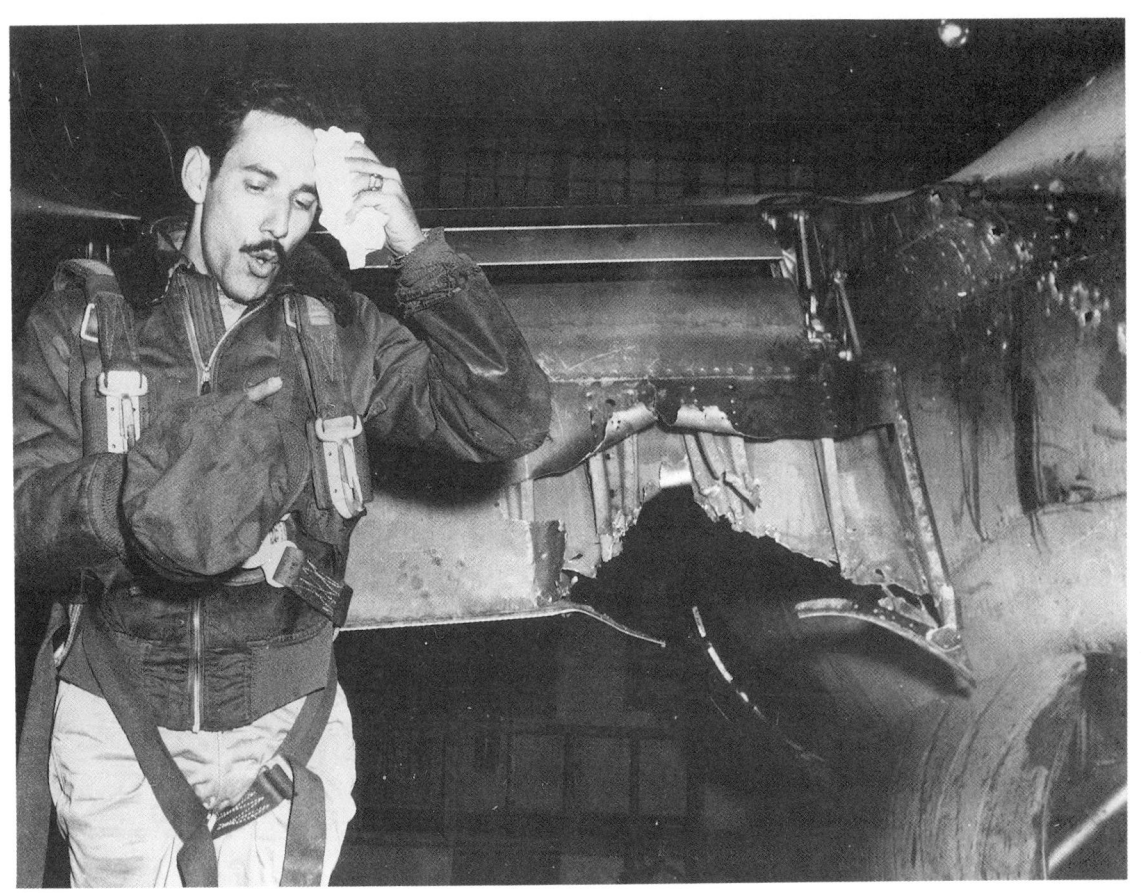

Sgt. Armand deLuna of Los Angeles ruefully regards perforated cap he was wearing when his B-26 was struck by enemy fire over Korea. That would have been a Douglas B-26 (A-26) Invader, not a Martin B-26 Marauder. (USAF)

1951, averaging about 20 miles north of the 38th Parallel (the 38th Parallel was the border between North and South Korea). That would be the position of the opposing forces when a truce was at last agreed upon on July 27, 1953.

The truce talks had dragged out for two years. Then Dwight Eisenhower became President of the United States in January 1953, and "Ike" sent a message to Moscow, Peking, and the North Korean capitol, Pyongyang, saying that if satisfactory progress toward an Armistice was not forthcoming, "... we intend to move decisively and without inhibition in our use of weapons, and will no longer be responsible for confining hostilities to the Korean Peninsula." That was the kind or "negotiation" the communists understood.

Total UN casualties in the Korean War exceeded 550,000, including almost 95,000 dead. U.S. losses numbered 142,091, of whom 33,639 were killed, 103,284 wounded, and 5,178 missing or captured. Most of the casualties occurred during the first year of the fighting. Enemy casualties, including prisoners, exceeded 1,500,000 of which 900,000 were Chinese.

An interesting sidelight of the war was Truman's firing of MacArthur in mid-war (April 11, 1951), when MacArthur publicly disagreed with his Commander-in-Chief over the conduct of the war. MacArthur wanted to invade China, but the President had no intention of widening the conflict. Strangely, the American public seemed to support MacArthur.

The U.S. Navy played a major role in the conduct of the Korean War, committing 11 attack carriers, one light carrier, and five escort carriers during the three-year period. The British carrier *Theseus* also participated.

This was the first jet-vs.-jet airplane war, the Navy's F9F Panthers and the USAF F-86 Sabres accounting for most of the air duels with enemy MiG-15s. Although greatly outnumbered, the F-86s of the 4th Fighter Wing achieved a 10-to-1 kill ratio over the MiGs. (Actually, both Britain and Germany sent jets into combat late in WWII.)

December 31—Total number of passengers carried on the world's scheduled airlines in 1950 was 31,200,000; the average per aircraft was 19.1.

1951

January 31—Capt. Charles Blair, a Pan Am pilot, flew a P-51 Mustang nonstop from New York to London in seven hours, 48 minutes. Then, on May 29, he flew from Bardufoss, Norway, over the North Pole to Fairbanks, Alaska, (3,375 miles) in 10 hours, 29 minutes. Two days later, he landed his Mustang at Idlewild (Kennedy) Airport after flying nonstop from Fairbanks (3,450 miles) in nine hours, 31 minutes.

March 15—A Boeing B-47 jet bomber was refuelled in flight by a Boeing KC-97A piston-engine tanker.

October 6—The Soviets shot down a U.S. Navy Neptune patrol craft of VP-6 over international waters off Siberia.

December 31—The world's scheduled airlines carried 39,900,000 passengers in 1951, averaging 21.9 per aircraft flight.

1952

March 9—Major James Jabara, USAF, the first jet ace with six MiG kills, said that the MiG pilots over North Korea spoke in Russian on their aircraft radios.

April 15—The Boeing YB-52 made its first flight. Although it was constructed after the XB-52, the YB-52 was the first to fly. Rollout was November 29, 1951.

May 2—The first scheduled service with pure jet airliners began by BOAC with deHavilland Comet is between London and Johannesburg. After several unexplained crashes, the Comets were taken out of service, and it was later found that metal fatigue had caused in-flight structural failures.

June 16—Soviet MiG-15 fighters shot down a Swedish Catalina that was searching for a Swedish Dakota (DC-3), also believed downed by the Russians.

July 15–31—The first helicopter crossing of the North Atlantic was accomplished by two Sikorsky S-55s flown by Capt. Vincent McGovern and Lt. Harold Moore, from Westover, Massachusetts, to Prestwick, by way of Labrador, Greenland, and Iceland, in 42 hours, 25 minutes flying time.

October 7—Soviet fighter planes shot down a USAF B-29 six miles off the coast of northern Japan.

October 22—Rolls-Royce released some details of its Conway bypass engine, the first of its kind. By diverting some intake air around the engine into the jetpipe, the exhausting gases were cooled and slowed, resulting in greater efficiency.

December 31—According to the ICAO, the world's scheduled airlines carried 45,000,000 passengers, averaging 23.2 per aircraft, in 1952.

1953

January 20—Gen. Dwight D. Eisenhower was sworn in the office of President of the United States.

May 18—A record speed of 652.5 mph over a 100-kilometer closed course was flown by Miss Jacqueline Cochran (Mrs. Floyd Odum) in an F-86E Sabre at Edwards AFB, California.

May 18—The Douglas DC-7, fitted with four Wright 3,250-hp engines, made its first flight.

May 25—The North American YF-100 Super Sabre, fitted with a P&W J-57 turbine engine, made its first flight.

June 18—The largest number of people killed to date in a single airplane died when a MATS C-124 Globemaster crashed near Tokyo with 129 aboard; none survived.

June 18—The British occupation of Egypt ends and Egypt is proclaimed a republic.

July 11—The first Naval aviator to become a jet ace was Marine Maj. John F. Bolt, who downed his fifth and sixth MiGs over Korea this date.

August 21—A new altitude mark was established when Marine Lt. Cl. Marion E. Carl flew the research craft D-558-2 Skyrocket to 83,235 feet over Edwards AFB, California.

October 24—The prototype YF-102 made by Consolidated first flew at San Diego, California.

December 31—The world's scheduled airlines carried 52,400,000 passengers in 1953, averaging 24.8 per aircraft.

1954

February 7—The Lockheed F-104 Starfighter first flew at Edwards AFB.

March 1; March 20—The United States detonated hydrogen bombs on these dates in the Marshall Islands.

June 24—Colorado Springs was selected as the site for the new Air Force Academy, authorized in a bill signed by President Eisenhower on April 1.

June 24—The Douglas A4D Skyhawk prototype made its first flight.

July 15—The Boeing 707 prototype first flew at Renton, Washington.

July 23—Chinese Communist fighters shot down a Cathay Pacific Airways DC-4, killing 10 of 18 aboard. Three days later, two U.S. Navy Skyraiders, searching for survivors, were attacked by two Chinese Communist fighters. The Americans shot them down.

Another of those good ideas that didn't work too well, the Aerocar had quick disconnects to leave its wings and tailboom at the airport and then operated on the street as a motorcar. It was fitted with a 150-hp 0-320 Lycoming, cruised in air at 105 mph, and could top 60 on the ground. It was built in Longview, Washington. Pusher prop was behind tail; a 1950s effort.

August 2—The Convair XFY-1 vertical takeoff aircraft made its first free vertical takeoff and landing. It was not produced. Ryan built a similar machine. Later, the British *Harrier* concept would prove more practical.

September 4—A U.S. Navy Neptune was shot down by Soviet fighters over the Sea of Japan. Nine of the crew of 10 were rescued.

September 29—The McDonnell F-101 Voodoo, developed from the XF-88, made its maiden flight at St. Louis.

October 23—The Western Powers ended occupation of West Germany (German Federal Republic), and West Germany joined NATO.

November 1—The last Boeing B-29 bomber was retired from service.

November 7—A photorecon version of the B-29 was shot down over the coast of Hokkaido, Japan, with the loss of one crewman.

November 23—Red China announced that 13 Americans had been sentenced to various jail terms for "espionage;" two having been shot down on November 29, 1952, and 11 being the crew of a B-29 shot down over Manchuria January 12, 1953.

December 31—The world's scheduled air carriers transported 59,000,000 passengers in 1954, the average per aircraft being 25.8.

1955

March 22—The U.S. Navy's worst heavier-than-air crash to date occurred when an R6D of VR-3, assigned to MATS, struck Pali Kea Peak 15 miles north of Honolulu at 2:03 A.M., killing 57 passengers and the crew of nine.

April 1—The German airline Lufthansa began domestic service with a Convair 340.

June 22—A U.S. Navy P2V-5 Neptune was shot down by Soviet MiGs in the Aleutian area, crash-landing on St. Lawrence Island with no fatalities.

June 29—The first Boeing B-52 to go operational was delivered to the 93rd Bomb Wing at Castle AFB, California.

July 27—A Lockheed Constellation of El Al Airlines was shot down by Bulgarian fighter planes near the Greece-Bulgarian border, killing all 58 persons aboard.

August 1—The Chinese said they would release the 11 Americans held since early 1953.

October 13—Pan Am announced that it had ordered 25 Douglas DC-8s and 20 Boeing 707s. National ordered six DC-8s three weeks later; American ordered 30 707s, and United ordered 30 DC-8s. KLM Royal Duth Airlines bought eight DC-8s, while Eastern bought 10 Super Constellations and took options on some additional Lockheed Electra propjets. Eastern ordered 18 DC-8s in December of that year, and Braniff Boeing 707s. Sabena Belgian Airlines had four 707s on order by the end of the year, while Air France placed an order for 10 707s (as well as 24 Caravelles, a French design). The U.S. airframe builders had orders in hand for more than one billion dollars worth of jet and propjet airliners by the end of 1955.

December 31—The world's scheduled airlines carried 69,000,000 passengers in 1955, averaging 27.4 per aircraft.

1956

February 10—RAF Marshal and Viscount "Boom" Trenchard, Billy Mitchell's mentor, died in London at age 83.

June 1—Pan Am placed Douglas DC-7C long-range airliners in service between the U.S. and Europe.

June 30—A TWA Super Constellation and a United DC-7 collided over the Grand Canyon, Arizona, killing all 128 persons in the two craft.

July 24—Capital Airlines' orders for 75 Vickers-Armstrong Viscount propjets brought the total number of Viscounts sold worldwide to 342.

August 31—The first production version of the USAF KC-135 jet tanker made its first flight at Seattle.

September 20—U.S. Secretary of Defense Charles Wilson announced that the Bell X-2 research rocket plane had flown 1,900 mph and to an altitude of 126,000 feet, piloted by (respectively) Lt. Col Frank Everest and Capt. Iven Kincheloe. A week later (27th), the X-2 crashed, killing USAF Capt. Milburn Apt.

October 11—The first British atomic device dropped from an airplane was released from a Valiant jet bomber flown by Squadron Leader E.J.G. Flavell at Maralinga, Australia.

October 11—The last of the big piston-engined airliners, the Lockheed 1649A Super Constellation, fitted with four Wright 3,400-hp compound engines, made its first flight at Burbank, California.

October 22-23—The Hungarians revolted against their Communist masters in Budapest, but Soviet tanks soon reaffirmed the Marxist doctrine which holds that political power comes from the barrel of a gun.

October 29-November 6—Following the British withdrawal from Egypt, strongman Gamal Abdel Nassar of Egypt seized the Suez Canal in a fit of anger after the United States refused to finance construction of the Asswan "High Dam" across the Nile. Nassar began a military buildup in preparation for an attack on Israel. The British and French secretly allied themselves with Israel and, after the small but highly-motivated and well-trained Israeli Army and Air Force quickly thrust across the Sinai Peninsula and destroyed the Egyptian Air Force, Anglo-French forces stormed ashore at Port Said and Port Fuad and struck southward to occupy Ismailia. At that point, the Soviets threatened war against the British, French and Israelis, whereupon the United States disowned its friends and pressured them into leaving the Egyptian territory they occupied.

A United Nations peacekeeping force moved in and remained until May 19, 1967, when Nassar asked that it be withdrawn so he could attack Israel. The third Arab-Israeli war resulted in an even more decisive victory for the Israelis. Meanwhile, the Soviets built the High Dam for Nassar. Eisenhower was U.S. president during this period, and the Soviet Premier and First Party Secretary was the crude Nikita Khrushchev.

December 31—The world's scheduled airlines carried 78,000,000 passengers during 1956.

1957

January 3—The last operational PBY-6A Catalina was retired.

March 15—A U.S. Navy blimp, ZPG-2, commanded by Cmdr. J.R. Hunt, returned to NAS Key West, Florida, after a flight to the African Coast for a world record in distance (9,448 statute miles) and duration (264 hours, 24 minutes), nonstop and without refuelling.

May 17—The U.S. Navy's last escort carrier, CVE-116 *Badoeng Strait*, was decommissioned at Bremerton.

June—The Convair-built Atlas missile makes its first flight. This 100-ton 80-foot rocket became operational in September 1959.

July 16—A Royal Dutch KLM Super Constellation fell into the sea near New Guinea; 56 were killed.

September 30—The USS *Saipan* (CVL-48), last of the light carriers, was decommissioned.

October 4—The first artificial satellite, the 184-pound Sputnik I, was boosted into orbit about the Earth by the Soviets.

November 3—The Soviets launch into Earth orbit the 1,121-pound satellite Sputnik II, carrying a dog named Liaika.

1958

January 1—The USAF Strategic Air Command (SAC) assumes responsibility for America's Intercontinental Ballistic Missile program as the 672nd Strategic Missile Squadron was activated this date.

January 31—America's first Earth-orbiting satellite, the 31-pound Explorer 1, was launched this date by Jupiter C booster. It discovered the Van Allen Radiation Belt.

February 1—A midair collision between a MATS C-118 and a Navy P2V Neptune over Los Angeles took the lives of 48.

July 15—U.S. Marines landed in Beirut to protect American lives and interests; the Sixth Fleet stood by with the *Essex* air groups providing a show of aerial force. Other U.S. forces joined the operation later; there were no serious incidents.

August 6—The Department of Defense Reorganization Act of 1958 was approved. Effective six months from this date, it provided more direct civilian control over military operations.

August 23—The FAA Act of 1958 created the Federal Aviation Agency, which had broad powers to regulate the airlines and general aviation. In the mid-1960s, Lyndon Johnson would strip the FAA of its agency status and stuff it into its new Department of Transportation as the Federal Aviation Administration.

August 29—The Lockheed Electra propjet airliner (the second Lockheed to be so named), selected in April 1958 as the airframe for the Navy's new long-range anti-submarine patrol craft, made its first flight as the P3V-1. The Navy called it the Orion, and slicked-up versions were still in use by the navies of the Free World in the late 1980s. Its airline service was limited after three Electras suffered in-flight structural failures, killing a total of 189 people. Under certain power settings, sympathetic vibration of severe magnitude caused the Number Three engine nacelle to violently rotate, failing the wing. The U.S. Navy has taken delivery of more than 400 Orions.

October 1—NASA was formed. The National Aeronautics and Space Administration replaced the NACA (National Advisor Committee for Aeronautics).

October 15—The first of three North American X-15 rocket research airplanes is rolled out. Following glide tests after release from a B-52 mother ship at 38,000 feet, the first powered flight would come on September 17, 1959, to begin a 10-year program that yielded valuable basic space flight data, plus speeds to 4,534 mph at altitudes to 354,200 feet (more than 60 miles).

October 26—The Boeing 707-120 made its first commercial flight, flying from New York to Paris with 111 passengers. (Its maiden flight had been on December 20, 1957.)

1959

January 1—Climaxing a guerilla action dating back to 1956, Fidel Castro and his followers overthrew the Cuban government of dictator Fulgencio Batista.

The North American X-15 space research airplanes there were three of them yielded valuable speed and altitude data during a 10-year program. Best speed was 4,534 mph, 2,534 mph, or 3,534 mph? (October 15, 1958.) (USAF)

April 20—America's first seven astronauts are selected for Project Mercury: USAF Capts. Gordon Cooper and Donald Slayton, ages 32 and 35; Navy Lt. Cmdrs. Alan Shepard and Walter Schirra, ages 35 and 36; Navy Lt. Scott Carpenter, 33; Marine Lt. Col. John Glenn, Jr., 37; and Virgil "Gus" Grissom, 33, USAF Captain.

June 8—The first living creatures to be rocketed into space and then returned to earth in good health were the monkeys Able and Baker. Sent aloft in the nose cone of a Jupiter missile from Cape Canaveral, they soared 360 miles into the cosmos and then parachuted into the Atlantic to be picked up by the U.S. Navy fleet tug *Kiowa*, commanded by Lt. Joseph Guion. (The Soviets had previously sent a dog into space in Sputnik II, but no attempt was made to recover it.)

June 16—Two Soviet MiGs attacked a Navy P4M Mercator over international waters off Korea, wounding one crewman.

June 19—The largest non-rigid airship ever built, the ZPG-3W, the first of four such blimps, was delivered to the NAS at Lakehurst.

September—Atlas D ICBM missiles were pronounced operational in new underground silos. By 1965, a mix of Atlas Ds and Titan Is was replaced by Titan IIs.

September 12—The Soviet unmanned Luna 2 impacted on the moon.

October—The Piper Pawnee, especially designed for the application of chemicals to crops, was introduced.

Significant Events in Aviation

The Pratt & Whitney J-57 turbine engine (foreground) with Double Wasps. The J-57 powered, among other aircraft, the first operational jet fighter for the USAF which was a true Mach 1 airplane, the North American F-100. (United Technologies)

November 9—Russia's Luna 3 spacecraft, a 614-pound unmanned vehicle, photographed the moon's far side.

November 30—USAF Capt. Joe Kittinger parachuted from a helium-filled plastic balloon at an altitude of 76,400 feet.

1960

January 10—Pratt & Whitney announced the end of production for the R-2800 Double Wasp twin-row radial engine. Between 1939 and 1960, 125,443 were built. (39,037 Wasp Junior R-985s were built before production stopped.)

May 1—A Lockheed U-2 spyplane, flown by civilian pilot Francis Gary Powers under contract to the CIA, was shot down over Russia. Incredibly, President Eisenhower publicly admitted that the U-2 was on a spy mission. Powers, who parachuted from his stricken aircraft, was later swapped for Soviet spy Col. Rudolf Able. Powers died in a helicopter crash several years later.

July 20—First launch of a Polaris missile from a submerged submarine, the USS *George Washington*.

August 18—First midair space capsule recovery was effected on September 16 as the 1,700-pound Discoverer 14, sent into orbit on August 18, re-entered Earth's atmosphere. Seven additional midair satellite retrievals were made, the last one on March 21, 1962.

December 16—A United Air Lines DC-8 and a TWA Super Constellation collided in midair over New York City, killing 134 passengers and crew members.

1961

March—The Bell UH-1B Huey helicopter entered service with the Army.

April 12—The Soviet space vehicle Vostok 1, manned by Cosmonaut Yuri Gagarin, completed one orbit of the Earth and re-entered for a landing 400 miles southeast of Moscow.

April 17—Bay of Pigs fiasco: An invasion of Cuba by Cuban exiles attempting to overthrow the Castro government was crushed. U.S. Army advisors to President Kennedy advised that the planned air support by mercenaries was not necessary.

May 5—First American in space (but not in orbit) was Cmdr. Alan B. Shepard, who rode a Mercury-Redstone (*Freedom 7*) spacecraft to an altitude of 115 miles and a distance of 302 miles in a 15-minute flight. On July 21, Virgil Grissom duplicated the achievement in a similar craft, *Liberty Bell 7*.

August 6—Vostok 2, carrying Gherman Titov, flew a 17-orbit 25.3-hour flight. During re-entry, Titov parachuted from the vehicle at 21,000 feet.

August 12-13—East Germany closed the border between East and West Berlin to stop the great exodus of East Germans to the West. Then the East Germans built a wall dividing East Germany from Free Germany.

October—The first of the long-lived Piper Cherokees entered the market.

October 31—The U.S. Navy's lighter-than-air branch was decommissioned as Fleet Airship Wing 1, and Patrol Squadrons ZP-1 and ZP-3 ceased operations.

November 25—The nuclear-powered USS *Enterprise* (CVAN-65) was commissioned at Newport News, Virginia, Capt. Vincent P. DePoix commanding.

December 8—The fourth oldest Naval Air Station at Anacostia was permanently closed at 5 A.M.

1962

February 20—John H. Glenn, Jr. became the first American to orbit the Earth, riding Mercury-Atlas 6 spacecraft on three orbits at an altitude of 100 to 163 miles.

March 4—A British Caledonian Airlines DC-7C crashed near Douala, Cameroun, with the loss of 111 lives.

March 16—A Flying Tiger Super Constellation disappeared over the western Pacific with 107 aboard.

May 24—Mercury-Atlas 7 (*Aurora 7*) manned by Scott Carpenter, flew a three-orbit 4.9-hour mission and was picked up from the Atlantic by a Navy helicopter.

August 31—The last flight of a Navy airship took place at Lakehurst, a nostalgic event closing out 45 years of lighter-than-air operations.

October 3—Walter M. Schirra, Jr. completed a six-orbit space flight in Mercury-Atlas 8, a 9.2-hour mission.

October 22–November 20—Cuban Missile Crisis: After USAF and Navy reconnaissance aircraft and other intelligence sources revealed a Soviet military buildup in Cuba, President Kennedy ordered a sea and air blockade of the island of military equipment. A meeting with Premier Khrushchev resulted in the dismantling of the Russian missiles. The quarantine was lifted on November 20.

October 26—The last Boeing B-52 (H model) was delivered to the USAF.

November—Dulles International Airport near Washington, D.C. was opened.

November 27—The Boeing 727 70-to-114 passenger jetliner was unveiled.

1963

May 15—Mercury-Atlas 9 (*Faith 7*), with L. Gordon Cooper aboard, made a 22-orbit space flight of 34.3 hours.

May 27—Frustrated by Defense Secretary McNamara's degradation of the F-111, the USAF ordered the McDonnell F-4C Phantom II, which made its first flight on this date. Originally a Navy fighter, the first Phantom II flew on May 27, 1958.

June 14–16—Russia's Vostoks 5 and 6 fly 81 and 48 orbits, respectively, with cosmonauts Bykovsky and Tereshkova.

August 22—The North American research rocket airplane reaches 354,200 feet altitude.

October 7—The first Lear Jet (later, "Learjet"): The Model 23 Lear Jet made its first flight. It received FAA certification July 31, 1964, and the first customer delivery followed on October 13, 1964.

December 5—Mach 6 was exceeded for the first time by an airplane with USAF Maj. Robert A. Rushworth at the controls. On October 3, 1967, USAF Maj. William J. Knight would reach 4,434 mph in an X-15.

December 17—(60th Anniversary of the world's first airplane flight)—The Lockheed fanjet C-141 Starlifter made its initial flight.

1964

July—President Johnson ordered the U.S. military mission in South Vietnam increased from 16,000 to 21,000 (American advisors in Vietnam numbered 685 in 1954, 2,000 in mid-1961, at which time President Kennedy had been in office five months, and 15,000 in November 1963, when Johnson took office upon the tragic death of President Kennedy).

July 28—The 806-pound unmanned Ranger 7 spacecraft impacted on the moon, sending back to Earth many pictures before its crash.

August 2—North Vietnamese torpedo boats attacked the U.S. destroyer *Maddox* and inflicted some damage. The incident took place in the Gulf of Tonkin.

August 4—President Johnson obtained the "Tonkin Gulf Resolution" from Congress, which, in effect, gave the President a blank check in the conduct of military operations in Southeast Asia.

September 21—The North American XB-70A Mach 3 research airplane made its maiden flight. Two were built; one was destroyed in a midair collision in 1965 with an F-104 chase plane. The other is currently preserved at the Air Force Museum, Wright-Patterson AFB, Ohio.

October 12—A Soviet 11,731-pound spacecraft, Voskhod 1, accomplishes 16 orbits of the Earth with three cosmonauts aboard.

December 22—Rollout of the Lockheed SR-71 spyplane.

December 31—The total space record, all nations, through this date was 357 spacecraft launch attempts—271 by the United States, 82 by the Soviets, two joint British-American, one Italian, and one Canadian. The U.S. had 69 failures. The total number of Soviet failures were unknown.

1965

January 1—American casualties in South Vietnam totaled 225 during the previous five years (Jan 1, 1960 to Jan 1, 1965). The American presence was strictly as advisors.

February 7—On this night, a large force of North Vietnamese communist guerilas (Viet Cong) made a surprise attack on the American compound at Pleiku, South Vietnam, killing eight Americans and wounding 126. Two additional attacks on American barracks occurred within the succeeding five days. The United States retaliated with air strikes against military targets in North Vietnam.

February 15—The first woman pilot to fly a helicopter, solo, transcontinental was Mrs. Gay Maher, who ferried a Hughes 300 from Culver City, California, to Medford, New Jersey.

March 19—Charles A. Lindbergh was elected to the board of Pan Am.

March 23—Gemini 3, the first two-man U.S. spacecraft, completed a three-orbit mission with astronauts Grissom and John Young aboard.

SIGNIFICANT EVENTS IN AVIATION

April 6—The largest civil aircraft program in history resulted when United Air Lines signed orders totalling $750 million for 144 airplanes to be bought, optioned, or leased: 40 737s plus 30 optioned, six DC-8-61s plus three optioned, six quick-change 727s, four DC-8s, and 20 Boeing 727s.

June 2—Gemini 4, with astronauts James McDivitt and Edward H. White aboard, completed 68 orbits of Earth in 97.9 hours, during which time White became the first American to step into space, spending approximately 21 minutes outside the capsule. Splashdown was in the Atlantic, 400 miles west of Bermuda.

July—President Johnson announced an increase of U.S. troops in South Vietnam from 75,000 to 125,000. (He had pledged during the presidential campaign in 1964 that he would never ". . . send American boys to fight a land war in Asia.")

July 5—Four of the Navy's new Grumman A-6A Intruders made their first combat strike in Vietnam, flying from the carrier *Independence*.

July 8—Paul Mantz, 61, famed Hollywood pilot, died in the crash of the *Phoenix*, a hybrid airplane built for a James Stewart motion picture.

August 17—The Air Force's Minuteman II ICBM was successfully launched for the first time from an operationally configured underground silo at Vandenberg AFB, California.

August 21—Gemini 5, boosted into Earth orbit by a Titan II missile, and manned by Gordon Cooper and Charles Conrad, flew a 128-orbit mission.

August 28—Ellen Church Marshall, the San Francisco nurse who became the nation's first airline stewardess (United Air Lines), died of injuries sustained in a horseback riding mishap.

September 27—The Navy's A-7A Corsair made its first flight at the Ling-Temco-Vought facility near Dallas.

November 14—The first round-the-world polar flight started at Palm Springs, California, and returned to Burbank on November 17. A Boeing 707 carried a group of scientists on the 27,000-mile flight.

December 4-December 18—U.S. spacecraft rendezvous. Gemini 7 was launched on a 14-day mission carrying Frank Borman and James Lovell. Then, on December 15, Gemini 6, with Walter Schirra and Thomas Stafford aboard, blasted off for a space rendezvous with Gemini 7 which brought the two craft to within three feet of one another.

December 31—Total U.S. aerospace (aviation and space) employment at the end of 1965 was 409,900, up from 46,768 at the end of 1960, reflecting the impact of the space program. Also, the world's scheduled airlines carried 177,000,000 passengers in 1965, of which 95,000,000 were flown by U.S. air carriers.

1966

January 7—The Mach 3 Lockheed SR-71 joined the Strategic Air Command at Beale AFB.

January 31—The Soviet Luna 9 spacecraft, unmanned, landed on the moon and returned photos of the lunar surface for three days.

March 16—Gemini 8, with Neil Armstrong and David Scott aboard, complete a space docking test in a 6.5-orbit mission.

May 23–May 26—The first Lear Jet Model 24 was flown around the world in 65 hours and 40 minutes elapsed time by factory pilots, establishing 18 international records for the 23,000-mile trip.

May 30—Surveyor 1, a 600-pound unmanned U.S. (NASA) spacecraft, landed on the moon and sent back photos until July 13.

June 3—Gemini 9, an 8,268-pound spacecraft is manned by Thomas Stafford and Eugene Cernan, who accomplish rendezvous and space-walk tests in a 47-orbit, 72-hour mission and are recovered from the Atlantic by the *Wasp*.

June 16—A-4 Skyhawks and F-8 Crusaders from the *Hancock* attacked North Vietnamese petroleum facilities near Thanh Hoa to begin a systematic effort to destroy the petroleum storage system of North Vietnam.

July 18—Gemini 10, piloted by Michael Collins and John W. Young, accomplished a 46-orbit, 70.8-hour mission. Gemini 10 docked with an Agena satellite and Collins worked outside the spacecraft. A helicopter from the USS *Guadalcanal* recovered the astronauts from the Atlantic.

August 1—U.S. forces in South Vietnam totalled 267,000.

September 12—Gemini 11, with astronauts Charles Conrad and Richard Gordon, completed several dockings with an Agena satellite during a 47-orbit mission that also included an altitude record of 850 miles and a Gordon walk in space.

November 11–15—Gemini 12, with James Lovell and Edwin Aldrin aboard, completed the Gemini program with a 63-orbit, 94.6-hour mission.

1967

April 23—Soyuz 1, a new Soviet spacecraft, flew 17 orbits of the Earth, but due to fouled parachutes crashed upon landing, killing cosmonaut V. Komarov.

April 28—McDonnell and Douglas merge.

May 3—The prototype of Lockheed's AH-56A Cheyenne rigid-rotor helicopter was rolled out.

May 5—The first all-British satellite, Ariel 3, was placed in orbit.

May 15—Gates Rubber Company of Denver purchased controlling interest in Lear Jet Industries to form the Gates Learjet Corporation.

June 12—The Soviet unmanned spacecraft Venus 4 ejected a capsule for a soft landing on the planet Venus.

July 1—The beginning of the B-1 bomber saga occurred this date with a contract definition (DSARC1). This program would be cancelled by Jimmy Carter on June 30, 1977. Four were built. The program was revived under President Reagan as the B-1B in 1981. Rollout of the first B-1B production aircraft was on September 4, 1984. Operational deployment began in the summer of 1985.

December 31—America's total space effort 1957 through 1967, both manned and unmanned, was 460 attempts, 77 failures, and 383 successes. More than two-thirds of the failures occurred during the first five years. There were no manned flights in 1967 as intense preparations went forward for the Apollo moon program.

1968

January 23—The North Koreans capture the USS *Pueblo* spy ship and the President calls the USAF Reserve and six carrier squadrons of the Naval Air Reserve to active duty.

February 14—The Lockheed Constellation's last flight on a U.S. scheduled airline: A model 1049G (s/n 4655) flew from Newark, New Jersey, to Washington National Airport. It belonged to Eastern Air Lines.

March 31—President Johnson announced that U.S. warplanes would not bomb north of the 20th Parallel in Vietnam as an inducement to the North Vietnamese to negotiate a peace. Since Johnson and his Defense Secretary, Robert McNamara, had not allowed bombing of meaningful strategic targets in the north, this was a hollow gesture.

June 30—The Lockheed C-5A Galaxy heavy lifter made its first flight.

August 10—The first Lockheed C-9 Nightingale (modified DC-9) hospital plane was delivered to the Military Airlift Command (MAC); 12 of these craft were eventually operational with the 375th Aeromedical Airlift Wing, Scott AFB, Illinois.

October 11—Apollo 7 (Apollos one through six were unmanned test vehicles) was sent into Earth orbit by a Saturn 5 booster carrying Walter M. Schirra, Donn F. Eisele, and R. Walter Cunningham on an 11-day mission. Helicopters from the *Essex* retrieved the astronauts from the water 285 miles south of Bermuda.

November 1—After the limited bombing moratorium of the previous March failed to produce a move toward peace, Johnson ordered the cessation of all bombing of North Vietnam.

November 6—The big airship hangar at Lakehurst was designated a National Historic Landmark by the National Park Service.

December 19—President Johnson, with just a month left in office, approved new trans-Pacific routes for TWA and Continental; Braniff got a Hawaii route, and the Flying Tigers a new all-cargo route to Japan. American Airlines was denied a trans-Pacific route, but given a new Hawaii route. After President Nixon took office on January 20, 1969, he cancelled all of the last-minute Johnson gifts.

December 21—For the first time in history, man broke free of Earth's gravity. Apollo 8's third stage booster, in a 302-second burn ignited over Hawaii, thrust astronauts Frank Borman, William Anders, and James Lovell to a velocity of 24,196 mph, leaving Earth orbit on an intercepting course for the moon. After circling the moon, Apollo 8 returned to planet Earth on December 27, splashing-down in the Pacific within three miles of the waiting USS *Yorktown*.

1969

January 1—The FAA reported 2,636 Experimental aircraft (homebuilts) registered in the United States, 1,251 in active flying status. During the late 1960s, the homebuilts increased at the rate of approximately 300 annually.

February 3—The Naval Air Systems Command issued a contract to Grumman for development of the F-14 Tomcat.

March 3—Apollo 9, crewed by James McDivitt, Russell Schweickart, and David Scott, orbited the moon in a 10-day mission.

April 14—The North Koreans shot down an unarmed Lockheed EC-121 Constellation on a routine reconnaissance patrol over the Sea of Japan. The U.S. response was to activate Task Force 71 to protect such flights over those international waters in the future.

April 30—The first woman airline pilot in the Free World was Miss Turi Widerose, 31, of Norway, who made her first scheduled flight as a First Officer for Scandinavian Airlines from Oslo to Arctic Norway.

May 18—Apollo 10, carrying Thomas Stafford, John Young, and Eugene Cernan, flew an eight-day mission to test the operation of the LEM (Lunar Excursion Module, which also came to be known as the "moon taxi").

June—The two-place Taylorcraft lightplane, production of which ceased in 1946, was revived by Charles Feris in Alliance, Ohio.

July 16—Apollo 11, crewed by Michael Collins, Neil Armstrong, and Edwin Aldrin, journeyed to the moon, where Collins orbited in the spacecraft ("minds the store," as he phrased it) as Armstrong and Aldrin descended to the moon's surface in the LEM.

October 22—The U.S. Naval Air Systems Command executed an agreement with the British, clearing the way for purchase of 12 Hawker-Siddely Harriers, Vertical Takeoff and Landing fighter airplanes.

November 14—Apollo 12, with astronauts Richard Gordon, Charles Conrad, and Alan Bean on board, took off for a second moon landing, returning to Earth on the 24th.

December 31—Total U.S. civil aircraft production during calendar year 1969 was 13,505, of which 332 were transports, 282 helicopters, and 9,996 general aviation airplanes. Exports totalled 2,895 units.

1970

February 10—Marine air units began withdrawal from Vietnam. On October 13, the last Marines left Chu Lai, a base from which they had operated since 1965.

April 11—Apollo 13 was launched on what turned out to be a four-day aborted mission to the moon. The crew was James Lovell, John Swigert, and Fred Haise.

September 25—As a result of a crisis in Jordan, caused by Palestinian guerillas attempting to unseat the monarchy in Amnan, the Sixth Fleet, joined by four additional attack carriers, was ordered to stand by in case U.S. military protection was required for the evacuation of Americans there.

December 21—The F-14A Navy fighter, piloted by Grumman test pilots Robert Smyth and William Miller, made its first flight at Grumman's Calverton, Long Island, plant.

December 31—A total of 383,000,000 passengers were carried by the scheduled airlines of the Free World, with a load factor of 55 percent.

SIGNIFICANT EVENTS IN AVIATION

The Saturn V second stage had five hydrogen-fueled engines, each of which produced 200,000 pounds of thrust. The Saturn Vs took us to the moon. Who was the first human to set foot on the moon? (July 16, 1969.) (Rocketdyne Photo)

1971

January 31—Apollo 14, crewed by Alan Shepard, Roosa, and Mitchell, began the practice of flying as many new astronauts as practicable.

March—The program for development of an American SST (supersonic transport, proposed by Boeing, and larger than the British-French Concorde) was refused further funding by the U.S. Congress. A Soviet SST was not successful, and the Concorde would prove uneconomical in operation. The Soviet SST, the TU-144, came apart in midair on June 4, 1973, during a demonstration flight at the Paris Air Show. It fell on a French village; 14 died.

April 1—The BD-5 homebuilt airplane, designed by Jim Bede, was announced as a series of kits to be made available on a pay-as-you-go basis. To be powered with a 40-to-70 hp engine

72 1001 Flying Facts and Firsts

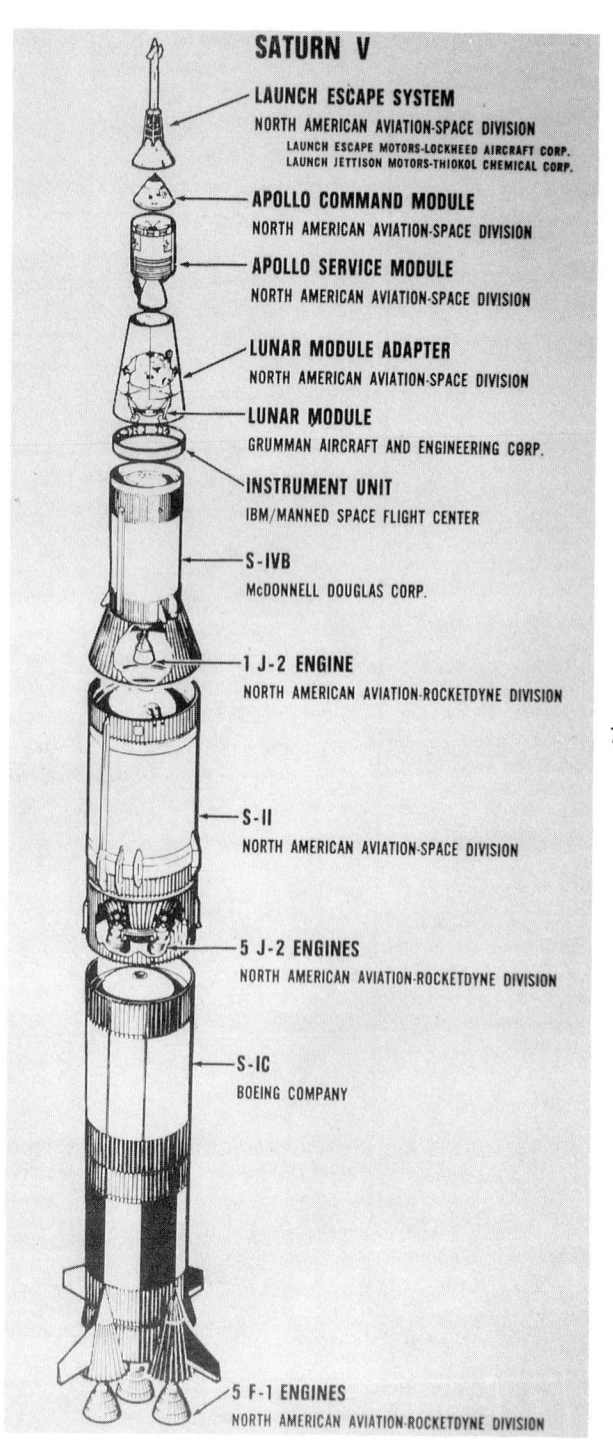

SATURN V

- **LAUNCH ESCAPE SYSTEM**
  NORTH AMERICAN AVIATION-SPACE DIVISION
  LAUNCH ESCAPE MOTORS-LOCKHEED AIRCRAFT CORP.
  LAUNCH JETTISON MOTORS-THIOKOL CHEMICAL CORP.

- **APOLLO COMMAND MODULE**
  NORTH AMERICAN AVIATION-SPACE DIVISION

- **APOLLO SERVICE MODULE**
  NORTH AMERICAN AVIATION-SPACE DIVISION

- **LUNAR MODULE ADAPTER**
  NORTH AMERICAN AVIATION-SPACE DIVISION

- **LUNAR MODULE**
  GRUMMAN AIRCRAFT AND ENGINEERING CORP.

- **INSTRUMENT UNIT**
  IBM/MANNED SPACE FLIGHT CENTER

- **S-IVB**
  McDONNELL DOUGLAS CORP.

- **1 J-2 ENGINE**
  NORTH AMERICAN AVIATION-ROCKETDYNE DIVISION

- **S-II**
  NORTH AMERICAN AVIATION-SPACE DIVISION

- **5 J-2 ENGINES**
  NORTH AMERICAN AVIATION-ROCKETDYNE DIVISION

- **S-IC**
  BOEING COMPANY

- **5 F-1 ENGINES**
  NORTH AMERICAN AVIATION-ROCKETDYNE DIVISION

The Saturn V space system. (Rocketdyne Photo)

SIGNIFICANT EVENTS IN AVIATION

(Bede was vague about the engine), it was promoted as a 200-mph pusher, single-place machine. The company went bankrupt before shipping all of the promised components.

July 26—Apollo 15, with Scott, Worden, and Irwin aboard, flew an 11-day mission in which a record 76,278 pounds were lifted into moon orbit.

November 24—A man identified as D.B. Cooper parachuted over Idaho from the aft stairway extended beneath a 727 airliner with $200,000 extorted from the airline. No trace of Cooper has been found to date.

Earlier, on January 20, 1971, Richard C. LaPoint commandeered a jetliner over Colorado and parachuted with $50,000 ransom, but was caught within hours. In April, Richard McCoy bailed out of an airliner with half a million dollars and was apprehended within 24 hours as a result of a tip to police.

The first aerial hijacking was in 1949, and by the end of 1971 there had been almost 150 such incidents committed by 200 nuts, terrorists, and crooks. Forty convictions had been obtained; 17 cases were pending, 15 were in mental institutions, 9 had been killed or had committed suicide, four cases ended in acquittals, a few cases had been dismissed, and 112 offenders remained fugitives, including terrorists who had destroyed three jumbo jets in the Jordanian desert in September 1970. All this had prompted President Nixon to establish a Sky Marshal Force in November 1970.

December 31—A total of 411,000,000 passengers were carried by the scheduled airlines of the Free World in 1971, with a load factor of 54 percent.

1972

April 16—Apollo 16, carrying Young, Duke, and Mattingly, took off for an 11-day moon mission that included a record 71-hour stay on the lunar surface, a record stay outside the spacecraft on the moon, as well as the greatest mass landed and lifted on and from the moon, 18,208 pounds and 10,949 pounds, respectively.

December 7—Apollo 17, the last and longest Apollo mission, crewed by Cernan, Evans, and Schmitt, spent most time in lunar orbit (141 hours, 41 minutes) during a 12-day mission.

December 18—The "Eleven-Day War": The largest B-52 operation over Vietnam, known as Linebacker II, was an 11-day assault by the Stratofortresses in night raids against strategic targets in North Vietnam. Fifteen B-52s were lost on approximately 700 sorties, but the effort brought the North Vietnamese to seriously negotiate peace for the first time. Navy and Marine fighters provided protective combat screens and struck at targets along the coast of North Vietnam.

December 31—A total of 450,000,000 passengers were flown (191,349,000 American) by the scheduled airlines of the Free World during 1972, with a load factor averaging 57 percent. Total aircraft production in the U.S. was 10,576 (civil) units; 79 transports, 319 helicopters, and 7,702 general aviation airplanes. The military aircraft production total was 2,530.

1973

April 11—The Gates Learjet plant at Wichita passed the 5,000,000 production man-hour mark without a disabling accident to a worker. This three-year achievement established an industry record.

May 25–June 22—Skylab 2, crewed by Conrad, Kerwin, and Weitz, was launched the first of three missions which carried out various experiments over extended time periods in Earth orbit. Skylab 3, carrying Bean, Garriott, and Lousma, remained in orbit from July 28 to September 25, and Skylab 4, with Carr, Gibson, and Pogue aboard, orbited from November 16 to February 8, 1974.

November—Installation of EVS (Electro-Optical Viewing System) in the active B-52 fleet was completed, greatly increasing night offensive capabilities.

December 31—A total of 489,000,000 passengers were flown by the scheduled airlines of the Free World during 1973, with an average load factor of 58 percent. The U.S. airlines carried 202,208,000 passengers of the above total. The total number of civil aircraft produced was 14,709 units, of which 143 were transports, 342 helicopters, and 10,482 general aviation airplanes. A total of 1,821 military aircraft was delivered.

1974

December 31—A total of 515,000,000 passengers were flown (207,458,000 American) by the scheduled airlines of the Free World during 1974, with a load factor of 59 percent. Total civil aircraft production in the U.S. was 15,326 units; 91 transports, 433 helicopters, and 9,903 general aviation airplanes. Military production totalled 1,513.

1975

February 12—Glider-eating dogs: According to Mr. Stan Schultz, a pack of unruly dogs attacked and devoured a Schweizer 2-33 sailplane on the night of January 15, the *ninth* such machine eaten at Skylark Field, Lake Elsinore, California, by these canines on Thursday nights during a full moon.

July 15—USA/USSR space linkup occurred during a nine-day Earth orbit mission when an Apollo, manned by Thomas Stafford, Donald Slayton, and Vance Brand, docked with a Soyouz spacecraft crewed by Aleksey Leonov and Valeriy Kubasov. Eleven records for duration, distance, mass, and altitude in "group spaceflight" were established.

NASA funding for space flights ran out with the American/Soviet space linkup, and President Nixon put America's manned space program on hold. The space shuttle program went forward at a slow pace under the Carter administration, and the next manned space flight by a U.S. space vehicle would come in 1981.

December 31—A total of 534,000,000 passengers were flown by the scheduled airlines of the Free World during 1975, with a load factor of 59 percent. The U.S. scheduled airlines carried 205,062,000 of that number. The total civil aircraft production in the U.S. was 15,251, of which 127 were transports, 528 were helicopters, and 10,804 were gen-av airplanes. Military deliveries totaled 1,779 aircraft.

1976

January 10—The USAF announced that 273 B-52H global bombers had been fitted with a "quick start" capability that allowed simultaneous starting of all engines for faster scramble in an emergency.

August 1—Around the world in a homebuilt airplane was accomplished by USAF Lt. Col. (Ret.) Donald P. Taylor in an elapsed time of 61 days from Oshkosh, Wisconsin and return.

The airplane was a Thorp T-18 fitted with a Lycoming 0-360 engine of 180 hp. The total distance was approximately 24,000 miles.

October 1—A week before President Ford was due to debate Democratic presidential contender Jimmy Carter, Ford's Defense Secretary Rumsfeld said that the Soviets possessed more than 1,500 ICBMs in land bases and 800 more in submarines, vs. 1,054 U.S. ICBMs land-based, plus 656 in submarines. (Strictly speaking, the submarine missiles were not ICBMs, of course, because they had about half the range of the 6,000-mile ICBMs.)

December 31—A total of 576,000,000 passengers were flown by the Free World's scheduled airlines during 1976, with a load factor of 60 percent. The U.S. scheduled airlines carried 223,318,000 of those passengers. U.S. civil aircraft production totaled 16,429 units: 64 transports, 442 helicopters, and 12,232 gen-av airplanes. The U.S. built 1,318 military aircraft that year.

December 31—The FAA published a new rule allowing all classes of Airman Medical Certificate holders to wear contact lenses.

1977

August 1—The FAA amended its rules to permit aircraft registration numbers as small as three inches on most light, single-engine aircraft with operating speeds of less than 180 knots. The markings could be displayed on the sides of the fuselage or the vertical tail.

September 23—Embry Riddle Aeronautical University spokesman declared that TCP (tricresyl phosphate) reduced spark plug lead fouling by as much as 68 percent in lightplane engines designed for 80 octane fuel but forced to use 100 octane ("low lead blue"), and also reduced valve burn/sticking problems. Not generally understood was/is the fact that LL100 blue av-gas is "low lead" only compared to 100/115 octane green; LL100 blue contains twice as much tetraethyl lead as 80 octane red.

December 31—A total of 610,000,000 passengers were flown by the Free World's scheduled airlines during 1977, with a load factor of 61 percent. The U.S. scheduled airlines carried 230,326,000 of those passengers. U.S. civil aircraft production totaled 17,913 units: 54 transports, 527 helicopters, and 13,441 gen-av airplanes. The U.S. military took delivery of 454 aircraft, while 680 military aircraft were exported.

1978

April 1—A Learjet 23, the world's first business jet aircraft ("bizjet"), went on permanent display in the National Air & Space Museum. The Model 24 had been certified for operation to 51,000 feet a year earlier, the first civil aircraft to receive such approval by the FAA.

August 7—The first production version of the Navy's F-18 fighter was delivered.

September 25—A Pacific Southwest Airlines 727 airliner let down on top of a Cessna 172 over San Diego, killing 144.

October 10—American Jet Industries, headed by Al Paulson, acquired the Grumman American Corporation for $32 million in cash and $20.5 million in AJI preferred stock. Under AJI, the company would be Gulfstream American.

December 31—A total of 679,000,000 passengers was flown by the Free World's scheduled airlines during 1978, with a load factor of 65 percent. The U.S. scheduled airlines carried 274,716,000 of those passengers. U.S. civil aircraft production totaled 18,962 units: 130 transports, 536 helicopters, and 14,346 gen-av airplanes. A total of 996 military aircraft were produced, with 529 being exported.

1979

January 29—Learjet Models 28/29 became the first production airplanes certified with winglets (wingtip "sails"). The 1,000th Learjet would be delivered on March 28, 1980.

July 1—Cessna's propjet Conquest was returned to service after two groundings (and one fatal accident in which seven died) due to faulty design of a trim tab control.

July 20—A city ordinance banning jet aircraft from the Santa Monica Airport was ruled unconstitutional in Federal District Court.

August 15—Cessna introduced the retractable-gear Cutlass, essentially a 172 with fold-up feet and 180 hp.

October 1—Bellanca announced that it would build the Eagle agricultural airplane, a large biplane with high-aspect ratio wings.

December 1—The long-rumored takeover of Beech Aircraft Corporation by the conglomerate Raytheon Corporation was confirmed, with stockholder approval assured by January 1, 1980. Mrs. Olive Ann Beech retired in May 1982.

December 31—A total of 754,000,000 passengers were flown by the scheduled airlines of the Free World during 1979, with a load factor of 66 percent. The U.S. scheduled airlines carried 316,863,000 of those passengers. U.S. civil aircraft production totaled 18,460 units: 176 transports, 570 helicopters, and 13,177 gen-av airplanes. A total of 837 military aircraft was produced in the United States, of which 306 were exported.

1980

March 1—The Aviation Maintenance Foundation announced the results of its nationwide survey of aviation mechanics' pay scales. Average shop rate was $20.10 per hour: highest was in Alaska, $35 per hour; lowest was in the Southwest, $10 per hour. Average starting wage was $5.33 per hour. The AMF predicted an A&P shortage of 50,000 by 1985.

April 4—Piper furloughed 5,200 workers for two weeks, following the layoff of 3,120 in mid-March. This affected three plants at the Lock Haven, Pennsylvania, complex as well as two at Vero Beach, Florida. The prime interest rate had reached 18 percent on this date.

April 24—President Carter sent six C-130 Hercules and eight RH-53 Sea Stallion helicopters (two choppers aborted, leaving six), with 90 specially trained troops, deployed from the carrier *Nimitz*, in an attempted rescue of U.S. embassy hostages held in Tehran by the outlaw government of the Ayatollah Khomeini. The attempt failed due to poor planning, and eight Americans died.

May 1—Cessna laid off 1,500 workers at Wichita and furloughed another 1,500. Cessna normally employed 8,300. Cessna had delivered 645 Citations since the first one was sold in 1972, but the certification of the Citation II would be delayed due to the softening market, a spokesman said.

Significant Events in Aviation

May 1—Attorney F. Lee Bailey, controlling stockholder, announced that the Enstrom Helicopter Corporation had been sold to Bravo Investments Corporation of the Netherlands.

May 24—Tesoro Petroleum Corp., of San Antonio, Texas offered a reported $125 million for Gulfstream American, and GA announced that International Transport & Earth Moving Equipment Company, Ltd., headquartered in Monte Carlo would produce the Tiger and Cheetah (single-engine descendants of the Bede Yankees) in the United Kingdom.

June 1—Armand Rivard, a fomer Lake amphibian dealer in Laconia, New Hampshire, purchased the Lake Aircraft Company in September of 1979 and announced on this date a number of improvements to the new LA-4 Buccaneer.

July 25—Bellanca filed a voluntary petition of bankruptcy under Chapter 11.

August 7—The first flight of the first solar-powered airplane, the *Gossamer Penguin*, covered 2.1 miles in 14 minutes, 21 seconds (it touched down once at 1.6 miles). Altitude ranged from 2 to 12 feet. Designed by Dr. Paul MacCready and sponsored by the Du Pont Company, it was flown by Janice Brown, a Bakersfield, California, schoolteacher.

August 26—The new Douglas DC-9-80 was certified by the FAA with a two-man (two-person?) crew—over strenuous objections by the Airline Pilots' Association.

December 31—A total of 748,000,000 passengers were flown by the scheduled airlines of the Free World during 1980, with an average load factor of 63 percent. The U.S. scheduled airlines carried 296,903,000 of those people. U.S. civil aircraft production totaled 13,637 units: 150 transports, 841 helicopters, 8,703 gen-av airplanes. A total of 1,047 military aircraft were produced by U.S. manufacturers, 422 of which were exported.

1981

January 15—Cessna discontinued production of the twin-engine centerline thrust Skymaster, promising that production would resume at Reims Aviation, Reims, France.

March 15—Members of the Professional Air Traffic Controllers Organization (PATCO) called off their threatened (illegal) strike. Their main demand was pay equal to that of similarly experienced airline pilots. Another strike deadline in June also passed without action. It seemed clear that FAA Administrator J. Lynn Helms, Secretary of Transportation Drew Lewis, and President Reagan would not go beyond the $40 million package offered. The controllers wanted a total of $700 million.

April 12—Space Shuttle 1 *Columbia*, with astronauts Young and Crippen aboard, lifted a record payload of 4,667 pounds into earth orbit in a two-day mission that lands successfully in New Mexico.

June—Howard "Pug" Piper, son of the founder of Piper Aircraft, died of cancer at age 63.

August 8—Some 11,500 air traffic controllers, members of the Professional Air Traffic Controllers Organization, struck for higher pay and better working conditions. Given 48 hours to change their minds, the union members were fired by the President when they did not. At the time, the average controller's pay was $33,000 per year for an average of 25 hours per week. They were demanding across the board raises of $10,000 per year. The government's final offer included raises of 11.4 percent over a three-year period. It should be noted that air traffic controllers are forbidden by law to strike.

August 19—Two Libyan fighter-bombers, Soviet-made SU-22 Fitters, attacked two U.S. Navy F-14 Tomcats over the Gulf of Sidra. The F-14s destroyed the Fitters with a couple of Sidewinder missiles within one minute.

September—The USAF Thunderbirds' team commander was killed during a flight demonstration at Cleveland. The Thunderbirds cancelled the rest of their appearances for 1981. On January 18, 1982, four Thunderbird pilots died following their leader into the ground after a mechanical malfunction in the lead airplane. That cancelled the 1982 season. The Thunderbirds would resume their 80 shows-per-year schedule in 1983, having exchanged their T-38s for F-16s.

September—Cessna halted production of the Model 404 Titan. The 310 had been discontinued in May 1981. Other models out of production were the 180 Skywagon, the R172 Hawk XP, 188 Ag Wagon, and 177RG Cardinal.

October—Beech announced that production of the two-place Skipper had been suspended after a total of 300 were built.

October—The Lockheed L-1011 TriStar jetliner was awarded FAA certification for Category IIIa automatic landings using a new Collins FCS-240 digital autopilot. The CAT IIIa approval specifies a minimum of 700 feet (200 meters) horizontal visibility and zero ceiling, and requires that airport facilities and aircrews be approved for CAT IIIa. (In practice, any given airline may or may not permit such minimums.)

November 12—Space Shuttle 2, crewed by Engle and Truly, flew a two-day mission.

December 31—A total of 752,000,000 passengers were flown by the scheduled airlines of the Free World during 1981, with an average load factor of 64 percent. The United States scheduled airlines carried 285,976,000 of those. U.S. civil aircraft production totaled 10,916 units: 132 transports, 619 helicopters, and 6,840 gen-av airplanes. A total of 1,062 military aircraft were produced, including 359 for export.

1982

January 10—A return to the 12-inch registration numbers, ordered by the FAA November 2, 1981, allowed aircraft owners until January 1, 1983 to comply. Antiques were/are exempt.

January 13—Air Florida Flight 90, a Boeing 737, carrying an unacceptable load of ice on its external surfaces, crashed into a bridge and fell into the Potomac River as it attempted takeoff from Washington National Airport, Washington, D.C. Seventy-eight died, including five in cars on the bridge; five passengers survived. Air Florida filed for bankruptcy in 1984.

March—Some 250 commuter airlines were operating 1,425 passenger aircraft in the 50 states and U.S. possessions, with average capacities of 16 seats per aircraft.

March 22—Space Shuttle 3, with Lousma and Fullerton aboard, flew an eight-day mission, landing at Northrop Strip, New Mexico.

April 2—Argentine military forces invaded the Falkland Islands, a possession of the United Kingdom. The British responded on May 21 with a landing force of 5,000 men in an operation involving 25,000 in ships. The Falklands War ended on June 14 when Argentine Gen. Mario Benjamin Menendez surrendered to British Gen. Jeremy Moore. Two hundred and fifty British soldiers, sailors, airmen, and Falklands civilians were killed; 775 Argentinians died. British

Prime Minister Margaret Thatcher was cheered in Parliament for her handling of the confrontation.

May—U.S. Naval Intelligence disclosed that the Soviets had put in service their fourth carrier configured for helicopter and vertical takeoff fighters. Recon satellite photos later revealed what appeared to be two conventional flattops in the 70,000-ton class under construction at Nikolayev shipyard on the Black Sea. Previously, the Russians had not possessed a carrier that would accommodate conventional fighters and fighter-bombers or craft requiring runway and/or catapult launch.

May—Braniff ceased operation, unable to pay its bills. Backed by the Hyatt Corporation, Braniff would resume operation on a much reduced scale in March, 1984.

June 6—The Army celebrated the 40th birthday of Army organic aviation for the field artillery. Established at Ft. Sill, Oklahoma, operations began with 23 L-2 (Taylorcraft), L-3 (Aeronca), and L-4 (Piper) reconnaissance airplanes. On October 13, 1955, the Army Aviation Center was permanently established at Ft. Rucker, Alabama.

June 27—Shuttle 4, manned by Mattingly and Hartsfield, fly a seven-day mission, establishing an altitude record for shuttles in the *Columbia* of 202.35 miles.

September 5—Varga production suspended (Kachina).

September 7—The Champion (Citabria) Aircraft line was purchased by B&B Aviation of Tomball, Texas, an FBO at David Wayne Hooks Memorial Airport near Houston.

September 7—Sir Freddie Laker, who launched his cut-rate New York to London service in 1977 and went broke in February 1982, told the press that he would soon return with another airline.

September 17—Bendix announced that it had bought controlling interest in Martin Marietta in a hostile takeover bid.

October 1—The FAA published FAR Part 103, which established the operating parameters for ultralight aircraft.

November 11—Space Shuttle 5, with Brand, Overmyer, Allen, and Lenoir aboard, flew a five-day mission in *Columbia*, establishing a record for the greatest mass lifted to altitude (235,635 pounds), landing at Edwards AFB.

December 31—A total of 764,000,000 passengers were flown by the scheduled airlines of the Free World during 1982, with an average load factor of 64 percent. The U.S. scheduled airlines carried 294,342,000 of those. U.S. civil aircraft production totaled but 5,085 units: 111 transports, 333 helicopters, and 3,326 gen-av airplanes. A total of 1,159 military aircraft were produced, including 469 for export.

1983

January 1—McDonnell-Douglas announced the Super 83, an extended-range addition to its Super 20 twinjet series. As of January 1st, the company had firm orders for 187 Super 80s; 100 had been delivered.

Although NASA spoke of "routine" launchings of their Space Transport System (STS), investigation following the Challenger *disaster revealed routine good luck instead, because a design weakness in the solid-fuel boosters was certain to manifest itself sooner or later. There were 24 successful launches prior to the January 28, 1986, tragedy.* (NASA)

April 4—Space Shuttle 6, carrying Weitz, Bobko, Peterson, and Musgrave, flew a five-day Earth-orbiting mission, establishing a record for the greatest mass lifted to the greatest altitude (45,049.4 pounds to 181.281 miles) in *Challenger*.

May 1—The FAA levied a fine of $4,000 against Lawrence R. Walters for operating an aircraft without an Airworthiness Certificate (among other things) as a result of his flight, July 3, 1982, from his San Pedro, California, home driveway, in a lawn chair supported by 42 weather balloons. Walters reached an altitude of 16,000 feet.

June 18—Space Shuttle 7, crewed by Crippen, Hauck, Fabian, Thagard, and Sally Ride, flew a six-day mission in *Challenger* establishing a circular orbit of 198.86 miles.

August 30—Space Shuttle 8, with Truly, Brandenstein, Gardner, Bluford, and Thornton aboard, flew a six-day mission.

September 1—Soviet fighter planes shot down a South Korean 747 airliner, killing 269 people. The airliner had strayed into Russian airspace over the Kamchatka Peninsula. The Free World assessed no serious penalty against the Soviets for the callous outrage. Canada suspended

Aeroflot (the Russian airline) service for 60 days. The U.S. had cancelled Aeroflot landing rights two years earlier to protest the imposition of martial law in Poland.

September 5—The USAF's Military Airlift Command contracted for the lease/purchase of 80 Learjets, designated C-21A, with option for 20 more.

October 1—The Howard Hughes estate announced that it was seeking a buyer for Hughes Helicopters, Culver City, California. Schweizer (the glider people) of Elmira, New York contracted to produce the Hughes 300 helicopter. In December, McDonnell-Douglas bought Hughes Helicopter for $470 million.

October 5—Board chairman Frank Borman (the former astronaut) told Eastern Air Line employees they would have to accept a 20 percent pay cut or the airline would face bankruptcy.

November 28—Space Shuttle 9, carrying Young, Shaw, Garriott, Parker, Lichtenberg, and Merbold, flew a 10-day mission to establish a duration record in *Columbia*.

November 30—The Experimental Aircraft Assocation (EAA) announced that it had obtained Supplemental Type Certificates (STCs) permitting the use of unleaded automobile gasoline in Cessna 120, 140, 180, and 182. An STC for the Cessna 150 was obtained in 1982, following exhaustive tests. Since 1983, many more such approvals have been added to the list. Meanwhile, the Illinois Department of Transportation revealed that it was operating a Cessna 182 on 190-proof ethanol, an alcohol distilled from corn.

December 31—A total of 795,000,000 passengers was flown by the scheduled airlines of the Free World during 1983, with an average load factor of 64 percent. The U.S. scheduled airlines carried 318,638,000 of those. U.S. civil aircraft production totaled 3,356: 133 transports, 187 helicopters, and 2,172 general aviation airplanes. A total of 1,053 military aircraft were produced, including 287 for export.

1984

February 1—Lear Siegler, Piper Aircraft's new corporate parent, announced that Piper would close its Lock Haven, Pennsylvania, facility in August 1984. Production would continue at the Florida facilities, including the new Piper Malibu, the first pressurized, cabin-class piston single, deliveries of which began in November 1983.

February 1—The Experimental Aircraft Association, the organization devoted to sport flying and the homebuilt airplane people, completed its move to Wittman Airfield, Oshkosh, Wisconsin, from Hales Corners.

February 10—Space Shuttle 10, crewed by McCandless, Brand, Stewart, Gibson, and McNair, flew an eight-day mission; they tested the manned maneuvering unit (MMU) in space.

February 13—United Air Lines is accused of cheating other airlines that contracted to use United's computer reservation system.

February 24—Department of Transportation Secretary Elizabeth Dole nominated Adm. (Ret.) Donald Engen as FAA Administrator after J. Lynn Helms resigned under fire. Engen took office April 10. Engen would leave in 1987, frustrated. (See August 1, 1987 entry.)

April 6—Space Shuttle 11, crewed by Crippen, Scobee, Hart, Nelson, and Van Hoften, flew a seven-day mission in which the satellite Solar Max was retrieved, repaired and redeployed.

May 1—The FAA reported that there were 5,987 unrestricted public landing sites in the United States at the end of 1983.

June 1—Cessna reported its first-ever annual loss for 1983, and announced a loss of $17.2 million for the first half of fiscal 1984. Cessna also reported the sale of its ARC Avionics Division to Sperry. A bright spot was the sale to Federal Express of 30 Cessna Caravans, plus an option for 70 more, with deliveries due December 1984 to December 1985.

August 30—Space Shuttle 12, crewed by Hartsfield, Coats, Mullane, Walker, Hawley, and Judith Resnik, flew the *Discovery* on a six-day mission, on which a non-astronaut was aboard (Charles Walker from McDonnell-Douglas).

October 5—Space Shuttle 13, carrying Crippen, McBride, Leestma, Scully-Power, Mare Garneau (Canadian), Sally Ride, and Kathryn Sullivan, orbited for eight days in the first mission with seven crewmembers, and the first flight with two U.S. women. *Challenger* was the vehicle.

November 8—Space Shuttle 14, with Hauck, David Walker, Allen, Gardner, and Anna Fisher, was in orbit almost eight days, during which time two disabled satellites were retrieved and brought back to earth for repair in *Discovery*.

November 20—The Provincetown-Boston Airline has its operating certificate revoked for gross safety violations.

December 31—A total of 832,000,000 passengers was flown by the scheduled airlines of the Free World during 1984, with an average load factor of 65 percent. The U.S. scheduled airlines carried 343,264,000 of those. U.S. civil aircraft production totaled 2,999: 102 transports, 143 helicopters, and 2,013 gen-av airplanes. A total of 930 military aircraft were produced, including 375 for export.

1985

January 1—Following the November 8, 1984, flight of *Discovery*, there were 10 more successful Shuttle missions through 1985. Because of the repetitious and "routine" nature of Shuttle missions 15 through 24, those will not be listed here. Of some interest was a *Discovery* mission in April that included Senator (R) Jake Garn among its six crew members, along with still another U.S. female astronaut, Rhea Seddon.

January 15—The NTSB said that, since 1947, a total of 235 airplanes have disappeared during flights over the U.S., 56 of those missing over Alaska.

January 15—Following evaluation of its new Airport Radar Service Areas (ARSA) at Austin, Texas and Port Columbus, Ohio, the FAA announced that it would begin establishing TRSAs at 130 of the nation's busiest non-TCA airports.

April 1—The FAA issued a proposal for a "Recreational Pilot License" designed to serve pilots who fly close to their home airports in good weather and avoid controlled airports. (As of this writing, that proposal appears to have died of malnutrition.)

April 1—Beech Aircraft announced that it had purchased Scaled Composites, the company that built the Starship prototype. Founded by Burt Rutan, the new division would be a Beech subsidiary with Rutan as president.

May 1—Pan Am sold its Pacific routes to United for $750 million. Financially troubled Pan Am had sold its Manhattan headquarters building for $400 million in 1980, and its Intercontinental Hotel chain for $500 million in 1981.

June 14—TWA Flight 847, bound from Athens to Rome, was hijacked by Lebanese Shiite terrorists. One American was murdered and the remaining 39 passengers held hostage for 17 days.

June 14—TWA agreed in principle to be acquired by Texas Air Corporation for $793.5 million. Texas Air already owned Continental and New York Air.

June 23—An Air India 727 crashed off the coast of Ireland, killing 329.

June 28—The first B-1B bomber to go operational stopped at SAC headquarters, Offutt AFB, Nebraska, on its way to Dyess AFB, Texas. A total of 100 B-1Bs was scheduled for delivery through 1988.

August 2—A Delta jetliner crashed at the Dallas-Ft. Worth Airport, killing 134, apparently as a result of flying into a thunderstorm-related wind shear at low altitude.

August 12—Civil aviation worldwide was experiencing its worst year in history as a Japan Air Lines crash killed 520 in the worst single-plane accident ever.

September—Great Lakes Aircraft of Claremont, New Hampshire, purchased Champion and said it planned to build Citabrias, Decathlons, and Scouts beginning in 1986.

Meanwhile, George Ruckle of Mackeyville, Pennsylvania, bought Taylorcraft and said new T-Crafts would be built in the former Piper plant at Lock Haven.

September 16—Famed exhibition and movie pilot Art Scholl, 53, died when his two-place Pitts went into the Pacific near San Diego after failing to recover from an inverted flat spin.

October 15—Boeing received its largest order in history from United Air Lines with a $3.1 billion contract for 110 737-300s and six 747-200s. Within days, Northwest Orient Airlines signed a $2 billion contract for the first 10 747-400s (world's longest-range commercial jet), 10 757-200s, and three 747-200s. The dash-400 would be configured for two-pilot operation.

December 12—An Egyptian Boeing 737 was held by terrorists and 58 of the 79 hostages died as commandos stormed the parked aircraft.

December 31—The FAA announced that, from 1981 through 1985, approximately 90,000 new Student Pilot permits were issued each year, while approximately 35,000 new Private Pilot Certificates and 9,000 new Commercial Certificates were issued each year. As of December 31, 1980, there was a total of 827,071 active Airman's Certificates (including Student Pilots). At the end of 1984, the total was 722,376. During those four years, the number of Private Pilots declined by 37,393, while the number of active Airline Transport Pilots increased by 9,623.

1986

January 1—The FAA said there had been 777 reports of near midair collisions (NMAC) in 1985, 758 of which were reported by pilots. The FAA's definition of an NMAC is the passing of aircraft within 500 feet of one another or any report given by a pilot. Of the 758 pilot-reported incidents, 205 involved an air carrier and another type airplane; 35 involved two airliners, and the rest were between 2 or more non-airliners.

January 3—The Beechcraft Starship I was rolled out and certification tests of the full-sized prototypes began.

January 15—Classic Aircraft Corporation of Lansing, Michigan, announced production of a new Waco F-5, built from original plans. Fitted with a 245-hp Jacobs radial, this open-cockpit fabric-covered biplane had a base price of $92,000.

January 18—Arrow Air, the Miami-based company whose DC-8 was ferrying home members of the 101st Airborne when it crashed at Gander, Newfoundland, on December 12, 1985, killing 248 servicemen and its crew of eight, had its fleet of 10 remaining DC-8s declared unairworthy by the FAA due to the use of parts not certified by the FAA.

January 28—Space Shuttle 25's boosters exploded one minute and 12 seconds after liftoff and the remains of the orbiter *Challenger*, with its crew of seven, fell from an altitude of approximately nine miles into the Atlantic. Apparently, all died instantly. They were: Francis R. Scobee, Michael J. Smith, Ronald E. McNair, Ellison S. Onizuka, Sharon Christa McAuliffe (selected from 11,146 teacher applicants to be the first to fly under NASA's Citizen-in-Space-Program), Gregory Jarvis, and Judith A. Resnik.

February 20—The U.S. Drug Enforcement Administration revealed that federal indictments were pending against 50 of Eastern Air Lines' baggage handlers in Miami for smuggling billions of dollars worth of cocaine into the U.S. aboard some of Eastern's 13 daily flights to Latin America.

March 24—Libya launched five or six SA-5 and SA-2 missiles at U.S. Navy aircraft over the Gulf of Sidra. Grumman EA-6B Prowlers diverted the missiles and A-6 Intruders and A-7 Corsairs from the U.S. 6th Fleet carriers *Yorktown*, *Saratoga*, *America*, and *Coral Sea* sank several Libyan attack boats and destroyed the radar site at Surt. Libyan MiG-25s refused to do battle.

April 14—Strike on Libya: After receiving positive evidence of Libyan dictator Muammar Gaddafi's sponsorship of terrorist operations in Europe and the Middle East, much of it directed against Americans by way of skyjackings and by explosives planted in airports, President Reagan directed that an attack be made by U.S. warplanes against military targets on the Libyan coast. Navy A-6 Intruders and Prowlers, flying from carriers offshore, attacked targets in the Benghazi area, while USAF F-111s struck at military installations around Tripoli. The F-111s operated from a base in England; one was lost.

June 1—During the first five months of 1986, Mooney delivered the most single-engine retractable-gear airplanes—41, compared to 34 Beechcrafts, 28 Pipers, and 27 Cessnas.

June 4—Burroughs bought Sperry for $4.8 billion.

July 15—Cessna's chairman, Russ Meyer, told the Senate Aviation Subcommittee that Cessna's premium for liability insurance had gone from $5,000 per airplane in 1983 to $90,000 in 1986 (three weeks earlier, Cessna had suspended production of all piston-engined aircraft). The Beech spokesman told the Subcommittee that its product liability premium for 1986 worked out to $80,000 per airplane. Piper, which had substantially retrenched in February, said it planned to resume production on all models of its singles.

September 5—Frontier Airlines, a subsidiary of People's Express, filed for protection from its creditors under Chapter 11 of the Bankruptcy Code. Concurrently, Delta offered $860 million for Western Airlines.

September 7—AeroMexico Flight 498, a DC-9, collided with a Piper Archer of Cerritos, California; 67 died in the two airplanes, along with 13 on the ground below. NTSB spokesman John Lauber instantly proclaimed, via the TV evening news, that the Archer was at 6,500 feet (anything above 7,000 feet would have been a legal altitude) and in violation of the LAX TCA. Actually, it was not possible to establish the Archer's altitude; the controller did not recall seeing it on his radar scope, and was away from his scope at the time of the collision.

September 12—Pan Am Flight 73, a Boeing 747 with 400 aboard, was skyjacked by Palestinian terrorists, and 17 passengers and crew were killed.

September 15—TWA acquired Ozark Air Lines for $250 million.

September 25—Texas Air bought People Express, including the bankrupt subsidiary, Frontier (and then offered $600 million for troubled Eastern Air Lines). Texas Air paid only $125 million for PE, plus $175 million for Frontier.

September 25—The 740 Flight Service Station positions cut from the FY 1987 budget were reinstalled. At the same time, the FAA announced that it would install five Loran-C transmitters ($43 million) to fill the mid-continent gap.

December 1—Blackhole Investments of Guelph, Ontario, Canada, began limited production of full-sized replicas of the Bucker Jungmann (two-place) and Jungmeister (single-place), priced at $60 to $70,000 without engines and instruments.

December 1—The DeVore Sunbird, a two-placer of composite construction built in Albuquerque and fitted with a two-cylinder, four-cycle air-cooled British engine of 60 hp, was undergoing certification testing. It was to be priced (hopefully) at $22,000. Early in 1987 the prototype crashed in test, but the program continued.

December 13—Piper Aircraft was purchased from Forstman, Little, & Company (which had bought Piper from Lear Siegler) by Romeo Charlie, a company formed in November by Stuart Millar.

December 14—The first round-the-world, nonstop, nonrefueled flight was accomplished by Dick Rutan, 48, and Jeana Yeager, 34, in *Voyager*, an airplane especially designed for that purpose by Dick's brother Burt, 43, one of America's most innovative designers and regarded as the father of the Beechcraft Starship I. Dick and Jeana, flying from Edwards AFB, completed their almost-26,000 mile odessey on December 23, effectively doubling all unrefueled nonstop distance records. Jeana was the holder of eight other world class air records, which she and Dick, in preparation for the world flight, established in 1986.

December 31—The FAA announced that the 526 fatalities on U.S. air carriers during 1986 translated into 1.09 for each 100,000 hours flown. Total U.S. civil aviation fatalities were 860.

Also revealed was that, since deregulation of the airlines in 1978, 150 had gone broke, and that eight major airlines now possessed 87 percent of the market. Deregulation clearly had two faces.

1987

January 1—General Dynamics announced that it had written off $420 million of the purchase price of Cessna, convinced that the gen-av market would show no improvement for several years.

January 12—Glen Odekirk, designer and builder of Howard Hughes' Hercules flying boat ("Spruce Goose") died at 81.

February 24—Astronomer Ian Shelton, a Canadian working at the Las Campanas Observatory in northern Chile, discovered the brightest exploding star in 383 years, and the first one visible to the naked eye since 1885. Located in the Large Magellanic Cloud, it exploded 170,000 years ago, and its light, travelling at 186,282 miles per second, at last reached planet Earth, one of nine satellites orbiting a rather common yellow star in a galaxy far, far away.

February 25—The Defense Advanced Research Projects Agency chose Scaled Composites (a Beech subsidiary headed by Burt Rutan) to build a 60 percent scale proof-of-concept machine for an advanced 14-passenger, 350-knot transport capable of operating from a 1,000-foot runway.

March 10—The Senate Commerce Committee voted to give the Secretary of Transportation 12 months to establish mandatory drug and alcohol testing of rail, aviation, and motor carrier industry employees.

April 1—The FAA said that it would require Mode C transponders (altitude reporting capability) for all aircraft operating in Group II TCAs by December 1, 1987, advancing that requirement by one year.

April 2—The Cessna Pilots Association announced that it had reached the 10,000-member mark. It was organized for single-engine Cessna owners. (Address is P.O. Box 12948, Wichita, KS 67277.)

May 1—The FAA issued an Airworthiness Directive requiring detailed inspection of the main spars and wing-root skins on most PA-28 Cherokees and some PA-32 Cherokee Sixes with 5,000 or more flying hours.

May 1—The USAF announced that it had selected Lockheed-California and Boeing Military Airplane Company, along with General Dynamics, to develop the YF-22A advanced tactical fighter.

May 6—Beech Aircraft Corporation announced that it would make a modification to the tails of approximately 5,300 of the 7,200 V-tail Bonanzas in service. The V-tails were built between 1947 and 1982. Beech's mod included a small fuselage-mounted brace positioned over the stabilizer leading edge on C35 through V35B model Bonanzas built between 1951 and 1982. An additional external stabilizer reinforcement was added to C35 through G35 models built between 1951 and 1956.

May 26—Beech Aircraft, a subsidiary of Raytheon, announced that it had "captured" (that's what they said) a contract to provide 19 T-34C trainers to the Navy for $19.8 million. The original T-34, which dates back to 1948, was fitted with a 185-hp Continental; the T-34A had the 225-hp Continental (O-470-13), and most of the Bonanza's airframe. The T-34C is powered by the timeless P&W PT6A-25 turboprop engine flat-rated to 400 shaft horsepower.

June 1—President of the Airline Pilots Association Henry Duffy, said there would be a severe shortage of pilots by the end of the 1980s, with more than 7,000 airline pilots facing mandatory (age 60) retirement.

June 4—Cessna Skyhawk to Moscow: June 4 was Border Guard Day in Russia, and at about 7:30 P.M. a blue-and-white Cessna 172 Skyhawk circled Red Square, then landed behind

St. Basil's Cathedral. The pilot was 19-year-old Mathias Rust, a computer operator and private pilot from Hamburg, West Germany. Rust had just flown untouched from Helsinki across some 400 miles of the supposedly best-guarded airspace in the world. The Soviets tossed Rust in jail, then fired Defense Minister Sergei Sokolov and Marshal of Aviation Alexander Koldunov.

July 1—Admiral Donald Engen resigned as Administrator of the Federal Aviation Administration, effective July 1. Robert Whittington was acting Administrator until T. Allan McArtor assumed the office on July 25.

July 15—Congressional critics charged that cost overruns could take the price of each of the Northrop Stealth bombers—132 planned—to $300 million.

August 16—A Northwest Airlines DC-9 (MD-80) failed to achieve flying speed on take-off from Detroit Airport and crashed, killing 154 aboard the airplane and four on the ground. The lone survivor was a four-year-old girl.

August 24—A protracted news media blitz about real and imagined "near misses" between airliners and "small planes" stampeded the FAA's new Administrator, Allan McArtor (a former military pilot), into adding more Terminal Control Areas (TCAs) around major airports, and calling a meeting with the chief pilots from the nation's airlines. No general aviation pilots were invited.

August 25—Automatic airline ticket dispensing machines were announced for installation in corporate offices.

II

Quiz of "Firsts"

Statements as to who or what was "first" in the saga of manned flight sometimes require a *however* or two. It would seem safe to say that the world's first scheduled airline was the Tampa-St. Petersburg Line established in January 1914. *However* (there's that word!), the Germans operated a dirigible airline between 1910 and 1914, and although you might object that the service was too dependent upon the weather to qualify as a "scheduled" operation, it did regularly fly to several cities on designated days—when possible.

Another example is the question of hinged ailerons. Who invented them? The Wrights used wing-warping to make coordinated turns. Well, it appears that French air pioneer Robert Esnault-Pelterie had ailerons in 1904 (which is why these flight surfaces have a French name). *However*, Esnault-Pelterie intended to use them for pitch control rather than lateral control—and, in any case, his machine was a failure.

Both Henri Farman, in France, and Glenn Curtiss, in America, used ailerons on their 1908 flying machines, by which time the Wrights' wing-warping system was understood (and protected by patents).

Interestingly, the U.S. Government paid a reported $100,000 to Dr. William Henry Christmas for his 1914 patent on "recessed ailerons." Dr. Christmas, whose rather weird *Christmas Bullet* of 1919 did not fly, claimed to have flown at Fairfax Courthouse, Virginia, March 8, 1908, in a machine featuring interconnected ailerons for lateral control.

Answers to the following True-False questions are to be found in Section I under the date referenced.

1. The first woman to fly across the Atlantic alone was Jacqueline Cochran. (*May 20, 1932*)
2. The first flight by a jet-propelled aircraft occurred in Germany. (*August 27, 1939*)

QUIZ OF "FIRSTS"

3. The U.S. Navy's first aircraft carrier was the *Saratoga*. (*July 11, 1919*)
4. More than 30 people were aboard the aircraft that made the first round trip across the Atlantic. (*July 2–13, 1919*)
5. The first float-equipped aircraft was piloted by Gabriel Voisin. (*June 8, 1905*)
6. The first nonstop flight around the world was accomplished in a USAF B-50 bomber. (*March 2, 1949*)
7. The first flight around the world was by U.S. Air Service pilots flying Douglas biplanes. (*April 6–September 28, 1924*)
8. The U.S. First Aero Squadron, stationed at Ft. Sill, Oklahoma, was equipped with Curtiss JN-2 aircraft. (*November 1915*)
9. The world's first airplane passenger was Charles Furnas. (*May 14, 1908*)
10. The first scheduled passenger service across the Pacific was by TWA. (*November 12, 1935*)
11. The world's first successful helicopter was flown by Igor Sikorsky. (*July 5, 1937*)
12. The Condor Legion was the first RAF squadron entirely manned by American pilots in WWII. (*October 8, 1940*)
13. The first American raid on Tokyo during WWII was by 16 B-29 Superfortresses flown from the carrier *Hornet*, and led by Lt. Col. Jimmy Doolittle. (*April 18, 1942*)
14. The young German private pilot who landed in Moscow's Red Square was flying a Cessna 152. (*June 4, 1987*)
15. The first production airplanes to be fitted with wingtip sails, or "winglets," were the Cessna Citation IIIs. (*January 29, 1979*)
16. The first space shuttle orbiter carried a woman crewmember. (*April 12, 1981*)
17. The first airplane to fly faster than Mach 6 was the SR-71 Blackbird. (*December 5, 1963*)
18. The first airline stewardess was Janice Brown, a former cocktail waitress from Santa Monica. (*May 15, 1930*)
19. The first humans to leave Earth orbit and fly an intercepting track to the moon were aboard Apollo 8. (*December 21, 1968*)
20. The first living creatures to be sent into space and then retrieved in good health were a sheep and a chicken sent aloft by the Soviets. (*June 8, 1959*)
21. The first American to orbit the earth in a space capsule was Alan Shepard. (*February 20, 1962*)
22. The first woman airline pilot in the Free World was Miss Turi Widerose of Norway. (*April 30, 1969*)
23. The first round-the-world flight in a homebuilt airplane was made by Don P. Taylor in a Thorp T-18. (*August 1, 1976*)
24. The name of the first space shuttle orbiter was *Challenger*. (*April 12, 1981*)
25. The Soviets possess four aircraft carriers similar to the U.S. *Nimitz*-class flattops. (*May, 1982*)
26. The first lawn-chair aeronaut ascended from Edwards AFB supported by 200 circus balloons of various colors. (*May 1, 1983*)
27. The world's first air combat took place over Paris during the Franco-Prussian War. (*1870–1871*)
28. The first crossing of the English Channel by air was accomplished by Louis Bleriot. (*January 7, 1785*)
29. Apollo 11, crewed by Michael Collins, Neil Armstrong, and Edwin Aldrin, achieved moon orbit, then Armstrong and Aldrin descended to the moon's surface in their Lunar Excursion Module to become the first humans to walk on the moon. (*July 16, 1969*)

30. The first round-the-world, nonstop, nonrefueled flight was accomplished by Dick Rutan and Jeana Yeager in *Voyager*, a twin-engine aircraft of composite construction. (*December 14–23, 1986*)
31. The first German flying bomb, the V-1, exploded in Britain. (*June 13, 1944*)
32. The first nonstop crossing of the U.S., from New York to San Diego, was accomplished by U.S. Army Air Service pilots J.A. Macready and O.G. Kelly. (*May 2–3, 1923*)
33. The first successful autogiro was the creation of Juan de la Cierva of Spain. (*January 9, 1923*)
34. The first coast-to-coast air mail flight was flown by Army Air Service pilots. (*February 22–23, 1921*)
35. The first automatic pilot was demonstrated by Sperry in a Navy flying boat. (*March 27, 1920*)
36. The first helicopter mercy mission was flown by Cmdr. Frank Erickson of the U.S. Coast Guard. (*January 3, 1944*)
37. The first combat jet acquired by the USAAF was the Bell Airacomet. (*January 9, 1944*)
38. The first American aircraft carrier lost in the Atlantic was the *USS Block Island*. (*May 29, 1944*)
39. The first commander of the Strategic Air Command (SAC) was Gen. George C. Kenney, who had been chief of the 13th and Far East Air Forces during WWII. (*March 21, 1946*)
40. The world's first successful parachute jump was accomplished from a balloon over Paris in the 18th century. (*October 22, 1797*)
41. The world's first official air mail flight was by balloon from Paris to Le Havre. (*August 17, 1859*)
42. The world's first four-stroke internal combustion engine was demonstrated in Germany. (*1876*)
43. The Wright Brothers' first aircraft had a wingspan of 33 feet. (*August 1899*)
44. The first zeppelin, 420 feet in length, flew more than three years prior to the Wrights' first successful powered flight. (*July 2, 1900*)
45. The first sea battle in history during which the opposing ships were never in contact was the Battle of Midway. (*May 4–8, 1942*)
46. The first Lockheed Constellation went into service with TWA. (*January 9, 1943*)
47. The first Navy blimp shot down lost a duel with a German U-Boat. (*July 18, 1943*)
48. The U.S. Navy received its first helicopter during WWII. (*October 16, 1943*)
49. The first directed suicide attacks by Japanese kamikaze pilots occurred off Leyte as Americans returned to the Philippines. (*October 10–November 25, 1944*)
50. The first war in which jet aircraft met in combat was WWII. (*June 30, 1950*)

III

Record Flights

The aviation and space records listed here are taken from the *World and United States Aviation & Space Records*, updated to January 1, 1988, distributed by the National Aeronautic Association,* the NAA being the U.S. official representative (since 1922) of the *Federation Aeronautique Internationale* (FAI), which was originally formed October 14, 1905, for the purpose of supervising and officially recording world aviation records. With headquarters in Paris, the FAI is today composed of the National Aero Clubs of 52 nations.

The NAA book of records named above contains more than 200 pages and includes many intercity records in various classes of aircraft, along with such imaginative achievements as an endurance/distance record flown below sea level (7 hours, 35 minutes; by Russell Saunders flying a Cessna 140 around Death Valley), the greatest number of consecutive inside loops (R. Steven Powell, 2,315 in a Decathlon), and the greatest number of different aircraft flown in one day (65, by USAF Col. (Ret.) Tom A. Thomas).

Which individual holds the greatest number of air records? Are you ready for this? It is Marie McMillan of Las Vegas, Nevada (mostly intercity records from nowhere to nowhere).

Absolute World Records

Great Circle Distance without Landing,
Distance over a Closed Circuit: 24,986.727 miles (40,212.139 kilometers)
    USA
    Richard Rutan, pilot; Jeana Yeager, pilot
    Voyager
    Continental 0-240 air-cooled, front; Continental 10L liquid-cooled, rear
    Mojave, California
    December 14–23, 1986

---

*Available for sale from the NAA, 1400 Eye St., NW, Suite 550, Washington, D.C. 20005.

Nonstop, Nonrefueled Flight around the World (Original Record): 115.65 mph (186.11 kph)
USA
Richard Rutan, pilot; Jeana Yeager, pilot
Voyager
Continental 0-240 air-cooled, front; Continental 10L liquid-cooled, rear
Elapsed time: 216 hours, 3 minutes, 44 seconds
Mojave, California
December 14–23, 1986

Altitude: 123,523.58 ft (37,650.00 meters)
USSR
Alexander Fedotov
E-266M (modified MiG-25)
RD Turbojets of 30,865 pounds thrust
Podmoscovnoe, USSR
August 31, 1977

Altitude in Horizontal Flight: 85,068.997 feet (25,929.031 meters)
USA
Capt. Robert C. Helt, USAF
Lockheed SR-71A Blackbird
Two P&W, 30,000 pounds thrust
Beale AFB, California
July 28, 1976

Altitude Launched from Carrier Airplane: 314,750.00 feet (95,935.99 meters)
USA
Maj. Robert H. White, USAF
North American X-15-1
One Reaction Motors XLR-99 (rocket)
Edwards AFB, California
July 17, 1962

Speed over a Straight Course: 2,193.16 mph (3,529.56 kph)
USA
Capt. Eldon W. Joersz, USAF
Lockheed SR-71A Blackbird
Two P&W, 30,000 pounds thrust
Beale AFB, California
July 28, 1976

Speed over a Closed Circuit: 2,092.294 mph (3,367.221 kph)
USA
Maj. Adolphus H. Bledsoe, USAF
Lockheed SR-71A Blackbird
Two P&W, 30,000 pounds thrust
Beale AFB, California
July 27, 1976

RECORD FLIGHTS 93

USAF pilots established world's records in the SR-71 Blackbird for altitude in horizontal flight, speed over a straight course, and speed over a closed circuit course, as well as speed over a 15/25-kilometer course.

1001 Flying Facts and Firsts

The above are absolute world records as of January 1, 1988. Following are world records listed according to type of aircraft.

Balloons

Altitude: 113,739.9 feet (34,668 meters)
    USA
    Cmdr. M.D. Ross, USNR, and Lt. Cmdr. V.A. Prother
    Lee Lewis Memorial
    Gulf of Mexico
    May 4, 1961

Duration: 137 hours, 5 minutes, 50 seconds
    USA
    Ben L. Abruzzo, commander
    Maxie L. Anderson, commander
    Larry M. Newman, radio operator
    Double Eagle II
    Presque Isle, Maine, USA, to Miserey, France
    August 12-17, 1978

Distance: 5,208.67 miles (8,382.54 kilometers), Class A
    USA
    Ben L. Abruzzo, pilot
    Larry M. Newman, copilot
    Rocky Aoki, pilot
    Ron Clark, pilot
    Raven Experimental
    Nagashima, Japan, to Covello, California
    November 9-12, 1981

Distance: 3,544.25 miles (5,703.03 kilometers), Sub-classes AA-10–AA-13
Also, first solo across the Atlantic in a balloon.
    USA
    Joseph W. Kittinger
    Yost GB55
    Caribou, Maine, to Cairo Montenotte, Italy
    September 15-18, 1984

Piston-Engine Airplanes

Altitude: 56,046 feet (17,083 meters)
    Italy
    Mario Pezzi
    Caproni 161
    Piaggio XI R.C.
    Montecelio, Italy
    October 22, 1938

RECORD FLIGHTS

The FAI is keeper of world aviation and space records, and the U.S. representative is the National Aeronautic Association, which designates the official observers for record attempts in America. Records are for "absolute" and by type and class of aircraft. For example, free balloons are Class A machines, and they are subdivided according to lifting agent (helium/hydrogen or hot air), and by size: In sub-class AX-2, 250-400 cubic meters capacity, the records for altitude, distance, and duration, 12,043 feet, 35,21 miles, and 2 hours 44 minutes 20 seconds, respectively, are held by Dr. Coy Foster of Plano, TX. The young lady in the photo is demonstrating—unwittingly, perhaps—the single greatest danger to this sport, high-tension utility wires.

Straight Line Distance: 11,235.6 miles (18,081.99 kilometers)
    USA
    Cmdr. T.D. Davies, USN
    Lockheed P2V-1 Neptune
    Two Wright R-3350
    Perth, Australia, to Columbus, Ohio
    September 29, 1946

Time to Climb to 3,000 Meters: 1 minute, 31.9 seconds
    USA
    Lyle T. Shelton
    Grumman F8F-2 Bearcat
    One Wright R-3350
    Thermal, California
    February 6, 1972

Speed over a 15/25 Kilometer Course: 517.1 mph (832.12 kph)
    USA
    Frank Taylor
    Dago Red, modified North American Mustang
    Once R-R Merlin V-1650-9
    Mojave, California
    July 30, 1983

Turboprop Airplanes

Straight Line Distance: 8,732.09 miles (14,052.95 kilometers)
    USA
    Lt. Col. Edgar L. Allison, USAF
    Lockheed C-130 Hercules
    Four T-56A15
    Ching-Chuan Kang, Taiwan, to Scott AFB, Illinois
    February 20, 1972

Altitude: 51,014 feet (15,549 meters)
    USA
    Donald R. Wilson
    LTV L450F
    One PT6A-34
    Greenville, Texas
    March 27, 1972

Time to Climb to 3,000 Meters: 1 minute, 48 seconds
    USA
    Charles "Chuck" Yeager, pilot
    Renald Davenport, co-pilot
    Piper Cheyenne 400LS
    Portland, Oregon
    April 16, 1985

Speed over a 15/25 Kilometer Course: 501.44 mph (806.10 kph)
    USA
    Cmdr. D.H. Lilienthal, USN
    Lockheed P3C Orion
    Four Allison T56-A014
    NAS Patuxent River, Maryland
    January 27, 1971

Speed over a 1,000 Kilometer Course w/25,000 Kg Payload: 541.449 mph (871.38 kph)
    USSR
    Ivan Soukhomline
    Tupolev TU-114
    Four TB-12
    Sternberg, USSR
    March 24, 1960

Propjet Speed Around the World: 304.8 mph (490.51 kph)
    USA
    Joe Harnish, pilot
    David B. Webster, pilot
    Gulfstream Commander 695A
    Two Garrett TPE-331-501K
    Elkhart, Indiana and return
    March 21-24, 1983

Time to Climb to 3,000 Meters, Single-Engine Propjet: 2 minutes, 45.28 seconds
    USA
    William C. Broadbeck
    Ayres S2R-T65 (ag-plane)
    One P&W PTSA-65AG
    Albany, Georgia
    November 27, 1985

Turbojet Airplanes, Unlimited

Straight Line Distance: 12,532.28 miles (20,168.78 kilometers)
    USA
    Maj. Clyde P. Evely, USAF
    Boeing B-52H Stratofortress
    Eight P&W TF-330-3
    Kadena, Okinawa, to Madrid, Spain
    January 10-11, 1962

Altitude: 123,523.58 feet (37,650 meters)
    USSR
    Alexander Fedotov
    E-266M (modified MiG-25)
    Two RD
    Podmoscovnoe, USSR
    August 31, 1977

Time to Climb to 3,000 Meters: 27.571 seconds
   USA
   Maj. Roger J. Smith, USAF
   McDonnell Douglas F-15 Eagle
   Two P&W F-100
   Grand Forks, North Dakota
   January 16, 1975

Speed over a 15/25 Kilometer Course: 2,193.16 mph (3,529.56 kph)
   USA
   Capt. Eldon W. Joersz
   Lockheed SR-71 Blackbird
   Two P&W
   Beale AFB, California
   July 28, 1976

Speed around the World, Turbojet: 512.853 mph (825.32 kph)
   USA
   Brooke Knapp
   Gulfstream III
   Two R-R Spey Mk511-8
   Washington, D.C. and return
   February 13-15, 1984

Speed around the World over Both Poles: 487.31 mph (784.31 kph)
   USA
   Capt. W. Mullikin; Capt. A. Frink; S. Beckett; F. Cassiniti, and E. Shields
   Pan Am Boeing 747SP
   Four P&W JT9D-7A
   San Francisco and return
   October 28-31, 1977

Rocket-Engine Aircraft

Altitude: 314,750 feet (95,935.99 meters) (launched from carrier aircraft)
   USA
   Maj. Robert M. White, USAF
   North American X-15-1
   Edwards AFB, California
   July 17, 1962

Altitude: 79,452 feet (24,217 meters) (launched from ground)
   France
   R. Carpentier
   SO Trident
   Two Turbomeca turbos plus two Sper rockets
   May 2, 1958

Jet Lift Aircraft

Altitude: 46,063 feet (14,040 meters)
    UK
    T. Leckie-Thompson
    Hawker Siddeley Harrier GR Mk 1
    One R-R Pegasus 10
    January 2, 1971

Time to Climb to 9,000 Meters: 1 minute, 44.7 seconds
    UK
    T. Leckie-Thompson
    Hawker Siddeley Harrier GR Mk 1
    January 5, 1971

Seaplanes

Distance in Straight Line: 5,997.462 miles (9,652.001 kilometers)
    UK
    Capt. D.C.T. Benneti
    Short-Mayo Mercury
    Four Napier Rapiers
    Dundee, Scotland to near Ft. Niloth, South Africa
    October 6-8, 1938

Altitude: 44,429 feet (13,542 meters)
    Italy
    Col. Nicola de Mauro
    Caproni 161
    Piaggio SI PC 100
    Vigna di Valle, Italy
    September 25, 1939

Speed over a Three-Kilometer Course: 440.681 mph (709.209 kph)
    Italy
    Francesco Agello
    Macchi-Castoldi MC-72
    Fiat AS 6
    Lake Garda, Italy
    October 23, 1934

Amphibians

Distance in a Straight Line: 3,571.65 miles (5,748.04 kilometers)
    USA
    Cmdr. W. Fenlon, USCG
    Grumman UF-2G Albatross
    Two Wright R-1820-76B
    October 25, 1962

Altitude: 32,883 feet (10,022.7 meters)
   USA
   Lt. Cmdr. Charles H. Manning
   Grumman HU-16B Albatross
   Two Wright R-1820-76D
   Homestead, Florida
   July 4, 1973

Speed over a Three-Kilometer Course: 230.413 mph (370.814 kph)
   USA
   Maj. Alexander P. de Seversky
   Seversky N3PB (P-35 prototype)
   Wright Cyclone
   Detroit, Michigan
   September 15, 1935

Helicopters

Straight Line Distance: 2,213.04 miles (3,561.55 kilometers)
   USA
   Robert G. Ferry
   Hughes YOH-6A
   One Allison T63-A5
   Culver City, California to Ormond Beach, Florida
   April 6–7, 1966

Altitude: 40,820 feet (12,442 meters)
   France
   Jean Boulet
   Alouette SA 315-001 Lama
   Artouste IIIB 735 KW
   Istres, France
   June 21, 1972

Time to Climb to 3,000 Meters: 1 minute, 22.2 seconds
   USA
   Maj. John C. Henderson, US Army
   Sikorsky CH-54B
   Two P&W JFTD-12
   Stratford, Connecticut
   April 12, 1972

Speed over a 15/25 Kilometer Course: 228.91 mph (368.4 kph)
   USSR
   Gourguen Karapetyan
   Mil A-10
   Two TB-3-117
   Podmoscovnoe, USSR
   September 21, 1978

Speed around the World: 35.40 mph (56.97 kph)
    USA
    H. Ross Perot, pilot; J.W. Coburn, copilot
    Bell 206 L-II Long Ranger
    One Allison 250-C28B
    Dallas, Texas and return; 28 days, 3 hours, 8 minutes
    September 1–30, 1982

Gliders

Distance in a Straight Line: 907.7 miles (1,460.8 kilometers)
    West Germany
    Hans Werner Grosse
    ASK12
    Luebeck to Biarritz
    April 25, 1972

Would you believe that the record for straight-line distance in a sailplane is 907.7 miles? It is currently held by Hans Werner Grosse of West Germany flying an ASK-12. Pictured is the similar ASW-12. These machines have so little drag they must use drag chutes to slow them for landing.

Distance to a Goal and Return: 1,023.25 miles (1,646.68 kilometers)
    USA
    Thomas L. Knauff
    Nimbus III
    Williamsport Airport from Ridge Soaring Gliderport, Pennsylvania
    April 25, 1983

Altitude Gained: 42,303 feet (12,894 meters)
    USA
    Paul F. Bikle
    Schweizer SGS-123-E
    Mojave, Lancaster, California
    February 25, 1961

Absolute Altitude: 49,009 feet (14,938 meters)
    USA
    Robert Harris
    Burkhart Grob G-102
    California City, California
    February 17, 1986

Multi-Place Gliders

Straight Line Distance: 617.52 miles (993.76 kilometers)
    New Zealand
    S.H. Georgeson, pilot; Helen Georgeson
    Janus C
    Alexandra to Gisborne
    October 31, 1982

Distance to a Goal and Return: 664.18 miles (1,052.74 kilometers)
    West Germany
    Erwin Muller, pilot; Carl Senne
    Janus C
    Bon Springs, Australia
    December 26, 1983

Altitude above Sea Level: 44,255 feet (13,489 meters)
    USA
    Laurence E. Edgar, pilot; Harold E. Klieforth
    Pratt Read PR-G1
    Bishop, California
    March 19, 1952

Man-Powered Aircraft

Straight Line Distance: 22.26 miles (35.82 kilometers)
Duration: 2 hours, 49 minutes
    USA
    Bryan Allen
    Gossamer Albatross
    Folkestone, UK, to Cap Gris Nez, France
    June 12, 1979

Speed over a Triangular Course of 1,500 Meters: 22.19 mph (35.7 kph)
    West Germany
    Holger Rochelt
    Musculair 1
    Neubiberg, West Germany
    August 21, 1984

Speed over a Closed Circuit: 27.54 mph (44.32 kph)
    West Germany
    Holger Rochelt
    Musculair II
    Oberschleissheim Airport, West Germany
    October 2, 1985

IV

Significant U.S. Military Aircraft

The United States possessed no combat aircraft when the nation went to war against the Central Powers (primarily, Germany) on April 6, 1917. The war in Europe—World War I—was then 32 months old, and had forcibly advanced aircraft development among the warring nations, while America, determined to stay out of the war, made no effort to develop modern warplanes or build an air force. That is why, when the U.S. at last joined the conflict, our combat aircraft had to be purchased from Britain and France.

The only American-built airplane that saw combat in WWI was the British deHavilland DH-4, a two-place observation and light bomber selected for production in America because it would accept the V-12 engine that Packard wanted to build. It should be noted that the automobile interests—very strong both financially and politically by that time—controlled the tiny aircraft industry, the principal pioneers (the Wrights, Curtiss, and Martin) having either sold out or lost control as they expanded as public corporations.

When WWII erupted 20 years after WWI ended, America again had a couple of years to shore up her leaky defenses while again pledging neutrality. We were forced into WWII following the attack on Pearl Harbor, and were better (although not adequately) prepared to defend our freedoms because we possessed some talented young aircraft designers, and because warplane orders from our future allies helped expand U.S. production facilities before our own hour of desperate need overtook us.

Some successful military designs, especially fighters, were produced in a number of versions, usually reflecting an evolutionary process that saw such machines as the P-51 developed as far as the P-51H. These changes normally meant more powerful engines and detail refinements to the airframe, along with, perhaps, changes in armament. Described here are the definitive production versions, which saw service in significant numbers.

SIGNIFICANT U.S. MILITARY AIRCRAFT

In the case of civil airliners, evolution has most often meant stretched fuselage versions of successful designs, and/or greater fuel capacity, as well as more efficient engines.

The descriptive format below lists, in the following order: Year the aircraft entered service in its original version / Wingspan / Length / Gross weight / Empty weight / Service ceiling / Range / Engine(s) / Armament / Maximum speed.

Each entry is numbered because a quiz is at the end of this list.

COMBAT AIRCRAFT

1. **Spad S.13**—1918 / 26 ft. 11 in. / 20 ft. 8 in. / 1,815 lbs. / 1,255 lbs. / 20,000 ft. / 240 miles / 200 or 220-hp Hispano-Suiza water-cooled V-8 / Two Vickers machine guns / 130 mph. The U.S. bought 893 in March 1918 to replace several versions of the French Nieuport originally—but briefly—flown in combat.

2. **DeHavilland DH-4**—1918 / 42 ft. 4 in. / 30 ft. 2 in. / 3,740 lbs. / 2,440 lbs. / 24,000 ft. / 350 miles / 400-hp water-cooled Liberty V-12 / Two fixed Brownings and two flex-mount Lewis in rear cockpit / 125 mph. U.S. production totaled 4,846. Some remained in Air Corps service until 1932. Surplus DH-4s were used by the Post Office Department as the standard air mail plane of the early twenties.

3. **Martin MB-2** and **NBS-1**—1920 / 74 ft. 2 in. / 42 ft. 8 in. / 12,027 lbs. / 7,232 lbs. / 8,500 ft. / 429 miles / Two 420-hp Liberty 12A / Five .30-cal., two front, two rear, and one through

Spad S.13, WWI fighter, purchased from France. U.S. insignia colors were red outer circle; blue; white center. Type of film used for this photo washes out the red on wings and next to the rudder post. (Peter M. Bowers)

floor, plus 2,000-lb. bombs / 98 mph. Crew of four; 133 procured. Used by Billy Mitchell in the 1921 bombings of war prize German battleships.

4. **Thomas Morse MB-3** and **MB-3A**—1920 / 26 ft. 0 in. / 20 ft. 0 in. / 2,485 lbs. / Empty weight not available / 19,500 ft. / 340-hp Wright-built Hispano-Suiza / One .50-caliber and one .30-caliber / 152 mph. Thomas Morse produced 50 in 1920, and Boeing received a contract for 200 of these single-place fighters (pursuits) in 1922.

5. **Boeing PW-9** (Army) and **FB Series** (Navy)—1925 / 32 ft. 1 in. / 22 ft. 10½ in. / 3,020 lbs. / 2,166 lbs. / 20,500 ft. / 437 miles / 430-hp Curtiss D-12 / Two .30-caliber / 165 mph. Single-place fighter; 111 procured. The Navy version, 39 total, 27 of which were the FB-5 models, had slightly different dimensions and were fitted with 525-hp Packard 2A-1500 engines (V-12s).

6. **Curtiss P-1** (Army) and **F6C Series** (Navy)—1925 / 31 ft. 7 in. / 22 ft. 10 in. / 2,846 lbs. / 2,046 lbs. / 21,000 ft. / 350 miles / 460-hp Curtiss D-12 (V-1150 military designation) (late models) / Two .30-caliber Brownings or one .30-caliber and one .50-caliber / 163 mph. Single-place fighter. These were the first Curtiss Hawks, produced through 1928, and the P-1F, totaling 178 of these popular biplane fighters, including 76 AT and P-3 versions fitted with 220-hp Wright Whirlwinds and 400-hp P&W Wasps. The Navy's versions, F6C-1 through F6C-4, totaled 75 machines and were almost identical to the Army Hawks.

The Curtiss P-1 was powered with the Curtiss D-12 engine of 400-460 hp. This airframe was also delivered with the 180-hp Hispano-Suiza V-8 as the AT-4 trainer. Re-engined with the D-12, it became the P-1D as shown. The bumblebee insignia indicates that this machine belonged to the 43rd School Sqdn. at Kelly Field, Texas.

SIGNIFICANT U.S. MILITARY AIRCRAFT 107

7. **Keystone Bombers**—1927 (LB-5 Model) / 67 ft. 0 in. / 44 ft. 8 in. / 12,155 lbs. / 7,024 lbs. / 8,000 ft. / 435 miles / 420-hp Two Liberty V-12s / Five .30-calibers, two for nose gunner, two for rear gunner, one through the floor (rear) / 107 mph. The Keystone B-6E was slightly larger and fitted with Wright R-1820-E Cyclones of 575-hp, resulting in a service ceiling of 14,100 feet, double the range, and a max speed of 128 mph. Bomb capacity was 2,500 pounds for both. A total of 140 Keystone bombers was built, and most of the LB models were re-engined with Cyclone radials to make them B models. A similar biplane bomber was the Curtiss B-2 Condor. Only 12 were built (1928).

8. **Boeing F2B, F3B**—1928 / 30 ft. 1 in. / 22 ft. 10½ in. / 2,830 lbs. / 2,014 lbs. / 21,500 ft. / 335 miles / 410–425-hp P&W R-1340 Wasp / One .30-caliber and one .50-caliber machine gun, plus five 25-lb. bombs / 158 mph. The U.S. Navy procured 107; they were also flown by Marine Fighting Squadrons VF-1 and VF-2 in dive-bombing demonstrations.

9. **Curtiss A-3 Falcon**—1927 / 38 ft. / 28 ft. 4 in. / 4,378 lbs. / 2,612 lbs. / 15,600 ft. / 630 miles / 430-hp Curtiss D-12 / Four fixed .30-caliber and two flex-mounted .30-caliber / 141

The Curtiss F7C-1 Seahawk went to the Marines. Pilot is Temple Joyce, who would later be a principal in the Berliner-Joyce Aircraft Company. Upper wing sweepback on biplanes often indicated a quick design fix for tailheaviness. There must have been a problem with the Seahawk somewhere or else the Navy would not have given brand new airplanes to the Marines.
(U.S. Navy)

mph. Two-place attack aircraft for close air support of ground troops. The Army bought 154 Falcons (A-3 series) and 74 of the O-1 series, designated as observation planes. The Navy bought 27 of the Falcons, Wasp-powered, as F8Cs and redesignated them OC-2s. These were the first Helldivers.

10. **Curtiss Hawk P-6 Series**—1929. These were essentially the same airframe as the P-1s, but fitted with the 600-hp Curtiss Conqueror (V-1570) V-12 designed for Prestone cooling. The U.S. Army received 21 P-6s, 10 of which were converted to P-6Ds with side-mounted superchargers, and two were originally P-11s fitted with an experimental H-1640 Chieftain engine. Last of the line and last Army biplane fighter was the P-6E, max speed 193 mph, of which 45 were delivered in 1932.

11. **Boeing F4B** (Navy) and **P-12** (Army)—1929 (F4B-4 version) / 30 ft. / 20 ft. 5 in. / 3,085 lbs. / 1,981 lbs. / 24,800 ft. / 190 miles / 500-hp P&W R-1340 / Two .30-calibers or one .30 and one .50-caliber, plus a mix of 150 lbs. of bombs / 184 mph. Single-place fighters. The U.S. Navy bought 188, F4B-1 through F4B-4; the U.S. Army procured 366, P-12 through P-12F, the last ones early in 1932.

The Boeing fighters, F4B Navy and P-12 Army, were the principal U.S. military fighters during the first half of the 1930s. Almost identical in Army or Navy dress, they ranged from the F4B-1 through F4B-4, Navy, and P-12 through P-12F, Army. Engines were the P&W R-1340 Wasps, 450 through 600 hp.

SIGNIFICANT U.S. MILITARY AIRCRAFT

12. **Curtiss Shrike, A-8** and **A-12**—1932 / 44 ft. / 32 ft. 3in. / 5,900 lbs. / 3,898 lbs. / 15,150 ft. / 455 miles / Wright Cyclone R-1820 of 690-hp for A-12 version, Curtiss Conqueror of 600-hp for the A-8; 46 of the former acquired, 13 of the A-8s / Six .30-caliber Brownings (including one in each wheel pant), 464 lbs. bombs / 175 mph.

13. **Curtiss F11C-2 Goshawk (BFC-2)**—1932 / 31 ft. 6 in. / 22 ft. 7½ in. / 4,120 lbs. / 3,111 lbs. / 24,000 ft. / 560 miles / 700-hp Wright R-1820-78 / Two .30-calibers or one .30 and one .50-caliber, plus 450-lb. capacity / 202 mph. Twenty-eight were procured and later designated BFC-2, for "bomber, fighter, Curtiss."

14. **Martin B-10** and **B-12**—1933 / 70 ft. 6 in. / 44 ft. 9in. / 14,731 lbs. / 9,681 lbs. / 24,000 ft. / 1,240 miles / Two 740-hp Wright Cyclones / 2,260-lb. bomb capacity, three .30-caliber Brownings / 213 mph. The 32 B-12s were fitted with P&W engines. A total of 119 B-10s was delivered to the Air Corps.

15. **Boeing P-26**—1933 / 28 ft. / 23 ft. 7½ in. / 2,935 lbs. / 2,914 lbs. / 27,800 ft. / 570 miles / 570-hp P&W R-1340-27 / Two .30-calibers or one .30 and one .50-caliber / 230 mph. The Air Corps' first all-metal low-wing fighter, 137 were procured.

16. **Grumman F2F** and **F3F**—1935 (F3F version) / 32 ft. / 23 ft. 3 in. / 4,116 lbs. / 2,990 lbs. / 28,500 ft. / 530 miles / 950-hp Wright R-1820 (the F2Fs had 650-hp P&W

This export version of the biplane Hawk series was known as the Hawk II; engine was the 710-hp Wright Cyclone R-1820-F3. Top speed was 210 mph. This Hawk II was one of 19 sold to Turkey in 1932. (NASM)

R-1535) / One .30-caliber and one .50-caliber Browning / 260 mph. In all, 164 F3Fs were delivered, 56 F2Fs, and 28 of the 1933 FF versions. All were biplane shipboard fighters with landing gear that retracted into the fuselage.

17. **Northrop A-17 Series**—1935 (A-17A version) / 47 ft. 9 in. / 31 ft. 8 in. / 7,543 lbs. / 4,990 lbs. / 19,400 ft. / 732 miles / 825-hp P&W R-1535 / Two .30-calibers in each wing and one .30-caliber rear flex-mount / 220 mph. The first 110 had fixed landing gear; the 129 A-17As had retractable gear, delivered 1937-1938.

18. **Seversky P-35**—1937 / 36 ft. / 25 ft. 4 in. / 5,599 lbs. / 4,315 lbs. / 30,600 ft. / 1,150 miles / 850-hp P&W R-1830-9 / One .30 and one .50-caliber (the P-35A, delivered in 1941, had a pair of .50s in the wings plus two .30s synchronized / 281 mph (the more powerful P-35A, 310 mph). In all, 76 P-35s and 60 P-35As were delivered.

19. **Curtiss P-36**—1937 / 37 ft. 3½ in. / 28 ft. 6 in. / 5,470 lbs. / 4,567 lbs. / 33,700 ft. / 825 miles / 1,050-hp P&W R-1830-17 / One .30 and one .50-caliber / 313 mph. In all, 241 were

A Curtiss P-36C of the 27th Pursuit Squadron, 1st Pursuit Group, in washable camouflage paint for the 1939 war games. (USAF)

Significant U.S. Military Aircraft

delivered to U.S. Army Air Corps; 778 were exported (Cyclone-powered), mostly to France as H-75As. Britain received about 235, which they called Mohawks.

20. **Douglas B-18 Bolo**—1937 (B-18A version) / 89 ft. 6 in. / 57 ft. 10 in. / 27,673 lbs. / 16,320 lbs. / 23,900 ft. / 1,100 miles (w/4,000 lbs. of bombs) / Two R-1820-53s of 1,000-hp each / Three .30-calibers, nose, dorsal, and ventral hatch / 216 mph. This was a DC-3 with bomber fuselage; 350 were procured.

21. **Curtiss P-40 Series**—1939 (E model) / 37 ft. 4 in. / 31 ft. 2 in. / 9,200 lbs. / 6,350 lbs. / 29,000 ft. / 700 miles / Three .50-calibers each wing / 354 mph. In all, 11,995 were built; 2,091 went to Russia and 3,633 to Britain and Commonwealth countries under Lend-Lease. F models and onward were Warhawks to the USAAF; E models and onward were Kittyhawks to the Commonwealth pilots, who called previous P-40s Tomahawks. For easy ident, small airscoop through P-40C (Tomahawks). Engines were V-1710 Allisons ranging from 1,040 to 1,150 rated hp (up to 1,470 hp war emergency), except for the F and L models, which had the low-altitude Merlin 28 (V-1650-1) of 1,080 hp.

22. **Lockheed Hudson** (RAF) and **A-28 / A-29** and **C-63** (USAAF)—1939 / 65 ft. 6 in. / 44 ft. 4 in. / 20,500 lbs. / 12,825 lbs. / 26,500 ft. / 1,550 miles / Two 900-hp Cyclone

The Curtiss P-40 series saw action in all theaters of WWII except over Germany, and was flown by the U.S., RAF, and all Commonwealth nations during WWII, as well as by the Soviets, who received about 2,000 of them. Pictured are machines of Royal Australian Air Force No. 84 Squadron.

R-1820-87s or GR-1820-G205As / Two .50-caliber dorsal turret, two .50-calibers fixed forward, and one .50 flex through rear door hatch / 253 mph. More than 2,500 were built; 1,302 were delivered to the USAAF. Hudsons were used extensively by Commonwealth nations.

23. **Boeing B-17 Flying Fortress**—1939 / **B-17G** specs: 103 ft. 9 in. / 74 ft. 9 in. / 65,500 lbs. / 36,135 lbs. / 35,600 ft. / 2,000 miles w/6,000 lbs. of bombs / Four 1,200-hp R-1820-97 / Two .50-cal. in chin, two free-mount nose guns, two .50-cals. each in dorsal and ventral turrets, one in each waist, and two in tail / 287 mph. Crew of 10. Total built: 12,677, mostly Fs (3,400) and Gs (8,680), the latter equipped with the chin turret.

24. **Grumman F4F Wildcat (FM-1 and Martlet)**—1940 (F4F-3 version) / 38 ft. / 28 ft. 9½ in. / 7,002 lbs. / 5,342 lbs. / 37,500 ft. / 845 miles / 1,200-hp P&W R-1830-76 / Two .50-caliber in each wing / 330 mph. The FM version, with tall vertical tail, was built by Eastern Aircraft Division of General Motors; the British flew this version as the Martlet.

25. **Douglas SBD Dauntless**—1940 / 41 ft. 6 in. / 31 ft. 8 in. / Combat weight 9,000 lbs. / Empty weight not available / 25,200 ft. / 1,565 miles / 1,000-hp Wright R-1820-60 / Two fixed .50-calibers forward, two flex-mounted rear / 250 mph. Total built was 5,396, plus 863 as A-24s for the USAAF.

26. **Consolidated (Convair) PBY-5 Catalina**—1940 / 104 ft. 0 in. / 63 ft. 10 in. / 30,700 lbs. / Empty weight not available / 1,405-mile range w/external ordnance (two torpedoes or

Douglas SBD Dauntlesses of the type that sank four enemy carriers during the Battle of Midway. These craft are returning to the new Yorktown, *October 1943.* (U.S. Navy)

Significant U.S. Military Aircraft 113

three depth charges of 325 lbs. ea.) / Two 1,200-hp P&W R-1830-92s / Three .30-calibers, two .50-caliber / 180 mph. As the PBY-5A, it was amphibious with retractable wheels; the U.S. Army bought 286 as OA-10s. Production for the Navy began in 1935 and ended in 1945; total built was 2,387.

27. **Douglas A-20 Havoc**—1940 / 61 ft. 4in. / 48 ft. 0 in. / 26,000 lbs. / 16,840 lbs. / 23,600 ft. / 1,100 miles w/2,000 lbs. of bombs / 1,700-hp Double Cyclone R-2600-29 / Six fixed forward .50-cal., two in dorsal turret, and one through ventral hatch / 320 mph. Havocs went to the French and British as DB-7s (Bostons); USAAF bought 206 Havocs.

28. **Bell P-39 Airacobra** and **P-63 Kingcobra**—1941, 1943 (P-39D) / 34 ft. 0 in. / 30 ft. 2 in. / 7,830 lbs. / 6,300 lbs. / 29,000 ft. / 350 miles / 1,150-hp Allison V-1710-35 / 355 mph. Four .30-cal. wing guns, two .50-cal. nose guns, one 37mm cannon / A total of 8,854 was delivered to the USAAF, but Lend-Lease machines were taken from that total, including 4,773 to Russia.

    The Kingcobra, delivered in 1943, had a new wing and two-stage supercharger, a top speed of 400 mph at 25,000 feet; of 3,303 built, most went to Russia.

29. **Consolidated B-24 Liberator**—1941 / 110 ft. 0 in. / 67 ft. 2 in. / 63,000 lbs. / 36,000 lbs. / 28,000 ft. / 2,100 w/5000 lbs. of bombs / Four 1,200-hp R-1830-65 / Eight to 10

The B-24 Liberator was built in greater numbers than any other American warplane; one variant, used by the Navy, was known as the Privateer. See #29.

114 1001 Flying Facts and Firsts

.50-calibers, two each in nose and tail, one each waist, one in ventral chute, and one to three in nose windows, nose turret on H and Gs / 303 mph at 25,000 ft. (B-24M). 18,188 were built, the highest number of any U.S. combat aircraft; Britain got more than 2,000 under provisions of Lend-Lease Act of March 1941. The U.S. Navy had a few single-tail versions known as Privateers.

30. **Lockheed P-38 Lightning**—1942 / 52 ft. 0 in. / 37 ft. 10 in. / 18,410 lbs. / 13,600 lbs. / 39,000 ft. / 1,425 miles / Two 1,500-hp Allison V-1710-F30 / One Hispano Suiza

This photo is for markings and insignia buffs. The "S" on the tails of these P-38 Lightnings identifies the little-known 6th Air Force, which spent WWII guarding the Panama Canal. (USAF)

20mm cannon and four .50-caliber Colt-Brownings / 415 mph at 29,600 ft. A total of 10,036 Lightnings was produced. Photorecon versions were F-5s.

31. **North American B-25 Mitchell**—1941 / 67 ft. 7 in. / 53 ft. 6 in. / 33,000 lbs. / 19,480 lbs. (bombardier nose versions) / 24,200 ft. / 1,350 miles w/3,000 lbs. of bombs / Two 1,350-hp Double Cyclone R-2600-13s / 275 mph. Armament varied widely on the Mitchells. The hardnose G and H models had a 75mm cannon, the latter with 12 .50-caliber machine guns, eight firing forward as fixed weapons. The USAAF took delivery of 9,815 Mitchells, but more than 2,000 of those went to Russia, Britain, China, Brazil, and the Netherlands.

32. **Martin B-26 Marauder**—1941 (B-26G version) / 71 ft. 0 in. / 56 ft. 1in. / 37,200 lbs. / 23,700 lbs. / 20,000 ft. / 1,300 miles at 225 mph w/3,000 lbs. of bombs / Two 2,000-hp P&W Double Wasp R-2800-43s / Two .50-cal. in dorsal turret, two in tail, four in package blisters forward of bomb bay, two in rear side hatches, and one in nose / 315 mph at 15,000 ft. The USAAF received 4,708 Marauders, of which 422 went to Britain.

33. **Grumman TBF and GM's Eastern Aircraft Division TBM Avenger**—1942 / 54 ft. 2 in. / 41 ft. 0 in. / 18,250 lbs. / Empty weight not available / 22,800 ft. / 1,130 miles / 1,450-hp Wright R-2600-8 / Two fixed forward .50-calibers, one flex .50 rear and one .30-caliber ventral aft of the bomb/torpedo bay / 270 mph. 2,546 were built by Grumman as TBFs, with 7,290 built by GM as TBMs.

34. **Curtiss SB2C Helldiver**—1943 / 49 ft. 8 in. / 36ft. 8 in. / 16,607 lbs. / 10,114 lbs. / 24,600 ft. / 1,100 miles w/1,000 lbs. of bombs / Wright R-2600-8 of 1,700 hp (takeoff) / Two .50-calibers rear flex, and four .50-calibers fixed forward, or two 20mm cannon fixed forward

After the unacceptable torpedo bomber losses at Midway it was clear that such machines should be differently used. The TBFs and TBMs also proved relatively ineffective early in the war due to the use of obsolete and faulty torpedoes. Changes in tactics and ordnance carried allowed the Grumman Avenger to prove its worth. (U.S. Marine Corps photo)

(wings) / 280 mph. 7,200 were built, including 1,000 built in Canada as SBWs; 900 were built as A-25s for the Army, and there were some Fairchild-built SBFs.

35. **Chance Vought F4U Corsair**—1943 / 41 ft. 0 in. / 32 ft. 10 in. / 14,003 lbs. / 8,982 lbs. / 36,900 ft. / 1,018 miles / 2,000-hp P&W R-2800-8 Double Wasp / Three .50-cal. in each wing / 415 mph at 21,000 ft. w/water injection. Corsairs remained in Navy service through the Korean War; 7,829 were delivered to the Navy, all models.

36. **Republic P-47 Thunderbolt**—1943 (P-47D-20 model) / 40 ft. 9 in. / 36 ft. 1 in. / 13,500 lbs. / 10,700 lbs. / approx. 36,000 ft. / 650 miles / 2,000-hp P&W Double Wasp R-2800-21 / Four .50-calibers in each wing / 433 mph at 30,000 ft. / 15,677 were built.

37. **Grumman F6F Hellcat**—1943 / 42 ft. 10 in. / 33 ft. 6½ in. / 12,800 lbs. (w/drop tank, 125 gal.) / 9,020 lbs. / 35,000 ft. / 1,495 miles w/drop tank and economy cruise (145 mph) / 2,000-hp P&W R-2800-10 / Three .50-calibers each wing, late models added one 20mm cannon inboard each wing / 380 mph. The U.S. Navy received 12,275 Hellcats.

The WWII Chance Vought Corsairs also fought again in Korea, largely with "retread" (ex-WWII) pilots at their controls. This one belonged to VMF-312, flying from the escort carrier Bairoko.

These are the kind of airplanes that sank four enemy carriers during the Battle of Midway. These craft are returning to the new Yorktown, October, 1943. Can you identify these machines? (See June 3-6, 1942, Section 1, and #25 Significant Combat Aircraft.) (Photo courtesy of U.S. Navy)

38. **North American P-51B Mustang**—1943 / 37 ft. 0 in. / 32 ft. 3 in. / Combat weight 9,800 lbs. (11,800 lbs. w/max fuel) / 7,390 lbs. / 41,800 ft. / 1,125 miles at 10,000 ft. w/269-gal. internal; 2,200 miles w/two 150-gal. drop tanks / U.S. Packard-built Merlin V-1650-3 of 1,450 hp (geared, two-speed, two-stage supercharger) at 19,800 ft. and 1,190 hp at 31,000 ft. / Two .50-calibers in each wing / 445 mph. Later versions (D, K) had bubble canopy, beefed-up airframe, dorsal fin, and the Merlin V-1650-11 with water injection which had 2,270 hp at 4,000 feet "war emergency," six .50-calibers, and up to 2,000 pounds external ordnance capacity. Originally designed for export to Britain, and apparently based upon the Curtiss XP-46 (not produced), the first 462 Mustangs (as the British called them; North American called them Apaches) were fitted with low-altitude Allisons. Those that followed were Merlin-powered; 13,603 were built altogether, plus 500 as A-36 attack craft fitted with Allisons.

An F6F Hellcat returns to the Intrepid, January 1944. This airplane was an all-around engineering triumph—superior performance, but a simple, uncluttered machine that was easy to fly and maintain. Grumman was the manufacturer responsible for its design.

A North American Mustang of the 354th FG lands at Ober Olm, Germany, April 17, 1945. That's a Cessna UC-78 raising dust in the background. Pilots and aviation writers have always favored the P-51 Mustang, but the 325th FG, which flew P-40s, P-47s and P-51s in turn, had better kill-loss ratios in the P-40 and P-47. (USAF)

Significant U.S. Military Aircraft   119

39. **Boeing B-29** and **B-50 Superfortress**—1944 (B-29A) / 141 ft. 3 in. / 99 ft. 0 in. / 134,000 lbs. / 70,140 lbs. / 31,850 ft. / 3,250 miles at 25,000 ft. w/20,000 lbs. of bombs / Four 2,200-hp Wright Cyclone R-3350-23 / 10 .50-calibers in four remote-controlled turrets and one 20mm cannon in tail / 358 mph. A total of 3,960 was built.

    The **Boeing B-50** was essentially a B-29 with more powerful engines and heavier skin. Fitted with the 3,000-hp P&W Wasp Major, it could do 380 mph at 25,000 feet, had a gross weight of 173,000 pounds, and could carry up to 30,000 pounds of bombs. Many were converted to tankers.

40. **Douglas A-26 (B-26) Invader**—1944 / 70 ft. 0 in. / 50 ft. 7 in. / 37,000 lbs. / 22,800 lbs. / 22,100 ft. / 1,400 miles w/4,000 lbs. of bombs at 284 mph / Two 2,100-hp P&W R-2800-79s / Up to 18 .50-calibers, with eight fixed in nose, three fixed under each wing, two each in dorsal and ventral turrets remotely controlled, plus 14 5-in. rockets / 373 mph. The A-26 Invader became the B-26 in 1948 after "Attack" designations were dropped and the Martin B-26 **Marauder** was stricken from inventory; 2,451 were built as A-26s.

41. **Northrop P-61 Black Widow**—1944 / 66 ft. 0 in. / 48 ft. 11 in. / 28,500 lbs. / 22,200 lbs. / 33,000 ft. / 600 miles or 2.5 hrs. at economy cruise / Two 2,000-hp R-2800-10 Double

This is a Boeing B-29? Sure is; General Motors hired Don Berlin (designer of the Curtiss P-36/P-40) in mid-war to try its Allison engines on the new Superfortress. Actually, the Army called it the XB-39, and the engines were V-3420 Allisons (double V-1710s). (Donovan R. Berlin)

This Douglas B-26 (A-26) Invader, with hydraulic system damaged by ground fire, makes a belly landing at Kimpo Airfield, Seoul, Korea, 1951. This is the "soft-nosed" version, originally an A-26C; the B models were "hard-nosed," most with eight .50-caliber guns in the nose. (USAF)

This early example of the Lockheed P-80, America's first operational jet fighter, was given multiple coats of paint to achieve a smooth skin, but the finishes available in 1945 would not withstand flight through rain at 500 mph, so subsequent production versions were delivered unpainted. (USAF)

Wasps / Four 20mm forward fixed cannon, two in turret on early versions / 369 mph. 706 were built.

42. **Lockheed F-80 Shooting Star**—1945 / 38 ft. 10½ in. / 34 ft. 6 in. / 11,700 lbs. / 8,000 lbs. / 40,000 ft. / 1,100 miles with tip tanks / G.E. J-33-GE9 / Six .50-calibers / 558 mph. The P-80 was the USAF's first service jet fighter.

Significant U.S. Military Aircraft

43. **North American F-82 Twin Mustang**—1945 / 51 ft. 3in. / 38 ft. 3 in. / 24,600 lbs. / 14,000 lbs. / 42,000 ft. / 1,600 miles / Two 1,500-hp Allison V-1710-119s / Six fixed forward .50-calibers; some versions eight more .50s in center section pod / 475 mph. 250 were delivered, 20 with Merlin engines.

44. **Grumman F7F Tigercat**—1945 / 51 ft. 6 in. / 46 ft. 11 in. / 22,091 lbs. / 17,518 lbs. / 37,300 ft. / 1,055 miles at 242 mph at 15,000 ft. / Two 2,350-hp P&W R-2800-34W / Four 20mm and four .50-cal. / 402 mph at 15,000 ft. Most of the 364 built went to the Marines as land-based night fighters.

45. **Grumman F8F Bearcat**—1945 / 35 ft. 6 in. / 28 ft. 0 in. / 8,788 lbs. / 6,733 lbs. / 33,700 ft. / 1,450 miles with drop tanks (normal, 955 miles) / P&W R-2800-22W (34W late models) / Two .50-calibers each wing / 424 mph at 17,300 ft. 1,263 were built.

46. **Douglas Skyraider AD-1** through **AD-7 (A-1J)**—1946 through 1956 / 50 ft. 0 in. / 39 ft. 0 in. / 25,000 lbs. / 12,000 lbs. / 1,400 miles with torpedo and bombs / 3,000-hp Wright R-3350-26W / Four 20mm cannon / 375 mph. 3,180 were built in 28 different versions.

The workhorse Douglas Skyraider (AD; A-1) was built in 28 different versions over a period of 10 years and remained in service throughout the Vietnam War. A total of 3,135 was built. This one is an AD-6 model. (McDonnell Douglas)

47. **Republic F-84 Thunderjet**—1947 / 36 ft. 5 in. / 37 ft. 2½ in. / 14,100 lbs. / 9,000 lbs. / 1,000 miles w/tip tanks / 4,000-lb. thrust Allison J35-A-15C / Six .50-caliber M3 machine guns / 550 mph. Later versions had Allison J35-A-29 engines of 5,000 pounds static thrust.

48. **Convair B-36**—1948 / 230 ft. 0 in. / 162 ft. 1 in. / 326,000 lbs. / Empty weight not available / 41,000 ft. / 10,500 miles w/extra fuel / Six 3,500-hp P&W Wasp Majors R-4360-41, plus four 5,200-lbs. thrust G.E. J47-GE-19 turbojets / Eight pairs of 20mm cannon in six retractable turrets, plus nose and tail guns / 435 mph. Unofficially, the B-36 was called the Peacemaker; 328 were produced.

49. **Northrop XB-35 and YB-49 Flying Wings**—1948; The prop-driven XB-35 Flying Wing bomber first flew in 1946 fitted with four 3,000-hp P&W R-4360s, had a range of 8,000 miles with 16,000 pounds of bombs; max speed was 391 mph at 35,000 feet, and service ceiling was 39,700 feet. Following a second XB-35 and a YB-35 came two jet-powered versions in 1947 and 1950, the YB-49 and YRB-49A. YB-49: 172 ft. 0 in. / 53 ft. 1 in. / 213,000 lbs. / 88,100 lbs. / 3,458 miles at 382 mph at 35,000 ft. w/30,000 lbs. of bombs / Eight 4,000-lbs. thrust Allison J35-A-5 / Armament never installed / 530 mph.

50. **McDonnell FH-1 Phantom**—1948 / 40 ft. 9½ in. / 38 ft. 9 in. / 10,035 lbs. / 6,683 lbs. / 43,000 ft. / 690 miles / Two Westinghouse J30-WE-20s of 1,600 lbs. thrust each / Four .50-cal. nose guns / 505 mph. The Navy's first all-jet service carrier fighter (not to be confused with the later F-4 Phantom), 60 were built.

51. **North American F-86 Sabre**—1949 (F-86F version) / 37 ft. 1 in. / 37 ft. 6 in. / 16,680 lbs. / 10,950 lbs. / 53,000 ft. / 1,250 miles / 5,970 lb. thrust G.E. J47-GE-27 / Six .50-calibers plus 16 5-inch rockets / 670 mph. USAF fighter; also built in Canada, Australia, and Japan.

52. **McDonnell F2H Banshee**—1949 / 41 ft. 6 in. / 39 ft. 11½ in. / 14,000 lbs. / 8,400 lbs. / 52,000 ft. / 1,200 miles / Two 3,150-lb. thrust Westinghouse J34-WE-30 / Four 20mm nose cannon / 642 mph. Navy fighter; 892 built.

53. **Grumman F9F Panther**—1949 / 38 ft. 0 in. / 42 ft. 0 in. / 17,000 lbs. / 8,860 lbs. / 53,000 ft. / 1,200 miles w/tip tanks / P&W J48-P-4 or P-8 of 6,250 or 7,250 lbs. thrust / Four 20mm in nose plus external rocket/bombs to 500 lbs. / 630 mph. The F9F-6 through F9F-8 Cougar was a swept-wing version of the Panther (F9F-2 through F9F-5) described above; 1,988 were procured by the Navy. Max speed was 690 to 712 mph; it had the same armament, but could carry up to 2,000 pounds of bombs/missiles. First deliveries were in 1952. In 1956, the Navy took delivery of 201 Grumman F11F-1 Tigers, supersonic versions of the Cougar with "area rule" fuselage design. The Tiger's main claim to fame was that one once accelerated into several rounds of ammunition it had fired and shot itself down.

54. **Cessna O-1 (L-19) Bird Dog**—1950 / 36 ft. 0 in. / 25 ft. 10 in. / 2,430 lbs. / Empty weight not available / 530 miles / 213-hp Continental 0-470-11 / 115 mph. 3,431 were built by Cessna; Bird Dogs were also built in Japan by Fuji.

55. **Lockheed F-94C Starfire**—1950 / 37 ft. 6 in. / 41 ft. 5 in. / 25,000+ lbs. / Empty weight not available / 49,000 ft. / 1,000 miles / 6,250-lb. thrust P&W J48-P-5 / 48 2.75-in. rockets in nose and wing launchers (no guns) / 600 mph. All-weather USAF fighter.

Significant U.S. Military Aircraft

56. **Martin B-57 Canberra**—1951 / 64 ft. 0 in. / 65 ft. 5 in. / 56,250 lbs. / 23,173 lbs. / 45,000 ft. + / 805 miles w/8,000 lbs. of bombs / 7,220-lb. thrust Wright J65-W-1 / Four 20mm cannon / 541 mph. About 300 of this British design (English Electric Co.) were built in the U.S.

57. **Boeing B-47 Stratojet**—1951 / 116 ft. 0 in. / 107 ft. 2 in. / 230,000 lbs. / 80,000 lbs. / 45,000 ft. / 3,000 miles w/10,000 lbs. of bombs / Six G.E. J47-GE-25s of 6,970 lbs. thrust each / Two 20mm cannon in tail / 600 mph. 2,384 were built.

58. **Northrop F-89 Scorpion**—1951 / 59 ft. 8 in. / 53 ft. 4 in. / 45,000 lbs. / Empty weight not available / 50,000 ft. / Two 5,450-lb. thrust Allison J35-A-35s / Six Falcon missiles, two Gemie nukes, or 42 2.75-in. rockets / 600 mph. Early F-89s had 20mm nose cannon; 1,052 were built.

The McDonnell F2H Banshee series, F2H-1 through F2H-4, served with 29 squadrons of Navy and Marines. They were committed to combat in Korea in August 1951, flying from the Essex as part of TF 77. A total of 892 was built. (McDonnell Douglas))

The Martin-built B-57 Canberra had an Australian name and was a British design. The USAF took delivery of about 300 of them. (USAF)

59. **Republic F-84F Thunderstreak**—1954 / 33 ft. 7½ in. / 43 ft. 4½ in. / 19,340 lbs. gross / 48,000 ft. / 1,700 miles / 7,200-lb. thrust Wright J65-W-3 / Six .50-calibers and up to 6,000 lbs. external stores / 700 mph. A redesign of the F-84 with swept wings, more powerful engine, etc.

60. **Chance Vought F7U Cutlass**—1954 / 39 ft. 8½ in. / 44 ft. 3½ in. / 27,340 lbs. / 18,210 lbs. / 40,000 ft. / Two Westinghouse J46-WE-8 of 6,100 lbs. thrust w/afterburner operating / 650 mph+. Tailless Navy fighter; 307 built.

61. **North American F-100 Super Sabre**—1954 / 38 ft. 0 in. / 47 ft. 0 in. / 50,000 ft. / Weights not available / 1,000 miles+ / P&W J57-P-21 of 16,000 lbs. thrust w/afterburning / Four 20mm cannon, plus missiles and rockets underwings / 825 mph. First USAF Mach 1 operational fighter; 2,294 built.

The Navy procured 307 of the 650-mph tailless Chance Vought F7U Cutlass fighters during the 1950s. Armament was four 20mm cannon and Mighty Mouse rockets. Service life was short because of instability problems. (Chance Vought)

62. **North American FJ-4 Fury**—1955 / 39 ft. 1 in. / 37 ft. 6 in. / 20,000 lbs. / 12,000 lbs. / 45,000 ft. / 7,800-lb. thrust Wright J65-W-16A / Four 20mm cannon, plus six Sidewinder or Bullpup missiles / 687 mph. FJ-1 through FJ-4 were Navy versions of the USAF F-86 Sabre; 1,137 built.

63. **Boeing B-52 Stratofortress**—1955 / B-52G specs: 185 ft. 0 in. / 157 ft. 7 in. / 488,000 lbs. / 170,000 lbs. / 55,000 ft. / 7,500 miles w/10,000 lbs. of bombs / Eight 13,750-lb. thrust P&W J57-P-43W (the H model has P&W TF-33 turbofans, which give a 15 percent increase in range) / Six-barrel Gatling in tail or radar-aimed Vulcan cannon / 665 mph. 744 Stratofortresses were built.

Final version of the Stratofortress was the B-52H, fitted with turbofans, thick skin, and a passel of gee-whiz electronics. Both the G and H models had cut-down vertical tail. (USAF photo by Sgt. Jerry A. Montrose)

64. **McDonnell F3H Demon**—1956 / 35 ft. 4 in. / 58 ft. 11 in. / 33,900 lbs. / 22,133 lbs. / Service ceiling and range not available / 9,200 lb. thrust Allison J71-A-2 / Four 20mm cannon, plus Sidewinder missiles / Mach 1+. 518 were produced, including 56 early versions with 8,000-lb. thrust J40-WE-22 engine.

65. **Douglas F4D-1 Skyray**—1956 / 33 ft. 6 in. / 45 ft. 8 in. / 27,000 lbs. / 16,024 lbs. / 52,000 ft. / 950 miles w/external drop tanks / 10,200-lb. thrust P&W J57-P-8B / Four 20mm wing cannon / Mach 1.05. Tailless, semi-delta fighter; 422 built.

66. **Convair F-102A Delta Dagger**—1956 / 38 ft. 1½ in. / 68 ft. 3in. / 27,000 lbs.+ / Empty weight not available / 54,000 ft. / P&W J57-P-35 of 10,900 lbs. thrust / Six Hughes Falcon missiles and 24 2.75-inch rockets / 825 mph. Approximately 1,000 Delta Daggers were built.

67. **Douglas B-66 Destroyer** and **A3D Skywarrior**—1956 / 72 ft. 6 in. / 75 ft. 2 in. / 83,000 lbs. / 42,788 lbs. / 45,000 ft. / 1,500 miles / Two Allison J71-A-13 of 10,200 lbs. thrust each / Two 20mm cannon in remote tail turret / 650 mph. The A3D version for the Navy had 9,700-lb. thrust P&W J57s and slightly shorter fuselage; 282 were built as B-66s and 294 as A3Ds.

68. **Douglas A4D Skyhawk**—1956 / 27 ft. 6 in. / 40 ft. 6 in. / 24,300 lbs. / 9,300 lbs. / 55,000 ft. / 2,000 miles / Curtiss-Wright J65-W-4B / 16A; last 194 fitted with P&W J52-P-8As / Two 20mm cannon / 710 mph. 1,540 were delivered.

Significant U.S. Military Aircraft

These Douglas A-4E Skyhawks of Attack Squadron 72 were flying from the carrier Independence *in the mid-1960s. Pilots liked this airplane very much and were sorry to see it being phased out during the mid-1980s.* (U.S. Navy)

69. **McDonnell F-101 Voodoo**—1957 / 39 ft. 8 in. / 67 ft. 5 in. / 50,000 lbs. + / Empty weight not available / 55,000 ft. / 800 miles combat radius / Two P&W J57-P-13 of 18,000 lbs. thrust each with afterburning / Four 20mm, three Falcon missiles, and 12 2.75-inch rockets / 1,210 mph, Mach limit 1.85 at 40,000 ft. / The F-101B two-place can carry Genies.

70. **Chance Vought F8U Crusader**—1957 / 35 ft. 8 in. / 54 ft. 2½ in. / Loaded weight about 27,000 lbs. / 55,000 ft. / P&W J57-P-12 of 17,500 lbs. thrust w/afterburning / Four 20mm cannon in fuselage sides, 32 2.75-inch rockets, four Sidewinder missiles / 1,000+ mph. Notable for its unique variable incidence wing, 1,524 of this first 1,000-mph Navy carrier fighter were delivered.

71. **Lockheed F-104 Starfighter**—1958 / 21 ft. 11 in. / 54 ft. 9 in. / 20,000 lbs. / 14,000 lbs. + / 60,000 ft. + / G.E. J79-GE-7 of 16,000 lbs. thrust w/afterburning / 20mm Vulcan cannon and four Sidewinders / 1,600 mph. More than 2,000 Starfighters were produced for 14 Free World nations.

72. **Republic F-105 Thunderchief**—1959 / 34 ft. 11 in. / 64 ft. 1 in. / 35,200 lbs. / 27,500 lbs. / 50,000 ft. + / 2,000 miles w/external fuel / P&W J75-P-19W of 26,500 lbs. thrust w/water injection / Vulcan six-barrel cannon, plus a mix of missiles, rockets, or bombs / 1,350 mph.

An RF-101 McDonnell Voodoo of the 460th Tactical Reconnaissance Wing, flown by Col. Edward Taylor, takes off from Tan Son Nhut Air Base in South Vietnam, May 1966. Top speed was above 1,200 mph; engines were a pair of P&W J57-P13s of 18,000 pounds static thrust each. (USAF)

The Lockheed F-104 Starfighter served 14 Free World nations. It was a slightly unbelievable machine with a wingspan of less than 22 feet and gross weight of 20,000 pounds, resulted in a wing loading of 112 lbs. sq./ft. A 1,600-mph fighter, more than 2,000 were built. (USAF)

Significant U.S. Military Aircraft

73. **Convair B-58 Hustler**—1959 / 56 ft. 10 in. / 96 ft. 9 in. / Max loaded weight 162,000 lbs. / 60,000 ft. / 3,000 miles / Four GE J79-GE-5B of 10,000 lbs. thrust each / One 20mm Gatling / 1,324 mph. A delta-wing Mach 2+ medium bomber; 80 were built.

74. **Convair F-106A Delta Dart**—1959 / 38 ft. 3 in. / 70 ft. 8½ in. / Loaded weight 35,000 lbs. / 60,000 ft. / 1,000 miles (approx.) / P&W J75-P-17 of 26,000 lbs. thrust w/afterburning / Two Genie and four Super Falcon missiles / 1,525 mph.

75. **McDonnell Douglas F-4 Phantom II**—1960 / 38 ft. 5 in. / 58 ft. 0 in. / 45,000 lbs. max loaded / 70,000 ft. / Combat radius 1,000 miles / Two G.E. J79-GE-2 of 16,150 lbs. thrust w/afterburning / Four Sparrow III and four Sidewinder missiles / Mach 2.4+. Originally a Navy fighter, the Phantom II also became a USAF fighter and proved so effective in both services that it was produced in many versions.

76. **Grumman OV-1 Mohawk**—1961 / 48 ft. 0 in. / 41 ft. 0 in. / 18,108 lbs. / 12,054 lbs. / 1,010 miles w/external tanks / Two Lycoming T53-L-701 turboprops of 1,150 shp / Six wing hardpoints for ordnance / 308 mph. An Army recce craft.

77. **Sikorsky H-3 Sea King (HSS-2)**—1961 / Rotor diameter 62 ft. 0 in. / 54 ft. 9 in. / 18,626 lbs. gross / 625 miles / Two G.E. T58-GE-8B turboshafts of 1,250 shp each / 850 lbs. of homing torpedoes, depth charges, etc. / 166 mph. 255 were built for the U.S. Navy; also flown by friendly foreign nations.

The High Hat Squadron, VF-14, was flying F-4 Phantoms from the attack carrier F.D. Roosevelt *in September 1966, when this photo was made in the Gulf of Tonkin. Twenty years later the High Hats were flying F-14 Tomcats as part of the air group aboard the* John F. Kennedy. (U.S. Navy photo by Neal Crowe)

The Army is limited in its acquisition of fixed-wing aircraft. Except for some Beech King Airs for the brass to ride around in, this OV-1 Mohawk is as large as is permitted by agreement with the Air Force. (Grumman)

78. **Lockheed P-3 Orion Series**—1961 / 99 ft. 8 in. / 116 ft. 10 in. / 142,000 lbs. / 61,491 lbs. / Mission radius 1,551 miles w/three hours on station at 1,500 ft. / Torpedos, mines, depth charges (including nukes) internal, 10 wing pylons for ordnance, for total weapons load of 20,000 lbs. A shore-based antisubmarine / recce aircraft originally based on the turboprop Electra II airliner; still in production, 1988.

79. **Grumman A-6A Intruder**—1961 / 53 ft. 0 in. / 54 ft. 9 in. / 60,625 lbs. / 26,350 lbs. / 47,200 ft. / Ferry range 2,378 miles / Two 8,700-lb. thrust each P&W J52P-8A / Wide variety of bombs and missiles may be carried externally / 563 knots. The KA-6D is a tanker version; the EA-6A is the Prowler, the electronic warfare version. Still in production, the A-6F version is next.

80. **Bell UH-1 Huey Helicopter**—1961 / UH-1B: Blade length 44 ft. / Chord 21 in. / 8,500 lbs. / 4,523 lbs. / 193 miles / Lycoming T53-L-5/9/11 of 1,100 shp / Armament varied; a 7.62mm minigun and 2.75-in. rocket system on each side was common / 111 knots.

81. **Boeing Vertol CH-47 Chinook**—1962 / Rotor diameter (each) 60 ft. 0 in. / Length 51 ft. 0 in. / 46,000 lbs. gross / Mission radius 115 miles at 160 mph w/13,450 lb. payload / Two Lycoming T55-L-712 turboshafts of 3,700 shp each / 190 mph. About 430 remain in U.S. Army service; also flown by RAF, RCAF, Egypt, and other friendly foreigns.

82. **Grumman E-2 Hawkeye**—1964 / 80 ft. 7 in. / 57 ft. 7 in. / 51,900 lbs. / 38,009 lbs. / 1,605 miles / Two Allison T56-A-422/425 turboprops of 4,910 shp / Unarmed; carries a large saucer-

SIGNIFICANT U.S. MILITARY AIRCRAFT

A Sikorsky SH-3D dips its sonar into the water to listen for enemy submarines. (Sikorsky)

shaped radome above fuselage as a carrier-borne early warning and fighter control aircraft / 348 mph. 145 of several versions built, latest in 1985.

83. **North American B-70 Valkyrie**—1965 / 115 ft. 0 in. / 170 ft. 0 in. / Max loaded weight 550,000 lbs. / 70,000 ft. / 7,600 miles / Four G.E. J93-GE-3 of 33,000 lbs. thrust each w/afterburning / 2,000+ mph. Three were built; one remains on display at the Air Force Museum. *Note*: The SR-71 Blackbird, in service with SAC, is not a combat aircraft and therefore not listed here. See Section III, Record Flights.

84. **Sikorsky S-65A Super Jolly** and **H-53 Sea Stallion**—1966 / Rotor diameter 72 ft. 2.75 in. / 67 ft. 2 in. / Gross weight 42,000 lbs. / 257 miles / Marine version has two 3,925-shp G.E.

Another seemingly ageless airplane is the Lockheed P-3 Orion, a Navy patrol/sub hunter that has been operational since 1961. The U.S. Navy plans to keep in service until the turn of the century. Packed with high-tech electronics and carrying Harpoon antiship missiles, this craft is also in use by many friendly foreigns. (Lockheed California Company)

T64-GE-413 turboshafts; Navy's RH-53Ds have two 4,380-shp T64-GE-415 engines / Fitted with special anti-mine gear / 196 mph.

85. **Cessna A-37 Dragonfly**—1967 / 35 ft. 10½ in. / 29 ft. 3½ in. / Gross weight 14,000 lbs. / 1,010 miles / Two 2,850-lb. thrust G.E. J85-GE-17A turbojets / One 7.62 minigun (Gatling type) and eight underwing hardpoints for 5,000 lbs. of ordnance / 507 mph. 538 were built; some saw action in Vietnam.

86. **LTV (Vought) A-7D Corsair II**—1967 / 38 ft. 9 in. / 46 ft. 1½ in. / 42,000 lbs. / 19,781 lbs. / 50,000+ ft. / Ferry range w/external tanks 2,871 miles / Allison TF41-A-1 turbofan of 14,250 lbs. thrust / One 20mm Gatling, plus 15,000 lbs. of ordnance (missiles, bombs, rockets, etc.) / 698 mph. 459 of the USAFs D-version were produced, with deliveries begun in 1973; the first A-7s were delivered in 1967.

87. **Bell HueyCobra AH-1G Attack Helicopter**—1967 / Rotor diameter 44 ft. 0 in. / Chord 27 in. / 9,500 lbs. / 5,809 lbs. / 7.62mm minigun and 40mm grenade launcher in turret, plus 2.75-in. rockets and TOW missile launcher / 129 knots. The AH-1S versions, delivered in 1978-1979, had 20mm Gatling guns and flat glass canopies, along with some stealth technology in an all-new fuselage.

Significant U.S. Military Aircraft

The Grumman A-6A Intruder. The taxpayers got their money's worth with the acquisition of this flying machine, which has been in service since 1965. (U.S. Navy)

88. **Cessna O-2 (Skymaster Model 337)**—1967 / 38 ft. 2 in. / 29 ft. 9 in. / 5,400 lbs. / 2,700 lbs. / 19,300 ft. / 1,350 miles / Two 210-hp Continental IO-360-CD / Four underwing pylons for flares, rockets, or gun pods. Used by USAF in Vietnam for forward air control (FAC) missions, 346 were acquired. Others were built by Reims Aviation in France.

89. **General Dynamics F-111**—1969 / 63 ft. 0 in.; fully swept 31 ft. 11½ in. / length 73 ft. 6 in. / 51,000 ft. / 91,500 lbs. / 46,172 lbs. / 3,165 miles w/internal fuel / One 20mm Gatling or two 750-lb. bombs in internal weapons bay; four swiveling and four fixed wing pylons with up to 25,000 lbs. ordnance capacity or fuel tanks / Mach 2.2. 437 were built, plus 76 as FB-111s for SAC.

90. **Northrop F-5E Tiger II**—1973 / 26 ft. 8 in. / 48 ft. 3½ in. / 24,080 lbs. / 9,558 lbs. / 53,000 ft. / 1,974 miles w/external tanks / Two GE J85-GE-21 of 5,000 lbs. thrust each / Two Sidewinders, wingtip launch; two 20mm nose cannon; plus up to 7,000 lbs. of ordnance carried

The UH series of Bell helicopters is tri-service with the military forces of more than 30 friendly nations. This is the Vietnam era Marine Corps version, UH-1E. Unarmed, it was called a "Slick." Others were fitted with a 7.62mm Gatling gun and 2.75-inch rocket launchers.

on underwing and fuselage hardpoints / Mach 1.5. More than 1,000 of this version were built. The design dates back to the early 1960s, originally conceived as a standard, low-cost NATO fighter.

91. **Lockheed S-3A Viking**—1974 / 68 ft. 8 in. / 53 ft. 4 in. / 52,539 lbs. / 26,650 lbs. / Combat range 2,300+ miles / Two G.E. TF34-GE-2 turbofans of 9,275 lbs. thrust each / As a four-place carrier-borne, anti-sub aircraft, torpedoes, mines, depth charges, missiles, etc., carried in bomb bays and under wings / 518 mph. 187 were procured initially; follow-ons are expected.

92. **Grumman F-14 Tomcat**—1975 / 64 ft. 1½ in. / 61 ft. 10½ in. / 74,348 lbs. / 38,930 lbs. / Two P&W TF30-P-414 afterburning turbofans of 20,600 lbs. thrust / One multi-barrel cannon (M61A1) front port side, four missile bays recessed under fuselage, and two wing pylons for fuel and/or Sidewinders / Mach 2.34. 491 were delivered to the U.S. Navy as A models; a contract for B models was cancelled.

93. **Fairchild A-10 Thunderbolt II**—1976 / 57 ft. 6in. / 53 ft. 4 in. / 46,270 lbs. / 19,856 lbs. / 30,500 ft. / 3,048 miles / Two 9,065-lb. thrust G.E. TF34-GE-100 turbofans / One 30mm Gatling-type cannon (GAU-8/A), 10 underwing hardpoints and one under fuselage for up to 16,000 lbs. of varied ordnance / 460 mph. 715 were built.

Significant U.S. Military Aircraft

The General Dynamics F-111 resulted from former Secretary of Defense Robert McNamara's order that the Navy and Air Force select similar fighter designs that could be manufactured with a maximum "commonality" of parts. The Navy did without rather than accept its version of this machine, while the Air Force has crippled along with theirs—which McNamara declared could serve as both fighter and strategic bomber. This one, an F-111F, was photographed at Willow Grove, PA, by Francis "Diz" Dean in 1975.

The Navy's newest sub hunter is the S-3A Viking built by Lockheed.

The McDonnell Douglas F-15 Eagle, America's Mach 2.5 air superiority fighter of the 1980s. (McDonnell Douglas St. Louis)

94. **McDonnell Douglas F-15 Eagle**—1976 / 42 ft. 9½ in. / 63 ft. 9½ in. / 40,000 lbs. / Absolute ceiling 66,900 ft. / Ferry range 2,800+ miles / One internally mounted 20mm Gatling-type cannon (M61A1), four Sidewinders and four Sparrow missiles externally; provision for up to 12,000 lbs. of varied ordnance on five hardpoints and electronic warfare pods outboard / Mach 2.5.

95. **General Dynamics F-16 Fighting Falcon**—1978 / 30 ft. 0 in. / 47 ft. 2 in. / 21,000 lbs. / 12,000 lbs. / 60,000+ ft. / ferry range 2,300+ miles / P&W F100-PW-100 turbofan of 25,000 lbs. thrust w/afterburning / One 20mm Gatling-type cannon in fuselage, infrared missile each wingtip, underwing hardpoints for other stores / Mach 2.

96. **Sikorsky UH-60A Blackhawk**—1978 / Rotor diameter 53.7 ft. / Length 53.7ft. / 20,250 lbs. / 10,900 lbs. / Two G.E. T700-GE-700 of 3,120 total hp / 160 knots. Slightly more than 1,000 are in service, designed to carry full equipped 11-man squads into battle.

SIGNIFICANT U.S. MILITARY AIRCRAFT

97. **McDonnell Douglas/British Aerospace AV-8B Harrier**—1981 / 30 ft. 4 in. / 46 ft. 4 in. / Max STOL, weight 28,750 lbs. / Radius of action 500+ miles / R-R Pegasus vectored thrust turbofan, F402-RR-404, of 21,500 lbs. thrust / Three under-fuselage and six underwing pylons for ordnance up to 9,200 lbs. / 740 mph. A vertical/short takeoff strike/recce aircraft for the U.S. Marines, 438 are planned.

98. **McDonnell Douglas (Hughes designed) AH-64 Apache Attack**—1985 / Rotor diameter 48 ft. / length 58.1 ft. / 20,700 lbs. / 10,600 lbs. / Two G.E. T700-GE-701s, total 3,388 hp / Carries, on four wing stations, over 6,000 lbs. of ordnance, including up to 16 Hellfires and six Sidewinders, or 76 2.75-inch FFAR rockets; chin turret contains 30mm Gatling-type cannon and advanced tech target acquisition systems, night vision, etc. 675 are planned, 264 were in service as of September 1, 1987.

99. **North American B-1B Bomber**—1985 / 137 ft. 0 in.; wings swept, 78 ft. 0 in. / 147 ft. 0 in. / 477,000 lbs. max gross / Unrefueled range is given by USAF as "intercontinental" / No service ceiling is given / Four G.E. F101-GE102 turbofans of 30,000 lbs. thrust / Principal weapons currently seen as air launched cruise missiles (ALCM) and the Boeing short range attack missile (SRAM), both nuke-tipped / Mach 1.2. The USAF hopes to acquire 100 B-1Bs, but late in 1987 Congress had funded only 50.

100. **McDonnell Douglas/Northrop FA-18 Hornet**—1986 / 37 ft. 6 in. / 56 ft. 0 in. / Takeoff weight 33,585 lbs. fighter mission, 47,000 lbs. attack mission / Combat radius 460 miles+ w/internal fuel only; over 633 miles in attack configuration / Two 16,000-lb. thrust G.E. F404-GE-400 turbofans / Seven weapons stations under wings and fuselage, plus wingtip missile shoes w/total capacity of 18,000 lbs. / Mach 1.8+. U.S. Navy originally asked for 1,377, but new Corsair II (A-7D) may prove too effective to be replaced by Hornets.

U.S. Combat Aircraft Quiz

Numbers in parentheses refer to aircraft profiles in this section.

1. What was America's first 10-engine bomber? (*48*)
2. Who manufactured the B-26? (*32, 40*)
3. The USAAF A-25 of WWII was known in the Navy as the _____? (*34*)
4. Where was the Bell P-63 most used in combat? (*28*)
5. Who or what was the "Bolo"? (*20*)
6. Identify the USAF Valkyrie. (*83*)
7. Which combat airplane was produced by the U.S. in greatest number? (*29*)
8. What was the first operational jet fighter procured by the USAF? (*42*)
9. What was the U.S. Navy's first all-jet carrier fighter? (*50*)
10. Was the Canberra an Australian-designed airplane? (*56*)
11. The USAF machine known as the Destroyer was the _____ in the U.S. Navy service. (*67*)
12. What is the Fighting Falcon? (*95*)
13. What ex-Army airplane was standard equipment on U.S. Air Mail routes during the early 1920s? (*2*)
14. Which manufacturer built the U.S. Navy's first and last Helldiver? (*9, 34*)
15. True or false: A Navy fighter once shot itself down. (*53*)
16. In what year did the Army Air Corps buy its last operational biplane fighter (pursuit)? (*10*)

17. Which Navy Corsair fought in two U.S. wars? *(35)*
18. Which is faster, the F-14 or the F-16? *(92, 95)*
19. What WWII U.S. fighter used the Rolls Royce Merlin engine in addition to the Mustang? *(21)*
20. What did the U.S. Navy call its version of the F-86? *(62)*
21. What was the first operational fighter with Mach 1 performance procured by the USAF? *(61)*
22. A USAF trainer, built by Cessna, was modified for use as an attack airplane in Vietnam; described by some as "a machine for converting kerosene into noise," it was the _____. *(85)*
23. In service with the U.S. Navy and many friendly foreigns is the Lockheed Orion. Name its primary mission. *(78)*
24. Initially, North American called the P-51 the Apache. The latest U.S. combat aircraft with this name is _____. *(98)*
25. What is the primary mission of the Grumman Hawkeye? *(82)*

V

Significant U.S. Civil Aircraft

Prior to the First World War, "commercial" flying was limited to exhibitions offered by pilot-entrepreneurs to a public willing to pay just to see "one of them contraptions take off and sail around just like a bird." True, there were visionaries even then who predicted the manner in which the flying machine would evolve, and the transportation revolution that it would inevitably foster, but not until the Douglas DC-2/DC-3 appeared in the mid-1930s did we possess a transport airplane capable of returning a profit from passenger revenues alone.

The first scheduled airlines in the United States, which managed to stay in business, grew from the air mail routes turned over to private operators by the Post Office Department during the late 1920s. These contractors survived because of the mail subsidies, and then expanded into passenger services with larger airplanes because (under the McNary-Watres Act of 1930) the Post Office began paying the operators for the "space available" in their airplanes. This was a deliberate ploy designed to encourage the acquisition of multiengine transports, which should promote the carrying of passengers, which in turn should eventually make the airlines self-sufficient, allowing an end to government subsidy.

It worked. Within two years, mail pay to the airlines went from an average of $1.10 per mile to $.55 per mile, while America's infant aircraft industry, aided by the concurrent "Lindbergh Boom," enjoyed a financial climate favorable to the development of more efficient airplanes. The first "big" airliners—the Ford, Fokker, and Stinson Trimotors—were less than efficient, but they provided the foundation (with help from the Post Office Department) for a domestic airline system second to none.

Meanwhile, private flying in America was almost exclusively represented during the 1920s by the gypsy barnstormers, flying from the nation's cow pastures in WWI-surplus Jennies and Standards. There was almost no market for new civil aircraft before the Post Office Department began contracting the mail routes early in 1926. Then, after Charles Lindbergh flew solo and nonstop from New York to Paris in May 1927, that bold and imaginative feat captured the fancy of the civilized world, dramatically demonstrating the reliability—and therefore the exciting promise—of "modern" air travel.

It was said that Lindbergh "sold" 10,000 airplanes overnight. Student pilot permits jumped from 575 in 1927 to 20,400 in 1929, and an industry that had produced a total of 60 new civil airplanes in 1924 turned out more than 6,000 in 1929.

The Great Depression of the '30s shot down the Lindbergh Boom, but many young, gifted Americans had been attracted to this fledgling industry, and their contributions would match the new challenges.

Although the Wrights and Glenn Curtiss had production facilities and offered airplanes for sale to civilian buyers before WWI, while exhibition pilots Clyde Cessna and Matty Laird built several machines that they sold to other pilots, the first commercially-produced airplanes for the U.S. civilian market appear to be the Curtiss Oriole, a two-place biplane with an OX-5 or C-6 engine, and Curtiss Seagull, a small flying boat, both of which appeared in 1920 and which found few buyers. The Laird Swallow, produced in Wichita the following year, was an OX-5-powered three-place biplane, and 43 were sold before Laird left that company and returned to his home in Chicago to start his own aircraft factory in 1923.

The Air Commerce Act of 1926 established Federal Aviation Regulations for the first time in the United States, and included the requirement that civil aircraft must henceforth meet certain standards of design and construction. Issuance of aircraft Approved Type Certificates began in 1927 (as did the awarding of pilots' certificates).

The descriptive format below lists, in the following order: Year the aircraft entered service in its original version / Brief description / Wingspan / Length / Gross weight / Empty weight / Service ceiling / Range / Engine(s) / Maximum speed.

1. **Boeing 40A**—1927 / Large biplane designed for flying the mail / 44 ft. 2 in. / 33 ft. 0 in. / 6,000 lbs. / 3,531 lbs. / 14,500 ft. / 650 miles / 410-hp P&W R-1340 Wasp (Model

Today's Boeing 747 jetliner can trace its ancestry back to this hefty biplane, the Boeing 40A, which flew the mail—and four adventuresome passengers at a time—between San Francisco and Chicago.

40B fitted with 500-hp P&W Hornet) / 128 mph. 25 were built for Boeing Air Transport, Contract Air Mail Route 18, San Francisco-Chicago. BAT later became United Air Lines.

2. **Waco Model 10**—1927 / Three-place biplane / 30 ft. 7 in. upper; 29 ft. 5 in. lower / 23 ft. 6 in. / 2,050 lbs. / 1,200 lbs. / 12,000 ft. / 385 miles / 90-hp Curtiss OX-5 V-8 liquid-cooled (WWI surplus) / 97 mph. Evolved from the 1925 Waco Nine, the first successful Waco. Later versions included the Waco Taperwing, which was a 10 with new wings and a large choice of engines. During the 1930s, Waco turned to cabin biplanes; all were fabric-covered.

3. **Stinson SM-1 Detroiter**—1927 / Six-place cabin monoplane, fabric-covered / 45 ft. 10 in. / 32 ft. 0 in. / 3,485 lbs. / 1,970 lbs. / 14,000 ft. / 700 miles / 220-hp Wright J5 Whirlwind / Max speed unavailable. The first of a long line of Stinson monoplanes.

4. **Travel Air Model 4000**—1928 / Three-place open biplane, fabric-covered / 34 ft. 8 in. upper; 28 ft. 8 in. lower / 23 ft. 6in. / 2,412 lbs. / 1,650 lbs. / 20,000 ft. / 450 miles / Originally fitted with the nine-cylinder Wright J5 Whirlwind, some had the later J6-7 or J6-9 Whirlwind radial of 225 and 300-hp respectively / 130 mph w/J5. Aerodynamically-balanced ailerons spawned the description "elephant-ear Travel Air." It was also called the "Wichita Fokker" because it portrayed a WWI Fokker D-VII in many war movies. The same airframe, originally with an OX-5 as the Model 2000, was available with a wide range of engines, as were most of the biplanes of that period. The Travel Air Company was formed in 1925 by Walter Beech, Clyde Cessna, and Lloyd Stearman.

5. **Lockheed Vega**—1928 / First of the wooden Lockheeds; wing plywood-skinned, fuselage built in concrete mold where a laminate of plywood veneer was held in place by an inflated rubber bag while the bonding agents cured; a five-place cabin design with a full cantilever wing, the Vega was popular with famous pilots of the "record-setting era" (Amelia Earhart's red Vega is in the NASM), and was normally powered with a J5 or J6-5 Whirlwind / 41 ft. 0 in. / 27 ft. 8 in. / 3,470 lbs. / 1,875 lbs. / 15,000 ft. / 900 miles / 138 mph. The Lockheed Company was formed in 1926 by Allan and Malcolm Lockheed (originally "Loughead") at Los Angeles. John K. "Jack" Northrop was chief engineer and Gerard "Jerry" Vultee his assistant.

The Lockheed Vega was a favorite of many famous pilots of the late 1920s and early '30s; those included Amelia Earhart, Wiley Post, Art Goebel, Roscoe Turner, and a host of others.

SIGNIFICANT U.S. CIVIL AIRCRAFT

6. **Fokker Tri-Motor F-10**—1928 / The first Fokker Tri-Motor was the F-7 of 1925, essentially the standard single-engine Fokker cabin monoplane with two additional engines. The trimotors were 10-place with fabric-covered fuselages and one-piece, all wood cantilever wings. The first ones were Whirlwind-powered; the F-10 described here had three 410-hp R-1340 Wasps / 79 ft. 2 in. / 49 ft. 11 in. / 12,500 lbs. / 7,390 lbs. / 16,500 ft. / 700 miles / 135 mph. The Fokker Trimotors were airliners and long-distance record setters.

7. **Curtiss-Robertson OX-5 Robin**—1928 / Three-place cabin monoplane / 41 ft. 0 in. / 25 ft. 10 in. / 2,217 lbs. / 1,489 lbs. / 10,200 ft. / 340 miles / 90-hp Curtiss OX-5 WWI surplus engine, water-cooled V-8 / 99 mph. Also produced with the 170-hp Curtiss Challenger engine, an air-cooled radial with six cylinders, and the 125-hp Warner Scarab air-cooled radial, as well as a couple of Whirlwinds.

8. **Ford 4-AT-B Tri-Motor**—1928 / The famed "Tin Goose" built by Henry Ford / 74 ft. 0 in. / 49 ft. 10 in. / 10,130 lbs. / 6,169 lbs. / 12,000 ft. / 520 miles / Three 225-hp J5 Whirlwinds; later versions used 300-hp J6-9s and 410-hp Wasps. Twelve to 14-place, a total of 199 (all models) was built. Production ended in 1932.

9. **Fleet Model 2**—1929 / Two-place, open-cockpit trainer (biplane) / 28 ft. 0 in. upper and lower / 20 ft. 9 in. / 1,575 lbs. / 1,010 lbs. / 14,300 ft. / 360 miles / 100-hp Kinner five-cylinder air-cooled radial K5 / 113 mph. Paul Mantz flew 46 outside loops in a Fleet Model 2 in 1930. Other versions of this design were fitted with a variety of air-cooled radials. Lawrence Bell was president and general manager of the plant in Buffalo, NY; Bell had begun with Glen Martin where he worked with Donald Douglas in 1919.

10. **Ryan Brougham B-5**—1929 / Six-place, high-wing cabin monoplane / 42 ft. 4 in. / 28 ft. 4 in. / 4,100 lbs. / 2,251 lbs. / 18,000 ft. / 720 miles / 300-hp Wright J6-9 / 140 mph. Fabric-covered, the Broughams were advertised as "sister ships to the *Spirit of St. Louis*," Lindbergh's NY-Paris machine. Several models with different engines were available; 255 Broughams were built.

11. **Great Lakes 2T-1**—1929 / Two-place open biplane / 26 ft. 8 in. upper and lower / 20 ft. 4 in. / 1,580 lbs. / 1,102 lbs. / 12,500 ft. / 375 miles / 85-hp Cirrus Mk 3, an air-cooled, four-cylinder in-line (upright) / 115 mph. Designed by Charles W. Meyers and Cliff Liesey as a sport-trainer; after WWII some were refurbished fitted with modern engines and used as aerobatic machines. About 650 were built.

12. **Laird Speedwing LCR-300**—1929 / Three-place open-cockpit high-performance biplane for the sportsman pilot / 28 ft. 0 in. upper; 24 ft. 0 in. lower / 22 ft. 7 in. / 3,010 lbs. / 1,922 lbs. / 17,000 ft. / 575 miles / 300-hp Wright Whirlwind J6-9 air cooled nine-cylinder radial / 155 mph; 175 mph w/NACA engine cowling.

13. **Boeing 80-A Tri-Motor**—1929 / 18-passenger tri-motor biplane airliner; fabric-covered / 80 ft. 0 in. upper; 64 ft. 10 in. lower / 56 ft. 6in. / 17,500 lbs. / 10,582 lbs. / 14,000 ft. / 460 miles at 90 gph fuel consumption / Three 525-hp P&W Hornets / 138 mph; 118 mph cruise. Entering service for United Air Lines between Chicago and San Francisco in 1930, 12 were built. The earlier Model 80 was Wasp-powered.

14. **Consolidated Model 16 Commodore**—1929 / 22-passenger flying boat / 100 ft. 0 in. / 61 ft. 8 in. / 17,600 lbs. / 10,550 lbs. / 11,250 ft. / 1,000 miles at 64 gph and 108 mph / Two 575-hp P&W Hornets / 128 mph. The twin-engine Commodore flew an 8,900-mile route

linking the Americas for the pioneering New York, Rio, Buenos Aires Line (NYRBA, called "near beer" by crews). Pan Am bought NYRBA and its 14 Commodores in 1930.

15. **Spartan C-3**—1930 / Three-place open biplane, fabric-covered with wings of equal span, not staggered; a solid, honest airplane in which your author got his first bootleg stick time. As with all biplanes of that era, one had a choice of several engines. The "best" was fitted with a 225-hp Wright J6-7. (The military called this engine the R-760, an indication of its cubic-inch displacement.) / 32 ft. 0 in. upper and lower / 23 ft. 3 in. / 2,700 lbs. / 1,740 lbs. / 15,000 ft. / 460 miles at 14 gph and 110 mph / 130 mph. Sold for $7,750 at Tulsa factory.

16. **Stinson SM-8A Junior**—1930 / Four-place high-wing cabin monoplane; fabric-covered / 41 ft. 8 in. / 28 ft. 11 in. / 3,195 lbs. / 2,061 lbs. / 14,000 ft. / 500 miles at 12 gph and 105 mph / 215-hp Lycoming nine-cylinder air-cooled radial R-680 / 125 mph. The Junior found 150 buyers during the first six months of 1930 due to its $5,775 price tag. Its principal competitor, the Travel Air 10-D, with a 225-hp Whirlwind, priced at $11,250, was forced to $8,495 in mid-year.

17. **Lockheed Model 8 Sirius**—1930 / Two-place, open-cockpit low-wing monoplane with fixed landing gear (the Lockheed Orion of 1931 was the first commercial airplane with fully retractable landing gear) / 42 ft. 10 in. / 27 ft. 6 in. / 4,600 lbs. / 3,060 lbs. / 20,000 ft. / 975 miles at 22 gph and 150 mph / 420-hp P&W Wasp R-1340 (this engine would be developed to 600 hp by 1940) / 175 mph. Lindbergh and his wife owned a Sirius which they fitted with a Cyclone engine and floats and flew across both oceans on airline survey flights.

18. **Monocoupe 110**—1930 / Small, two-place, high-wing cabin monoplane / 32 ft. 0 in. / 20 ft. 4 in. / 1,611 lbs. / 991 lbs. / 16,000 ft. / 480 miles at 7 gph and 112 mph / 110-hp Warner Scarab / 142 mph w/wheel pants and engine speed ring. Designed for the sportsman pilot, the 110 evolved from the very successful Monocoupe 90, which in turn came from the Model 113, fathered by the Model 70 of 1928. Don Luscombe was the president of Mono Aircraft Corporation at Moline, Illinois, until 1933, when he left to build airplanes under his own name. John Livingston flew a clipped-wing Model 110 to victory in many air races, reaching a speed of 220 mph with a 145-hp Warner engine installed.

19. **Stinson SM-6000 Airliner**—1930 / Tri-motor 10-place, fabric-covered, high-wing monoplane / 60 ft. 0 in. / 42 ft. 10 in. / 8,400 lbs. / 5,575 lbs. / 15,000 ft. / 345 miles at 36 gph and 115 mph / Three 215-hp Lycoming R-680 / 138 mph. Stinson and Lycoming were in the Aviation Corporation (AVCO) orbit, along with American Airways (later American Airlines), hence Stinson's extensive use of Lycoming engines. The company was located at Wayne, Michigan, and Eddie Stinson was president.

20. **Northrop Alpha**—1930 / The first practical low-wing all-metal cabin monoplane to go into production; seated six plus pilot; featured Northrop's stressed-skin construction / 41 ft. 10 in. / 28 ft. 5 in. / 4,500 lbs. / 2,590 lbs. / 19,300 ft. / 600 miles at 22 gph and 145 mph / 420-hp P&W R-1340-C / 170 mph. Northrop had left Lockheed in 1928 to build airplanes on his own, with Donovan Berlin as his chief engineer (Berlin would later go to Curtiss-Wright, where he designed the P-36/P-40). After Boeing bought Northrop and merged it with Stearman in Wichita, Jack Northrop left the company to start still another Northrop company. Douglas bought that one, and again Northrop left to start still another Northrop company. The Alpha saw service on several airlines, including TWA. At least 20 Alphas were built.

SIGNIFICANT U.S. CIVIL AIRCRAFT

E.L. Cord, the wheeler-dealer automobile magnate, used this Stinson tri-motor on his "Century Airlines" in the early 1930s.

21. **Aeronca C-3 Duplex**—1931 / Two-place sportplane / the two-place C-3 / 36 ft. 0 in. / 20 ft. 0 in. / 875 lbs. / 466 lbs. / 14,000 ft. / 200 miles at 2½ gph and 65 mph / Aeronca 36-hp two-cylinder air-cooled four-stroke / 80 mph. A child of the Great Depression, the Aeronca C-2/C-3 series (the 2 was single-place and had 10 less hp) offered minimum cost fun flying and flight training—an operator could make money selling solo time for $5 per hour in either. At least 500 were built into 1937 by Aeronautical Corporation of America (hence AERONCA) in Cincinnati.

22. **Curtiss-Wright Junior CW-1**—1931 / Two-place sportplane / 39 ft. 6 in. / 21 ft. 3 in. / 975 lbs. / 570 lbs. / 12,000 ft. / 200 miles at 3 gph and 70 mph / 45-hp Szekely air-cooled engine mounted as a pusher / 80 mph. Another low-cost two-placer born of the depression, the C-W Junior had a parasol wing and was produced by C-W at their St. Louis facility, where Walter Beech was president (of the Airplane Division) after selling Travel Air to C-W in 1929. Ralph Damon was general manager. About 270 Juniors were built before production ended in 1932.

23. **Gee Bee Sportsters**—1931 / Single-place sportplanes / 25 ft. 0 in. / 16 ft. 9 in. / 1,400 lbs. / 912 lbs. / 19,000 ft. / 570 miles at 7 gph and 127 mph / 110-hp Warner Scarab seven-cylinder air-cooled radial / 148 mph. The Gee Bee production models were the little single-place low-wing C, D, and E, fitted with, respectively, the four-cylinder, inline, inverted air-cooled 95-hp Menasco, 125-hp Menasco, and the 110-hp Warner Scarab air-cooled radial. Intended for the private "sportsman" pilot, these craft seemed to be used chiefly for racing. The one-of-a-kind pure Gee Bee racers—Models Z, Y, R-1, and R-1 rebuilds/derivatives—set records and were world famous during the early 1930s. They were built by the Granville brothers in Springfield, Massachusetts.

24. **Buhl Bull Pup LA-1**—1931 / Single-place, economy private airplane, shoulder-wing cabane-strut wire-braced / 30 ft. 0 in. / 19 ft. 0 in. / 842 lbs. / 550 lbs. / 14,000 ft. / 240 miles at 3 gph and 80 mph / 45-hp Szekely three-cylinder air-cooled radial / 95 mph. Buhl also produced the six-place cabin sesquiplane, the Buhl Air Sedan.

25. **Pitcairn Autogiro PCA-3**—1931 / Rotor diameter 45 ft. 0 in. / Fixed wing span of 30 ft. 0 in. / 3,063 lbs. / 2,121 lbs. / 15,000 ft. / 300 miles at 16 gph and 100 mph / 300-hp P&W R-985 / 120 mph. Although Kellett built some excellent autogiros, it was Harold F. Pitcairn who introduced these unique machines to America. Invented in Spain in 1923 by Juan de la Cierva, the autogiro was built and further developed in America by Pitcairn, and later Kellett. A couple of smaller versions preceded the PCA-3, a three-placer (other models of the Pitcairn autogiros followed; the PCA-3 is representative). It should also be mentioned that the R-985 Wasp Junior was up to 450 hp by 1940.

26. **Lockheed Orion Model 9** and **9E**—1933 / Cabin monoplane / 42 ft. 9 in. / 27 ft. 6 in. / 5,400 lbs. / 3,664 lbs. / 20,000 ft. / 800 miles at 25 gph and 205 mph. / 450-hp P&W Wasp SC-1 / 228 mph. The E version's cabin was quickly convertible to cargo, part cargo, or six passengers. The 9E / Explorer hybrid carried Wiley Post and Will Rogers to their deaths in Alaska. TWA flew three 9Es. Only 195 wooden Lockheeds were built—Vega, Air Express, Sirius, Orion, Altair, Explorer, and a couple of hybrids—but they figured in so many record flights, flown by famous pilots, it has always seemed there were a lot more of them.

27. **Stinson Reliant SR** and **SR2**—1933 / 43 ft. 3 in. / 27 ft. 0 in. / 3,155 lbs. / 2,070 lbs. / 14,000 ft. / 460 miles at 12½ gph and 115 mph. / 215-hp Lycoming R-680 / 130 mph. The SR2 had the 240-hp Lyc; both versions were four-place.

28. **Boeing Model 247**—1934 / The first "modern" airliner—all-metal, low-wing, twin-engine, carrying 10 passengers and a crew of three, including stewardess / 74 ft. 0 in. / 51 ft. 4 in. / 12,650 lbs. / 8,370 lbs. / 18,400 ft. / 600 miles at 60 gph and 161 mph. / Two 550-hp P&W Wasps / 182 mph. Had Boeing not reduced the size, and therefore seating capacity, in a major planning decision, the Douglas DC-3 might never have achieved the success it was soon to enjoy. About 60 247s were built, mostly for United Air Lines.

29. **Curtiss-Wright T-32 Condor**—1933 / Twin-engine, fabric-covered, 17-place biplane airliner (sleeper version had eight berths and five reclining seats) / 82 ft. 0 in. upper; 74 ft. 0 in. lower / 48 ft. 10 in. / 16,800 lbs. / 11,235 lbs. / 15,500 ft. / 580 miles at 70 gph and 145 mph / Two 670-hp Wright Cyclone GR-1820-F11s / 170 mph. An anachronism when it appeared, it nevertheless remained in service with American and Eastern for a couple of years because those lines were part of the "Curtiss-Keys" combine (all the airline-manufacturing alliances were broken up by federal law in 1934). An earlier Condor, powered by Curtiss Conqueror V-12 engines, in service with Eastern, was little more than a converted Air Corps bomber. At least 60 T-32 and AT-32s were built.

30. **Waco Model UKC**—1934 / Cabin biplane / 33 ft. 3 in. upper; 28 ft. 3 in. lower / 25 ft. 3 in. / 2,850 lbs. / 1,745 lbs. / 14,000 ft. / 500 miles at 13 gph and 128 mph / 210-hp Continental R-670-A / 140 mph. The UKC was typical of the Waco four-place cabin biplanes produced during the 1930s. There were an amazing number of them, the three-letter designators supposedly descriptive of the airplane, first letter indicating kind of engine and its hp rating; second letter, wing design and third letter the type of airframe. In this case, "U" was for the 210-hp Continental; the "K" wings were shared by most of the cabin Wacos, and "C" was a four-place cabin built into 1936.

31. **Fairchild 24**—1934 / Cabin monoplane / 36 ft. 4 in. / 23 ft. 9 in. / 2,400 lbs. / 1,390 lbs. / 18,200 ft. / 505 miles at 8½ gph and 120 mph / 145-hp Warner seven-cylinder Super Scarab / 138 mph. One of the most popular private airplanes built prior to WWII, the 24

This is the 1946 model of the Fairchild 24R powered by an inverted, inline air-cooled 200-hp Ranger engine, manufactured by TEMCO. All Fairchild 24s built prior to WWII were built by Fairchild at Hagerstown, MD.

Nothing so epitomized the glamor age of air travel as the Pan American Airways "Clippers." Pan Am had 10 of these Sikorsky S-42 flying boats on its South American routes during the 1930s. See C32. (Pan Am photo)

began life in 1932 as a two-place (side-by-side) cabin monoplane fitted with the 95-hp inverted, four-cylinder Cirrus engine. The C8A, which followed in 1933, had the 125-hp Warner Scarab radial. Described here is the Model 24-C8C fitted with the 145-hp Warner, a three-placer. The four-place 24R of 1939-40 was powered with the 175-hp inverted, air-cooled six-cylinder Ranger. The 24W, which appeared in 1939 and was produced into 1947, had a 145 or 165-hp Warner. The 24Rs and 24Ws were four-place.

32. **Sikorsky S-42 Flying Boat**—1934 / Four-engine seaplane / 114 ft. 2 in. / 67 ft. 8 in. / 38,000 lbs. / 21,945 lbs. / 16,000 ft. / 1,280 miles at 150 gph and 154 mph. / Four 700-hp P&W Hornet S5D1G; later versions had 750-hp Hornets / 181 mph. Pan American Airways S-42s entered service August 16, 1934, flying South American routes (the famed Martin M-130 "China Clippers" went across the Pacific in 1935). The S-42 was a parasol monoplane with four engines which carried 32 passengers and crew of six; 13 were built.

33. **Lockheed Electra Model 10**—1934 / 12-place, all-metal twin-engine airliner / 55 ft. 0 in. / 38 ft. 7 in. / 10,100 lbs. / 6,325 lbs. / 550 miles at 48 gph and 195 mph / Two 450-hp P&W R-985-SB3 / 210 mph. A highly successful design, more than 100 were built.

34. **Stinson Model A Airliner**—1934 / Tri-motor airliner / 60 ft. 0 in. / 36 ft. 10 in. / 10,200 lbs. / 7,200 lbs. / 17,000 ft. / 490 miles at 42 gph and 170 mph / Three 260-hp Lycoming R-680-5 / 180 mph. A low-cost, low-wing, fabric-covered tri-motor that carried eight passengers, a stewardess, and two pilots, the Stinson Model A had good performance but was obsolescent when it appeared; 35 were built.

35. **Beech Model 17 Staggerwing**—1934 / Cabin biplane / 32 ft. 0 in. upper and lower / 24 ft. 6 in. / 3,150 lbs. / 1,800 lbs. / 15,500 ft. / 560 miles at 13.2 gph and 152 mph / 225-hp Jacobs L-4 / 175 mph. Walter Beech resigned from Curtiss-Wright in 1932 and returned to Wichita to form Beech Aircraft Corporation with wife Olive Ann. Their first production airplane was the Model 17L, a four-place cabin biplane, fabric-covered, with lower wing staggered ahead of the upper. The ''Staggerwing'' (an unofficial name) was eventually offered with six different engines; 781 were built, 276 of those with the 450-hp P&W R-985. Production continued into 1948. About 40 of the Model 17Ls were built.

36. **Wiley Post Model A**—1935 / Sport biplane / 28 ft. 6 in. upper / 24 ft. 6 in. lower / 19 ft. 9 in. / 998 lbs. / 605 lbs. / 10,000 ft. / 110 miles at 4 gph and 70 mph / 40-hp Ford Model A engine, four-cylinder, water-cooled / 82 mph. Originally built in Wichita as the ''Straughan A,'' this little fabric-covered biplane with side-by-side seating for two was produced in Oklahoma City with Wiley Post as president. Price was $1,692; between 12 and 15 were built.

37. **Ryan STA**—1935 / Sporty low-wing, two-place, open-cockpit trainer and fun airplane with metal-covered fuselage and fabric-covered wings / 29 ft. 11 in. / 21 ft. 6 in. / 1,600 lbs. / 1,035 lbs. / 17,500 ft. / 350 miles at 8.4 gph and 127 mph / 125-hp Menasco C-4 inverted, inline air-cooled four-cylinder / 150 mph.

38. **Cessna Model C-34**—1935 / Cabin monoplane / 33 ft. 10 in. / 24 ft. 7 in. / 2,200 lbs. / 1,220 lbs. / 18,900 ft. / 550 miles at 9 gph and 143 mph / 145-hp Warner / 162 mph. A very clean, fabric-covered, four-place, cabin high-wing (fully cantilever) monoplane, the C-34 was offered through 1941 with 145 or 165 hp; 185 were built during those years to keep Cessna afloat. Cessna was one of a relative handful of private airplane manufacturers to survive the Great Depression. Clyde Cessna retired to his Kansas farm in 1936 (he died in 1954) and Clyde's nephew, Dwane Wallace, ran the company until it was acquired by General Dynamics 50 years later.

39. **Rearwin Sportster 7000**—1935 / Light high-wing cabin monoplane with fabric covering and seating for two in tandem / 35 ft. 0 in. / 22 ft. 3 in. / 1,410 lbs. / 853 lbs. / 14,000 ft. / 480 miles at 4.75 gph and 100 mph / 70-hp LeBlonde 5DE five-cylinder air-cooled radial / 110 mph.

40. **Stinson Reliant SR-7**—1936 / Cabin monoplane / 41 ft. 7 in. / 27 ft. 0 in. / 3,375 lbs. / 2,260 lbs. / 12,300 ft. / 475 miles at 14 gph and 136 mph / 225-hp Lycoming R-680-4 nine-cylinder air-cooled / 144 mph. The SR-7 was the first of the gull-wing Reliants, which ranged through the SR-10F, fitted with engines of 225 hp through 450 hp—plus the military AT-19 which became (refurbished) the V-77 Model of 1946 with 300 hp. All were fabric-covered, high-wing monoplanes seating four or five.

148   SIGNIFICANT U.S. CIVIL AIRCRAFT

Note the family resemblance between the 1937 four-place Cessna C-34 and the all-metal 190 and 195, which followed after WWII.

The 1936 Arrow Sport F was certified to fly with the Ford V-8 automobile engine. It seated two side-by-side.

41. **Arrow Sport Model F**—1936 / Low-wing, open-cockpit with side-by-side seating for two / 36 ft. 7 in. / 21 ft. 4 in. / 1,675 lbs. / 1,172 lbs. / 12,000 ft. / 300 miles at 5½ gph and 86 mph / 82-hp Ford V-8 water-cooled of 82 hp / 86 mph.

42. **Douglas DC-3**—1936 / Twin-engine airliner / 95 ft. 0 in. / 64 ft. 6 in. / 24,000 lbs. / 15,300 lbs. / 20,800 ft. / 1,260 miles at 93 gph and 188 mph / Two 850-hp Wright Cyclones, GR-1820-G2 (930 takeoff hp) / 212 mph. A refinement of the DC-2, of which 191 were built between May 1934 and July 1936 (the prototype DC-1 flew late in 1933), a sleeper version known as the DST entered service in June 1936 with American Airlines. The first DC-3 was delivered to AA on 18 August 1936. In September, United Air Lines received the first DC-3A, fitted with P&W Twin Wasp engines. The DC-3 carried 21 passengers, three crew, and 320 pounds of baggage/mail. Follow-on models had more power and slightly better performance. A total of 10,655 was built, 609 civilian orders, and 10,046 military. A high percentage of the latter were converted to airline use after WWII.

43. **Beech Model 18 ("Twin Beech")**—1937 / All-metal twin-engine, low-wing monoplane seating six passengers and crew of two / 47 ft. 8 in. / 31 ft. 11 in. / 6,500 lbs. / 4,100 lbs. / 20,000 ft. / 760 miles at 35 gph and 190 mph / Two 320-hp Wright R-760-E2 seven-cylinder air-cooled radials / 202 mph. In production until late 1969, the Twin Beech (a universal if unofficial name) was produced in 32 versions, with engines ranging from the 320-hp Wright (in the first one) to the 500-hp Continental. More than 9,000 were built, 5,000 for the military; the last ones had tricycle landing gear. The definitive version would be the post-WWII D-18S fitted with 450-hp P&W R-985 Wasp Juniors. Specs above are for the 1937 Model 18-A. Specs for the D-18S of 1946: 47 ft. 8 in. / 34 ft. 0 in. / 8,500 lbs. / 5,609 lbs. / 22,000 ft. / 1,200 miles at 35 gph and 200 mph / Two 450-hp P&W R-985 Wasp Juniors / 230 mph.

44. **Lockheed Model 14 Super Electra**—1937 / Twin-engine airliner / 65 ft. 6 in. / 44 ft. 4 in. / 17,500 lbs. / 10,300 lbs. / 24,300 ft. / 1,500 miles at 84 gph and 227 mph / Two 750-hp P&W Hornet S1E-G / 247 mph. The success of the Lockheed 10, followed by the scaled-down Model 12, pointed to a heftier machine for the feeder airlines, thus the 14, of which 52 were built. It was also the basis for WWII's famed Hudson patrol bomber.

45. **Piper J-3 Cub**—1937 / Sport monoplane / 35 ft. 3 in. / 22 ft. 3 in. / 1,100 lbs. / 635 lbs. / 12,000 ft. / 250 miles at 4 gph and 80 mph / 65-hp Continental A-65 four-cylinder, air-cooled, opposed / 92 mph. The Piper J-3 evolved from the Taylor E-2 and J-2 after Gilbert Taylor left the fledgling company (in 1935) to build airplanes on his own (Taylorcrafts) and his partner and financial angel William Piper took charge. The Cub's original engine, the 40-hp Continental, was replaced by 50-hp—Continental, Lycoming, or Franklin—and by 1940 the 65-hp Continental (mostly), which seemed the best for it. A lot of Cub variants followed, including the Cub J-4 Coupe, with side-by-side seats and engines up to 75 hp 1938-1941, and the Cruiser J-5 of 75-100 hp (the first Lycoming 0-235) in 1940-1941. The J-3-65 was produced as the L-4 during WWII, and then another 2,900 were built for the civil market in 1946-47.

46. **Howard DGA-11**—1937 / High-wing cabin monoplane seating five / 38 ft. 0 in. / 25 ft. 5 in. / 4,100 lbs. / 2,450 lbs. / 26,000 ft. / 800 miles at gph and 203 mph / 450-hp P&W Wasp Junior (R-985) / 196 mph.

47. **Aeronca Chief**—1938 / Two-place side-by-side fabric-covered high-wing monoplane / 36 ft. 0 in. / 21 ft. 1 in. / 1,130 lbs. / 670 lbs. / 270 miles at 3.75 gph and 90 mph / 50-hp

If you can't identify this one, you'll have to turn in your Junior Birdman's wings.

Continental A-50-1 / 100 mph. Like the Cub and Taylorcraft, the Chief progressed apace with small aircraft engine development.

48. **Luscombe Model 8** and **Silvaire**—1938 / Sport monoplane / 35 ft. 0 in. / 20 ft. 0 in. / 1,400 lbs. / 810 lbs. / 17,000 ft. / 490 miles at 5½ gph and 115 mph. / 90-hp Continental C-90 / 125 mph. First equipped with the 50-hp Continental, this two-place, side-by-side high-wing monoplane progressed through 65, 75, 85, and at last 90 hp in 1948. Wings were fabric-covered prior to WWII, and the craft was all-metal from mid-1946. It was briefly built by TEMCO 1949–50, and by a Colorado company 1955–60. Called the "Silvaire" from 1941 onward, the specs above are for the 8F Silvaire.

49. **Boeing Clipper Model 314**—1939 / Seaplane airliner / 152 ft. 0 in. / 106 ft. 0 in. / 84,000 lbs. / 49,149 lbs. / 14,000 ft. / 5,000 miles at 280 gph and 180 mph / Four 1,350-hp Wright Double Cyclone 709C-14AC1 / 199 mph. Scheduled passenger service across the North Atlantic by Pan Am began June 28, 1939, in the Boeing 314 flying boat *Dixie Clipper*. These large flying boats carried 34 passengers and 15 crew; 12 were built. Franklin Roosevelt, first American president to fly, went to the Casablanca Conference during WWII in the *Dixie Clipper*.

50. **Ercoupe, Model 415-C** through **415-G**—1940 / Two-place sportplane / 30 ft. 0 in. / 20 ft. 2 in. / 1,360 lbs. / 800 lbs. / 13,000 ft. / 450 miles at 5 gph and 102 mph. / 75-hp Continental C-75-12 / 117 mph. A two-place side-by-side low-wing (with fabric on wing and 65-hp 1940 415-C model; mid-'46 on all-metal, 75 and 85 hp) the Ercoupe was unique because it was non-spinnable, with limited-travel flight control surfaces and rudder-aileron interconnect which eliminated rudder pedals. Trailing-arm mainwheels allowed crosswind landings. Originally produced by the Engineering Research Corporation in Riverdale, MD, the design passed

through the hands of Hyattsville's Sanders Aviation ('48–'51); revived ('56–'60) by Forney Aircraft of Ft. Collins, CO with 90 hp; acquired by Alon ('63–'67) of McPherson, KS; finally sold to Mooney in 1967, where it was criminally redesigned and died a merciful death. Altogether, about 6,000 were built, the last ones with rudder pedals.

51. **Piper Cub Cruiser, J-5**—1940 / Tube-and-fabric, three-place, high-wing monoplane, "just like the J-3 except more so;" J-5 designation encompassed the J-5A, B, and C models, the J-5C being fitted with the new Lycoming 0-235 of 100 hp at 2550 rpm / 35 ft. 6 in. / 22 ft. 6 in. / 1,550 lbs. / 855 lbs. / 15,000 ft. / 385 miles at 6½ gph and 100 mph / 110 mph. In all, 1,289 were built at Lock Haven, PA.

52. **Boeing Stratoliner, Model 307**—1940 / Four-engine airliner / 107 ft. 3 in. / 74 ft. 4 in. / 45,000 lbs. / 31,200 lbs. / 23,800 ft. / 1,300 miles at 200 gph and 222 mph / Four 900-hp Wright Cyclone GR-1820-G105A / 250 mph. Although only nine were built—four for Pan Am, five for TWA—and those spent most of their lives in military service during WWII, this machine is significant because it was the first pressurized airliner (Lockheed experimented with cabin pressurization in 1935 with a modified Electra).

53. **Culver Cadet**—1940 / Low-wing sportplane / 27 ft. 0 in. / 17 ft. 8 in. / 1,305 lbs. / 750 lbs. / 17,000 ft. / 500 miles at 4½ gph and 130 mph / Franklin 4AC-176-F3 of 80-hp at 2500 rpm / 142 mph. Maximum performance with minimum power characterized the Cadet, a two-place, low-wing cabin monoplane designed by Al Mooney as a follow-on to his Culvert Dart of 1938. Powered with 75-hp, then 80-hp in 1941, Cadets were built in Wichita as the PQ-series of radio-controlled drones during WWII by a company controlled by Charles Yankey and Walter Beech. The design was built as late as 1966 as the 90-hp Helton Lark.

54. **Aeronca Champion, 7AC, 7BC, 7CC**—1945 / High-wing cabin monoplane seating two in tandem; primarily a trainer / 35 ft. 2 in. / 21 ft. 6 in. / 1,220 lbs. / 710 lbs. / 12,600 ft. / 250 miles at 4½ gph and 85 mph / 65-hp Continental A-65 / 100 mph. The above figures are for the 7AC; the 7BC and 7CC had 85-hp; more than 7,000 were built before production stopped in 1951. A new company bought the assets of the Middletown, Ohio, firm and briefly produced the Tri-Traveler and DX-ER with tri-gear in the mid-1950s. The Champion Citabrias, clearly based on the Aeroncas, entered the market in 1964, produced by Champion Aircraft Company of Oceola, Wisconsin. (The Champions will be listed separately.)

55. **Douglas DC-4 Skymaster (C-54)**—1946 / 52-passenger airliner / 117 ft. 6 in. / 93 ft. 10 in. / 66,500 lbs. / 40,409 lbs. / 26,000 ft. / 4,240 miles at 226 gph and 192 mph / Four 1,450-hp P&W Twin Wasps (R-2000) / 270 mph. 1,084 were built as C-54s and 79 as DC-4s.

56. **Stinson Voyager** and **Station Wagon, 108**—1946 / Four-place high-wing cabin monoplane with fabric cover; the 108 had the 150-hp Franklin; 108-2 the 165-hp Franklin, and the 108-3 "big tail" also 165 hp / 34 ft. 0 in. / 24 ft. 6 in. / 2,230 lbs. / 1,265 lbs. / 490 miles at 9½ gph and 124 mph / 135 mph. More than 5,000 were built.

57. **Lockheed Constellation**—1946 / Four-engine airliner / 123 ft. 0 in. / 95 ft. 1 in. / 86,500 lbs. / 55,345 lbs. / 25,500 ft. / 3,400 miles at 368 gph and 275 mph / 320 mph. The original 49-seat L-049 had added power as the L-649; the L-749 was long-range. The Super Connie L-1049 of 1951 was 18 ft. 4 in. longer and had R-3350s of 3,250 (takeoff) hp. The design eventually went through the L-1049H and L-1649A in 1956 with R-3350 compounds, seating up to 78 passengers. Also known as the C-69 and C-121 in military dress, 221 049/069/079s were built, along with 297 1049/1649s. Specs above are for L-049.

152   SIGNIFICANT U.S. CIVIL AIRCRAFT

58. **Globe (Temco) Swift, GC-1A** and **GC-1B**—1946 / Low-wing, cabin personal sportplane / 29 ft. 4 in. / 20 ft. 11 in. / 1,710 lbs. / 1,118 lbs. / 14,200 ft. / 420 miles at 8 gph and 132 mph / 125-hp Continental C-125 of 125 hp / 145 mph. Seating two side-by-side, the Swift was originally underpowered with 85 hp but became a very nice machine with 125 hp. Developed by Globe, production was taken over by Texas Engineering & Manufacturing Company (Temco) in 1947.

59. **Cessna 140/120**—1946 / Two-place trainer / 32 ft. 10 in. / 21 ft. 6 in. / 1,450 lbs. / 860 lbs. / 15,500 ft. / 420 miles at 6 gph and 105 mph / 85-hp Continental C-85-12F / 120 mph. A two-place, side-by-side trainer with metal fuselage, the high-wing was fabric-covered with two lift struts and featured spring-steel landing gear struts. The 120 was the economy version, without rear window and flaps. The 1949 140A had an all-metal wing with a single strut.

60. **Republic Sea Bee, RC-3**—1946 / Four-place amphibian for private flying / 37 ft. 8 in. / 28 ft. 0 in. / 3,150 lbs. / 2,100 lbs. / 12,000 ft. / 360 miles at 13½ gph and 105 mph / 215-hp Franklin 6A8-215-B8F / 120 mph. The Sea Bee was the result of an extensive market survey to determine average civil pilot's ''ideal'' personal airplane; 1,060 were built.

61. **Taylorcraft BC-12D**—1946 / Side-by-side, two-place high-wing cabin monoplane, a pre-WWII design / 36 ft. 0 in. / 22 ft. 0 in. / 1,200 lbs. / 750 lbs. / 15,000 ft. / 300 miles at 3½ gph and 95 mph / 65-hp Continental A-65 of 65 hp / 100 mph.

62. **Curtiss-Wright CW-20 (C-46)**—1947 / Twin-engine airliner / 108 ft. 0 in. / 76 ft. 4 in. / 49,600 lbs. / 26,000 lbs. / 25,000 ft. / 1,600 miles at 190 gph and 225 mph / Two 2,000-hp Double Wasps, R-2800-75 / 260 mph. The largest twin piston-engine ever placed in production, the C-46 was built for the military during WWII and converted to airline and air freight service postwar from surplus. It was fitted with both Wright and Pratt & Whitney engines in its several versions. Specs above are for the C-46E modified for civil use; approximately 3,200 were built.

63. **Johnson Rocket**—1947 / Fabric-covered, two-place high-performance cabin low-winger / 30 ft. 10 in. / 21 ft. 10 in. / 2,550 lbs. / 1,775 lbs. / 14,000 ft. / 690 miles at 11 gph and 160 mph / 185-hp Lycoming 0-435-A / 180 mph. Built in Ft. Worth, fewer than 20 were produced.

64. **Beech Bonanza Model 35**—1947 / Low-wing sportplane. Built in three versions, actually: the V-tail Model 35, conventional tail former Debonair Model 33, and the stretched six-place Model 36. Since there were 22 models of the V-tail during its 35 years of continuous production, there is not space to detail each one here, but the story is largely contained in a comparison between the specs of the first and last Model 35: 32 ft. 10 in. / 25 ft. 2 in. / 2,250 lbs. / 1,558 lbs. / 18,000 ft. / 650 miles at 8.6 gph and 172 mph / 165-hp Continental E-185-1 / 184 mph. V35B: 33 ft. 5½ in. / 26 ft. 4½ in. / 3,400 lbs. / 1,960 lbs. / 17,500 ft. / 600 miles at 13½ gph and 163 mph / 285-hp Continental I0-520-B. The Models 33 and 36 Bonanzas are listed according to their production years, 1960 and 1968 respectively. In 1988, only the F33A remained in production.

65. **Piper Super Cruiser, PA-12,** and **Family Cruiser, PA-14**—1947 / The Cub concept expanded a little more; tube and fabric high-wing monoplanes, the PA-12 seated three; the PA-14 was a four-placer. Both used the 108-hp Lycoming engine. PA-12 specs: 35 ft. 6 in. / 23 ft. 1 in. / 1,750 lbs. / 950 lbs. / 12,600 ft. / 600 miles at 6 gph and 103 mph / Lycoming 0-235-C or C1 of 100 and 108 hp / 114 mph. Family Cruiser, PA-14: 35 ft. 6 in. / 23 ft. 2 in. / 1,850

The Beech Model 35 was introduced in 1947, the first ones priced below $8,000 in anticipation of a sales volume that did not develop (other lightplane makers at the time made similar mistakes). The price went up and the Bonanza grew heavier, plusher, and more powerful—and sold steadily for 35 years. Pictured is a 1970 model of the V-tail. (Beech)

lbs. / 1,000 lbs. / 12,000 ft. / 500 miles at 7 gph and 110 mph / 108-hp Lycoming 0-235-C1 / 123 mph.

66. **Douglas DC-6**—1947 / 58-passenger pressurized airliner / 117 ft. 6 in. / 100 ft. 7 in. / 97,200 lbs. / 53,600 lbs. / 27,400 ft. / 4,000 miles at 380/400 gph and 307 mph / Four 1,800-hp P&W Double Wasp R-2800-CA15 / 362 mph. 538 were built, plus 167 for the military as C-118 and R6D.

67. **North American Navion**—1947 / All-metal, four-place cabin low-wing monoplane for the private sector / 33 ft. 5 in. / 27 ft. 6 in. / 2,850 lbs. / 1,897 lbs. / 18,000 ft. / 500 miles at 13½ gph and 170 mph / Lycoming GO-435-C-2 of 240 hp (260 hp takeoff) / 178 mph. About 800 were built by North American, then the design was sold to Ryan, who built another 1,240 of the 185-hp models, along with some 240-hp versions through 1951. A Texas company returned the Navion to production in 1961, retrofitting older ones with bigger engines, and building new ones of 260 and 285 hp as Rangemasters. Ryan built 163 for the U.S. Army as L-17s.

68. **Cessna 190/195**—1947 / Large four-place business airplane; the 190 was fitted with the 240-hp Continental air-cooled radial R-670-23, the 195 was powered by the 300-hp Jacobs

The Douglas DC-6 was designed during WWII, and the first one to fly, February 15, 1946, was designated XC-112A. Civil production began shortly afterwards, and United put the first one into service in April 1947. A total of 538 was built, plus 167 for the Army Air Forces and Navy as C-118s and R6Ds. (Pan Am)

R-755-A2 / Specs for 195: 36 ft. 2 in. / 27 ft. 4 in. / 3,350 lbs. / 2,050 lbs. / 18,000 ft. / 700 miles at 16 gph and 159 mph / 180 mph. In all, 1,123 were built, plus 83 195s for the military as LC-126s.

69. **Martin 202/404**—1947 / Twin-engine airliners / 93 ft. 3 in. / 71 ft. 4 in. / 43,000 lbs. / 27,060 lbs. / 22,600 ft. / 2,000 miles at 165 gph and 281 mph at 12,000 ft. (this airliner non-pressurized) / Two 1,800-hp P&W Double Wasp R-2800-CB16 / 312 mph. The 202 taken out of service due to structural failure after 25 were built. The 40-passenger 404 entered service with TWA in 1950; 103 were delivered, with Piedmont and Southern Airways also significant users. Specs are for 202A.

70. **Cessna 170**—1948 / Four-place sportplane / 36 ft. 0 in. / 25 ft. 0 in. / 2,200 lbs. / 1,205 lbs. / 500 miles at 8½ gph and 120 mph / 145-hp Continental C-145 of 145 hp / 140 mph. Four-place cabin high-wing monoplanes with all-metal fuselages and fabric-covered wings (170); the 170A and 170B had metal-skinned wings and a single strut on each side. Specs are for 170A; 5,136 170s of all models were built.

Here is the most fun airplane for the money ever built, and if you have never flown one from a quiet grass field on a dewy-fresh spring morning, you are not qualified to argue about it. Its manufacturer called it a PA-17; we all know and love it as the Piper Vagabond.

71. **Piper Vagabond, Models PA-15 and PA-17**—1948 / High-wing sportplanes / 29 ft. 3 in. / 18 ft. 8 in. / 1,150 lbs. / 650 lbs. / 12,000 ft. / 250 miles at 4½ gph and 92 mph / 102 mph. Another of the first-generation Pipers, a tube-and-fabric high-wing cabin two-placer, but the most delightful of all the early Pipers. The PA-15 had the 65-hp Lycoming and was the economy version (not even a floor mat!); the PA-17 had the Continental 65-hp engine, shocks, dual controls, and all the accessories the PA-15 lacked, including landing lights. Specs are for PA-17.

72. **Mooney Mite, M-18**—1949 / Single-place fun airplane, low-wing, with sliding canopy and retractable gear, partly plywood covered / 26 ft. 11 in. / 17 ft. 7 in. / 780 lbs. / 500 lbs. / 19,400 ft. / 360 miles at 3½ gph and 122 mph / Lycoming 0-145-B2 of 65 hp at 2,550 rpm / 138 mph. Originally tried with the 26-hp Crosley automobile engine, about half of the 250 or so built had the 65-hp Lycoming and half the Continental A-65. Specs are for M-18L.

73. **Convair 240/340/440/540/580/600/640/T-29/C-131A**—1948 / Twin-engine airliner / 105 ft. 4 in. / 79 ft. 2 in. / 53,200 lbs. gross / 21,000 ft. / 905 miles w/max payload of 12,986 lbs. / Two Napier Eland 504A turboprops of 3,500 hp each / 325 mph. The twin-engine Convair has proven to be a most durable airliner, turboprop versions still in scheduled service in 1988. The first one, Model 240, carried 40-passengers and was powered with 2,400-hp P&W R-2800 CA18s. AA bought the first 75 of the 571 built through 1957 (many were completed as T-29 aircrew trainers for the USAF, and C-131 transports); 176 were civil. In 1951, the 340 appeared with 13 feet 7 inches more wingspan, improved engines, and 4 feet 6 inches added length to seat 44; 209 were built. The 440 received the R-2800-CB17

The Convairliner was successful as a piston-engine aircraft from the time it appeared in 1948. Conversion to turbine power began about 1958, and many of those, the 580s and 640s, remain in service as this is written.

engines, plus detail improvements for 52 passengers, and 186 were built. The 540 and onward were conversions to turboprops: the 540 with British-built Napier Elands; 580 with Allisons; 600 and 640 with Rolls-Royce Darts. The 580 entered service in 1964, the others in 1965. Specs are for the 540.

74. **Boeing Stratocruiser, Model 377**—1948 / Four-engine airliner / 141 ft. 3 in. / 110 ft. 4 in. / 142,500 lbs. / 83,500 lbs. / 25,000 ft. / 4,600 miles at 467 gph and 315 mph / Four P&W Wasp Major R-4360-TSB3G or TSB6G of 2,800 hp (3,500 hp takeoff) each / 340 mph. About 900 Boeing KC-97 and C-97s were built for the USAF employing the wings, tail, landing gear and engines of the B-50 bomber, and the pressurized Stratocruiser was cloned from them with little effort as a 100-passenger airliner; 55 were produced.

75. **Varga Kachina/Morrisey/Shinn Model 2150**—1950 / Two-seat sportplane / 30 ft. 0 in. / 21 ft. 0 in. / 1,817 lbs. / 1,125 lbs. / 22,000 ft. / 525 miles at 9 gph and 135 mph / 150-hp Lycoming 0-320-A / 148 mph. This tandem-seat two-place low-wing sport/trainer was designed by WWII pilot Bill Morrisey, who sold a few before selling out to the Shinn Company. They built as many as 50 during the early 1960s. The design was revived in 1974 by George Varga of Chandler, AZ. (A Kachina is a Hopi Indian doll.)

76. **Beech Twin Bonanza, Model 50**—1951 / Business twin / 45 ft. 11½ in. / 31 ft. 6½ in. / 7,300 lbs. / 4,460 lbs. / 29,150 ft. / 1,095 miles at 10,000 ft. and 207 mph / Two 340-hp Lycoming IGSO-480-A-IB6 / 235 mph. A roomy four-to-five passenger business twin with an amazing bench seat for the copilot and his dog; 974 were produced. Specs are for 1962 J50.

The Aero Commander is the progenitor of the modern light twin, and is a Ted Smith design. It has always been slower than most other twins in its class, but is nice to fly and has a roomy cabin. Its configuration is so distinctive that it can't be confused with other makes. (Jim Gunter photo)

77. **Rockwell Aero Commander, 500/600/Shrike**—1951 / Business twin / Specs for 1978 Shrike Esquire II: 49 ft. 6 in. / 36 ft. 10 in. / 6,750 lbs. / 5,136 lbs. / 19,400 ft. / 850 miles at 32½ gph and 203 mph / Two 290-hp Lycoming IO-540-E1B5 / 215 mph. Aero Commander expanded its Ted Smith high-wing, cabin twin concept from the original 1951 Model 520 (with a pair of 260-hp piston engines) through the Model 560 (with 275-hp engines), the Model 680 (with two 320-hp Lycomings), the 1974 Shrike Commander 500s (with 290-hp IO-540 Lycs) the Commander 685 (with turbocharged Continentals of 435 hp each), the Turbo Commander 690A, a turboprop with 700 shp on each side, and even took a brief shot at the pure jet market with the 1966 Jet Commander with G.E. CJ610-1s rated at 2,850 pounds static thrust each. A pressurized Grand Commander was also introduced in the mid-1960s. The 500 series, which includes the Shrikes, were usually five-to-seven passenger; the 600 series carried seven to nine passengers.

78. **Piper Pacer, Tri-Pacer, and Colt**—1951 / High-wing sportplanes / 29 ft. 4 in. / 20 ft. 6 in. / 2,000 lbs. / 1,100 lbs. / 15,000 ft. / 500 miles at 9 gph and 125 mph / 150-hp Lycoming O-320 / 139 mph. The last of the fabric-covered Pipers, from the PA-15 Vagabond onward, these were known as the "short-wing Pipers." The PA-16 Clipper, with the 115-hp O-235-C1, may be described as a four-place Vagabond appearing early in 1949. It was replaced within a year by the PA-20 Pacer, offered with the 125-hp O-290-D Lycoming or the 135-hp O-290-D2. The PA-22 Tri-Pacer was the tri-gear version of the PA-20, introduced in 1952 with the same choice of engines. By 1959, the Tri-Pacer was offered with the 160-hp Lycoming O-320-B, along with the more popular 150-hp engine in the Tri-Pacer Caribbean model. The PA-22-108 Colt entered production in 1960, and was a two-place Tri-Pacer with the 108-hp O-235-C1B. Specs above are for the Caribbean. 7,668 Tri-Pacers were built, plus 1,822 Colts; production ended in 1963.

158 SIGNIFICANT U.S. CIVIL AIRCRAFT

This neat Tri-Pacer is owned by Dale Andrews of Littleton, Colorado, and its red/white/gold finish really gets your attention. This one has a full IFR panel and a radio stack that is downright embarrassing.

79. **Piper Super Cub, PA-18**—1949 / Two-place sportplane / 35 ft. 4 in. / 22 ft. 6 in. / 1,750 lbs. (normal overload 2,070 lbs.) / 930 lbs. / 19,000 ft. / 460 miles at 9 gph and 115 mph / 150-hp Lycoming O-320 / 115 mph. The two-place tandem-seat Cub was returned to production with 90 hp, flaps, and wing fuel tanks in 1949 and soon gained more power. The 125-hp and 150-hp versions were the most popular, although 115 and 135-hp versions were available throughout the 1960s. Piper sold the design to a Texas firm in 1984. In 1975, the 150-hp PA-18 was priced at $15,920.

80. **Cessna 180, 182, 185**—1953 / Utility sportplane / 35 ft. 10 in. / 28 ft. 2 in. / 2,950 lbs. / 1,645 lbs. / 17,700 ft. / 690 miles at 13½ gph and 160 mph / 230-hp Continental O-470-R / 168 mph. When introduced in 1953, the 180 had almost 40 percent more power than the 170, yet weighed only 350 pounds more; it would sell steadily for the next 28 years with a minimum of changes. It gained 100 pounds empty and 250 pounds gross weight, along with a mere five hp over the years. About 9,000 were built, and Cessna called the 180 the Skywagon, along with the 185 Model that came along in 1961 with 260 hp and 500 pounds more useful load. The 182 Skylane was introduced in 1956 at the same time the first 172 appeared. Actually, the Skylane version followed in 1958 and is the "uptown" version of the 182 just as the Skyhawk is the fully-equipped version of the 172. Specs are for the 1974 Skylane and are typical.

81. **Cessna Models 310 and 320**—1954 / Four to six passenger business twin / 36 ft. 11 in. / 29 ft. 3 in. / 5,500 lbs. / 3,251 lbs. / 19,750 ft. / 709 miles at 26½ gph and 222 mph / Two

This is the 1979 model of Cessna's first light twin, the 310, which first appeared back in 1954—actually, prior to both the 150 and 172. (Cessna Aircraft)

285-hp Continental IO-520-M / 238 mph. Originally powered by the Continental O-470-M of 240 hp, the 310J of 1966 had gained 500 pounds gross with the 260-hp IO-470-U, and in 1975 it received 285-hp Continentals, along with a 32-inch extended nose and the usual detail changes. In 1969, the 320 Skynight, the stretched 310, was replaced by the Turbo 310, and it, in turn, was replaced by the Model 340. Representative specs are for the 1975 Model 310. More than 5,000 were built of all models.

82. **Piper Apache, PA-23** and **Aztec**—1954 / Business twin / 37 ft. 0 in. / 27 ft. 1 in. / 3,500 lbs. / 2,180 lbs. / service ceiling not available / 1,200 miles at 15½ gph and 170 mph w/108 gal. including aux. tanks / Originally with 150-hp engines and barely four-place, the Apache received 160 hp on each side in 1957, and the 235-hp Lycoming O-540 in 1963; by then, the new Aztec, with 250-hp engines and an honest six-seat capacity, was more airplane for the money. Specs above are for the 1957 Apache. Specs for the 1975 PA-23 Aztec: 37 ft. 2 in. / 31 ft. 2 in. / 5,200 lbs. / 3,042 lbs. / 21,000 ft. / 1,210 miles at 25 gph and 190 mph / Two 250-hp Lycoming IO-540-C4B5 / 216 mph.

83. **Douglas DC-7**—1955 / Four-engine airliner / 127 ft. 6 in. / 112 ft. 3 in. / 143,000 lbs. / 72,150 lbs. / 25,000 ft. / 4,250 miles at 357 mph / Four Wright R-3350 compounds of 3,400 hp each (takeoff) / 405 mph. The DC-7, seating up to 95 passengers, appeared in 1955; the slightly larger and more powerful DC-7C ''Seven Seas'' a year later was the first airliner capable of flying nonstop, in both directions, between New York and California. Three versions of the DC-7 were built in approximately equal numbers for a total of 336.

84. **Mooney M-20 Series**—1955 / Four-place sportplane / 36 ft. 1 in. / 25 ft. 5 in. / 2,900 lbs. / 1,933 lbs. / 24,000 ft. / 1,446 miles at 195 mph and 10 gph / 210-hp Continental

A much improved version of the Piper Apache, the six-place Aztec has a little more power than late model Apaches. With lighter controls and electric trim, it's easier to fly.

TSIO-360-GB4 / 231 mph. Specs are for the 231. The wood-winged Mooney M-20 established the shape and concept of all Mooneys from its introduction in 1955 to the present Mooney 252. The M-20B of 1961 was the first all-metal Mooney; it had 1800 hp and was known as the Mk 21. The Super 21 of 1964 went to 200 hp. The first stretched version was the 200-hp Executive 21 of 1967; the 180-hp version was called the Ranger from 1968 onward and the stretched Ranger became the Statesman 1968–69. Until 1978 the Chaparral, Executive, and Ranger, with 200, 200, and 180 hp respectively, were the product line, plus the '71 Aerostar. There was no production during '72–'73. The 201 announced in 1977 is a cleaned-up version of the Executive, and the 231, which followed in 1979, is a 201 with turbosupercharging. The Mooney Master, with fixed gear convertible to retractable, was offered '63–'65. The M22 pressurized Mustang and other poor management decisions broke the company by 1969. Butler Aviation bought the assets in 1970, produced a few airplanes in '71, and closed the doors. Republic Steel bought Mooney in October '73 and resumed production in '74.

85. **Cessna 172, 175 Skylark/Powermatic, Skyhawk, Skyhawk II,** and **Hawk XP**—1956 / Four-place sportplanes / 35 ft. 10 in. / 26 ft. 11 in. / 2,300 lbs. / 1,350 lbs. / 13,100 ft. / 650 miles at 8 gph and 138 mph / 150-hp Lycoming O-320-E2D / 144 mph. The four-place, all-metal 172/Skyhawk (the Skyhawk is the deluxe version of the 172 basic machine), along with the WWII Messerschmitt Me.109, have been built in greater numbers—well over 30,000—than

The Mooney 201 gets 195 mph cruise from 200 hp, burning about 18 gals. of fuel per hour. The Mooney M20 series has always been noted for efficiency, and the company, until recently, was poorly managed. In 1987 Mooney was the top producer of single-engine lightplanes.

any other airplanes in history. The 172/Skyhawk engine was the 145-hp Continental O-300 until 1968, when a switch was made to the 150-hp Lycoming O-320-EZD. The 172 began production in 1956; the Skyhawk version followed in 1961. Significant changes since include the swept rudder and big rear window added in 1964, conical wingtips in 1970, tubular steel gear legs in 1971, modified wing airfoil for better slow-flight characteristics in 1973, Clark Y propeller airfoil in 1974. The 1977 Skyhawk received the 160-hp Lycoming O-320-H2AD rated for 100 octane fuel, and the 1978 model was given a 28-V electrical system. The Skyhawk II, introduced in 1974, was merely a standard Skyhawk with factory-installed nav/comm package, beacons, and ELT. The Hawk XP model appeared in 1977 fitted with the 195-hp Continental IO-360-K and constant-speed propeller. The Model 175 Skylark was produced in 1958–1963, the last ones called Powermatics. It was a Skylane airframe of the period powered with the Continental geared GO-300-E of 175 hp. Specs are for the typical 1975 model 172/Skyhawk.

86. **Lake Buccaneer, LA-4-20**—1958 / Four-place all-metal amphibian, originally produced as the Colonial Skimmer during the 1950s with the 180-hp O-360 Lycoming; latest ones fitted with the 200-hp IO-360 / 38 ft. 0 in. / 24 ft. 11 in. / 2,690 lbs. / 1,555 lbs. / Ceiling not available / 650 miles at 12.8 gph and 150 mph / Max speed not available.

87. **Beech Travelair, Model 95**—1958 / Four-place light twin / 37 ft. 10 in. / 25 ft. 11 in. / 4,200 lbs. / 2,650 lbs. / 18,100 ft. / 1,035 miles w/reserve at 20.3 gph and 195 mph / Two 180-hp Lycoming IO-360-B1B / 210 mph.

88. **Piper Comanche, Model PA-24, 180, 250** and **260**—1958 / Four-place sportplane / 36 ft. 0 in. / 25 ft. 3 in. / 2,900 lbs. / 1,630 lbs. / 1,108 w/90 gals. at 15 gph and 180 mph / 250-hp Continental O-540-E / 190 mph. The four-place Comanche entered production in 1958 powered with the 180-hp Lycoming O-360-A1A hp or the 250-hp O-540-A1A5. The 180 was dropped in 1965 and the choice was then between 250-hp O-540-E Continental or the 260-hp IO-540-D. Given an additional window on each side, this version became the Comanche B. The ''C''

followed in 1969 with a stretched nose; the Comanche C was available with turbocharging. A 400-hp version was offered for a short time, but reportedly had cooling problems. Comanche production ended in 1972 when a flood at the Lock Haven facility destroyed the tooling. Specs are for the 1966 Model 250.

89. **Cessna 150 and 152**—1958 / Two-place trainer / 33 ft. 2 in. / 23 ft. 11 in. / 1,600 lbs. / 1,111 lbs. / 14,000 ft. / 390 miles at 6½ gph and 122 mph / 100-hp Continental O-200-A / 125 mph. Cessna introduced the 150 late in 1958, almost eight years after the last 140 was built. It was always offered in three versions: Standard, Trainer, and Commuter, the differences being a matter of equipment, mostly avionics and cabin comfort items. The large rear window was added in 1964; the swept rudder, bigger doors, and larger tires in 1966. Conical wingtips began with the 1970 model, and 1971 saw tubular gear legs, new nose plate with landing light, extended prop shaft and new dorsal fin. In '73 the seats were lowered, and the Aerobat model got a new prop with Clark Y airfoil, a feature added to the 150 the next year, along with increased vertical tail area. The Aerobat version became available in 1970, with quick-release doors, a G-meter and airframe stressed for 6 Gs positive and 3 Gs negative flight loads. In 1977, after building almost 24,000 150s, the 152 was announced for 1978. It was a 150 with the Lycoming O-235-L2C, which would burn LL100 blue av-fuel and was rated at 110 hp. Performance remained almost identical to that of the recent 150s. Specs are for 1977 Model 150.

90. **Boeing 707 and 720**—1958 / Four-jet airliner / 130 ft. 10 in. / 136 ft. 9 in. / 234,000 lbs. max gross / 42,000 ft. / 4,155 miles w/43,117 lbs. payload / Four P&W JT3D-1 turbofans of 17,000 lbs. thrust each / 611 mph. The first U.S. jetliner in scheduled service was the 707-120 (October 26, 1958), followed by the 707-320 Intercontinental (August 26, 1959). The 120, with 13,500 pounds static thrust per engine, soon had 18,000 pound thrust turbofans as the 120B, but a lighter version with 15,800 pound thrust engines was the 707-220 built for Braniff, while BOAC required R-R Conway turbofans for its 707s, resulting in the 707-420. The 707-720 entered service with United October 6, 1960, and was slightly smaller than the 120 with a new wing featuring leading-edge slats. The 720B followed in 1961 with turbofans.

91. **Lockheed Electra, L-188**—1959 / Four-engine airliner / 99 ft. 0 in. / 104 ft. 8 in. / 116,000 lbs. max gross / 27,000 ft. / 2,500 miles w/22,000 lbs. payload / Four Allison 501-D13A turboprops of 3,750 shp each / 405 mph. The first U.S.-designed and built turboprop airliner was first in service with Eastern January 12, 1959; a total of 170 of the 99-passenger Electras was built, and they served as the basis for the U.S. Navy's P-3 Orion sub-hunters.

92. **McDonnell Douglas DC-8 and DC-8 Super Sixty**—1959 / Four-engine airliner / 148 ft. 5 in. / 157 ft. 5 in. / 335,000 lbs. max gross / 6,000 miles w/47,355 lbs. payload / 600 mph. The DC-8 was built in five basic versions, two domestic and three intercontinental; the former were dash-10s and dash-20s, with JT3C6 and JT4A3 engines of 13,500 and 15,800 pounds thrust respectively. The intercontinental dash-30s came with either of the above-mentioned engines; the dash-40s had R-R Conway 509s of 17,500 pounds thrust, and the DC-8-50s have JT3D-3 fans. The first DC-8-10s entered service September 18, 1959, with United and Delta. A DC-8-40 was the first jet airliner to exceed the speed of sound when it reached Mach 1.012 (667 mph) in a shallow dive, August 21, 1961; 294 DC-8s were built. The Super Sixties, the first of which was introduced in 1966, are the DC-8-61, -62, and -63, all of which are powered with JT3D-7s of 19,000 pounds thrust. The -61 has a stretched fuselage (up to 259 passengers); the -62 has a new wing and redesigned engine pods, and the -63 combines the

The Beech Queen Air, a six-to-nine place cabin class twin, with 340-hp turbo Lycomings, was the replacement for the Model 50 Twin Bonanza. The first one, which appeared in 1958, had a slab tail; pictured is the '66 model. (Beech Aircraft photo)

93. **Beech Queen Air, Models 65, 70, 80,** and **88**—1959 / Cabin-class twins / 45 ft. 10½ in. / 33 ft. 4 in. / 7,700 lbs. / 4,850 lbs. / 31,300 ft. / 800 miles at 36 gph and 200 mph / 239 mph. The six-to-nine place 65 was fitted with 340-hp IGSO-480-A1E6 Lycomings; the Model 70 with the same engines seats seven to 11. The 80 and 88 have 380-hp IGSO-540-A1D Lycomings, and the Model 88 is pressurized. (Piston engine designations are descriptive; above, the "I" means fuel-injection; "G" means geared; "S" is for supercharged, and "O" denotes an opposed-type engine configuration. The suffix letters/numbers describe accessories. Specs above are for 1966 Model 65.

94. **Cessna 210** and **Centurion**—1960 / Cabin monoplane / 36 ft. 9 in. / 28 ft. 2 in. / 3,800 lbs. / 2,168 lbs. / 17,300 ft. / 1,005 miles at 18 gph and 190 mph / Continental IO-520-L of 285 hp (300 hp takeoff) / 200 mph. A high-wing cabin monoplane seating four to six,

The E33 Bonanza was called a Debonair early in life. Fitted with a 225-hp 0-470 that fed upon 80 octane fuel, it was a bargain even in 1960 dollars, when introduced at $20,000. It was offered in a "limited edition" in 1987 and 1988 for $131,750 with the 285-hp Continental as the F33A.

the 210 entered the market in 1960 with 260 hp, received big rear window and four inch wider cabin in '62, became the 210 Centurion in '64 with new wing, larger tail, and 285 hp, and got a full cantilever wing in '67. In 1969, dihedral was reduced to 1½ degrees, the nosewheel strut was shortened and the nosewheel housing made flush; the cabin was 25 percent larger in '70 with later version engine. A pressurized version was introduced in '78 in addition to the Centurion and Turbo Centurion. Specs are for 1978 210 Centurion.

95. **Beech Debonair, Model 33** and **Bonanza 33**—1960 / Cabin monoplane / 33 ft. 5½ in. / 26 ft. 8 in. / 3,400 lbs. / 2,056 lbs. / 17,500 ft. / 600 miles at 15 gph and 200 mph / 208 mph. Probably the most Beech for the money ever offered, during the early 1960s, at $19,995, the Debonair was priced $5,300 below the M35 V-tail on the same assembly line. Fitted with the 225-hp IO-470-J and K as the Model 33, A33, B33, and C33 through 1967, it also had the 285-hp Continental IO-520-B as the C33A in '66–'67. In '68 and '69 it became the E33 Bonanza. The E33B and E33C are aerobatic versions. In 1970, the F33 was offered with 225 hp. The F33A Bonanza, '70–'88, has the 285-hp IO-520-BA, and was available in 1987 for the special price of $131,750. Beech built 100 of them and was tentatively accepting orders for 100 more in 1988. The V-tail went out of production in 1984. Specs are for F33A.

96. **Beech Baron, Models 55** and **58**—1961 / Four-to-six passenger business twin / 37 ft. 10 in. / 29 ft. 10 in. / 5,400 lbs. / 3,215 lbs. / 17,800 ft. / Range w/reserve and 168 gal. 1,220 miles / Two 285-hp Continental IO-520-C / 242 mph. Starting in 1961 as a Travelair with more muscle, the first Baron had 260-hp engines, Fowler flaps, and a swept tail. The B55 of '63 had a longer nose and fuel capacity up to 143 gallons; the '65 C55 went to 285 hp. The turbo version came in 1967 to achieve 290 mph at 25,000 feet. Club seating was introduced with the stretched Model 58 in '69, and the 58P pressurized Baron followed in 1976 with 310 hp. Also in '76 the 58TC turbo was added using the 58Ps engines and wings. Then,

By 1978 Beech offered five versions of the Models 55 and 58 Baron series, including the pressurized 58P pictured. Engines ranged from 260 to 310 hp. All models have a 7,000-feet single-engine pressure-altitude capability.

in '79, the 58TC and 58P received 325-hp Continental TSIO-520-WB engines. Representative specs are for the 1975 Model 58 Baron.

97. **Beech Musketeer, Sundowner, Sierra, etc.**—1962 / Two and four-place sportplanes / 32 ft. 9 in. / 25 ft. 8½ in. / 2,750 lbs. / 1,711 lbs. / 14,300 ft. / 440 miles at 10½ gph and 150 mph / 200-hp Lycoming IO-360-A1B / Max speed not available. The Model 23 Musketeer entered the market in 1962 and did amazingly little with 160 hp. The Musketeer II followed in '64 with fuel injection and 165 hp, and in 1965 there appeared three Musketeers, the Sport III, Custom III, and Super III, a two-place 150-hp, and 165 and 200-hp four placers. The Custom III got 180 hp in '68; the Super R retractable of 1970 replaced the Super III, and then became the A24R Sierra in 1972 when the name Musketeer was dropped. It became the B24R in 1974 with installation of the 200-hp Lycoming IO-360-A1B. Meanwhile, the Custom III evolved into the Sundowner and the two-place version, the B19 Sport—none of which helped a whole lot; Beech never got a handle on this end of the market. Above specs are for the Sierra 200 (1974).

98. **Maule M-4 and M-5 Rocket**—1962 / Four-place STOL / 30 ft. 10 in. / 23 ft. 0 in. / 2,300 lbs. / 1,400 lbs. / 25,000 ft. / 457 miles at 15.6 gph and 170 mph / Max speed unavailable. A four-place STOL, the Maule was originally offered with 145 hp; this was upped to 210

This is the original 1962 Beech Model 23 Musketeer from which the Sport, Sundowner, and Sierra evolved.

hp in 1965 as the M-4. In 1967 the Franklin-powered M-4 went to 220 hp (a 180-hp version was tried briefly in 1970). The M-5 appeared in 1975 with the 210-hp Continental, and in 1976 it was given the derated 235-hp O-540-J Lycoming.

99. **Aero Commander 200 (Meyers)**—1962 / High-performance four-placer / 30 ft. 6 in. / 24 ft. 4 in. / 3,000 lbs. / 1,985 lbs. / 18,500 ft. / 1,060 miles at 16½ gph and 210 mph / 285-hp IO-520-B / 212 mph. Originally built as the Meyers 200, fitted with 240, 260, and 285-hp engines, about 150 were produced altogether. The design was acquired by Aero Commander in 1965.

100. **Piper Cherokee PA-28s**—1961 / Two-place trainer; four-place sportplane / 35 ft. 0 in. / 23 ft. 9 in. / 2,325 lbs. / 1,301 lbs. / 12,700 ft. / 690 miles at 9.65 gph and 133 mph (50 gal.) / 150-hp Lycoming O-320-E3D / 135 mph. The first Cherokee was introduced in 1961, a low-wing, four-place fixed-gear sport-trainer of 150 hp. It remained for years as the 140, 140B, Flite Liner, and Cruiser. In 1964, this basic airframe was offered with four different engines, resulting in the (150-hp) 140B, 160, 180, and 235, the latter three named for engine

hp. In 1966, the 140 continued as the B Model two-place trainer, while the Cherokee C with this airframe was available with 150, 160, and 180 hp as a four-placer. The 235B was the '66–'67 model. In 1967, the tribe consisted of the 140B, 150, 180D, and 235C, plus the new Cherokee Arrow, PA-28R-180—essentially, the 180 with fold-up feet and a new third window (the PA-32 Cherokee Six had been introduced in 1966). This line-up remained unchanged into 1969 except that the Arrow went to 200 hp that year. The 1972 Cherokees gained a redesigned rudder and new dorsal fin. The 140B remained, along with a stripped version called the Flite Liner, while the 150 Model became the Cruiser. The 150-hp Warrior appeared in 1973, and the 235C was renamed Charger 235—and the following year was again renamed Pathfinder 235. The 180D, which had become the Archer 180 in '74, got the Warrior's new tapered wing in 1976 and became the Archer II. The Warrior wing was the most significant development among the fixed-gear Cherokees since their introduction. Specs above are for Cherokee Warrior.

101. **Piper Twin Comanche, PA-30 and PA-39**—1963 / The PA-39 was the PA-30 with counter-rotating propellers on this light twin known as the Twin Comanche C/R: 36 ft. 0 in. / 25 ft. 2 in. / 3,600 lbs. / 2,270 lbs. / 20,000 ft. / 1,110 miles at 13.8 gph and 188 mph (90 gal.) / 205 mph.

102. **Cessna Skymaster, Model 337**—1963-81 / High-wing twin / 38 ft. 2 in. / 29 ft. 9 in. / 4,440 lbs. / 2,660 lbs. / 19,300 ft. / 1,060 miles at 190 mph / Two 210-hp Continental IO-360-G / 199 mph. Featuring one tractor and one pusher engine on the centerline and counter-rotating props, early Skymasters had fixed landing gear. The pressurized model appeared

The twin-engine ("push-pull") Cessna Model 337 Skymaster is a good short-field performer but range is limited with more than four people aboard. The first ones had a fixed landing gear; last ones are pressurized and retractable. Single-engine service ceiling is 6,000 or 7,000 feet pressure altitude, depending upon which fan is stopped. Pictured is a pressurized 1975 model. (Cessna photo)

168 SIGNIFICANT U.S. CIVIL AIRCRAFT

in 1972 and the turbo version dropped until '78. The Super Skymaster of 1970 is representative; specs above.

103. **Champion Citabria Series** and **Other Aeronca Derivatives**—1964 / High-wing sportplane / 33 ft. 6 in. / 22 ft. 8½ in. / 1,650 lbs. / 1,034 lbs. / 12,000 ft. / 690 miles at 6 gph and 112 mph / Lycoming O-235-C1 of 115 hp (originally approved w/100 hp) / 119 mph. The original Aeronca went out of production in 1951, and was revived in 1955 by the Champion Aircraft Company of Oceola, WI (which was mostly Mr. Bob Brown, a WWII pilot) as the 90-hp Champion Traveler 7EC; there followed the Tri-Traveler, Tri-Con, Sky-Trac, DXer, and Challenger, all tri-gear. The DXer had 135 hp as the 7HC; the Challenger 7GCB had 150 hp (Brown also offered a high-wing, two-place twin called the Lancer). In 1964 Brown built the Citabria, a beefed-up and modernized Aeronca Champ fitted with the 100-hp Continental O-200-A (the Cessna 150 engine) and called it the 7ECA. The 7GCA with 150 hp followed, along with a 115-hp version. Bellanca bought Champion in 1970 and added the Decathlon, essentially, the 150-hp Citabria with constant-speed prop and aerobatic wing. Also offered was the 180-hp Super Decathlon 8KCAB, and the Scout bush airplane, the 8GCBC. Between 1970 and '73, about 70 ''cheap Champs'' were sold for $4,995 fitted with 60-hp two-cylinder Franklins. This was the 7ACA Champion. The specs above are for the Champion Model 7ECA (1975).

104. **Boeing 727**—1964 / Three-jet airliner / 108 ft. 0 in. / 133 ft. 2 in. / 160,000 lbs. (191,000 for stretched versions) / 37,400 ft. / 1,900 miles with 29,000-lb. payload / Three P&W JT8D-7 turbofans of 14,000 lbs. thrust each / 605 mph. The biggest jet transport success to date, the standard production model in the late 1960s was the 727-100, an 88 to 131-seater. Eastern was the first to fly a 727, on February 1, 1964. The 727-200 of 1967 was 20 feet longer and seated 189. By 1971 the 727 was the fastest-selling jetliner in the world, and by the end of 1984 1,696 were in service, 1,161 of those in the U.S. Specs are for 727-130.

105. **Beech King Air Series**—1964 / Business twin and airliner / 50 ft. 3 in. / 35 ft. 6 in. / 9,650 lbs. / 5,765 lbs. / 30,700 ft. / 1,100 miles at 89½ gph and 256 mph / Two P&W PT6A-21

Beech has led the industry with its propjet King Airs since the first one was introduced back in 1964; almost 4,000 have been delivered worldwide. Pictured is the 1984 King Air 300. (Beech photo)

turboprops of 550 shp each / 365 mph. The King Air Model 90 evolved from the Queen Air series (introduced in 1959), and its success prompted the addition of bigger and more powerful models. All are turboprops. By 1976 there were five King Air: Super King Air, King Air A100, King Air B100, King Air E90, and the economy leader, King Air C90. Size of engines and commensurate performance, along with relatively slight differences in span/length/weights, separated these six to 15-seat business aircraft (about 80 were in airline use about the world in 1985). By 1983, the King Air series consisted of the B200 with engines of 850 shp and 15-seat capacity, the B100 with 715-shp engines and 15-seat capacity, the F90 with 750-shp engines and 10-seat capacity, and the still popular C90 with 550-shp. In 1987, the new top-of-the-line King Air was the Super 300 with a gross weight of 14,000 pounds, a 35,000-foot service ceiling, 365-mph max speed, and max range of 2,255 miles. Specs above are for the 1980 model King Air C90.

106. **Gates Learjet, Models 23, 24, 25, 35 / 36,** and **Longhorns**—1964 / Business jets / 39 ft. 6 in. / 48 ft. 8 in. / 18,000 lbs. / 9,154 lbs. / 45,000 ft. / Two AiResearch TFE-731-2-2B turbofans of 7,000 lbs. thrust each / .83 Mach above 24,000 ft. The six-passenger Model 23 entered service October 13, 1964; the stretched versions 24 and 25 followed late in 1964 and in 1967, respectively. The company was acquired by Gates Rubber Company in 1967. The turbofan Learjets 35 and 36 appeared in 1974, and the eight-to-10-passenger Longhorns were introduced in 1980. Typical specs above are for a Learjet Model 36A.

The Model 35/36 Learjet (pictured) is powered by AiResearch turbofans, and received FAA certification in mid-1974. Bill Lear pioneered the bizjet market in the mid-1960s, when few people believed there was such a market. Cessna and all the rest were followers. (Gates Learjet photo)

107. **McDonnell Douglas DC-9**—1965 / Jet airliner / 89 ft. 5 in. / 104 ft. 5 in. / 90,700 lbs. gross / Service ceiling not available / 1,310 miles w/50 passengers / Two P&W JT8D-1 turbofans of 14,000 lbs. thrust / 561 mph. The first U.S. twin-jet transport to employ tail-mounted engines, the first DC-9 entered service with Delta on November 29, 1965. The series 10 seated 90, the stretched series 30 seats up to 115; the series 40 is a farther stretch for 125 passengers (1968). The C-9 variant for the USAF is a hospital airplane. Latest versions were the 80s, fitted with P&W JT8D-217 engines; 1,021 DC-9/MD-80s were in service worldwide at the end of 1984, 594 in the U.S. Specs are for DC-9-10.

108. **Cessna 205, 206, 207 Stationairs**—1965 / High-wing utility / 35 ft. 10 in. / 28 ft. 3 in. / 3,616 lbs. / 1,988 lbs. / 27,000 ft. / 775 miles / Continental TSIO-520-M of 285 hp (310 hp for takeoff) / 200 mph. The Cessna Skywagons actually began with the 180, of course, and the first model 206 Super Skywagon, directly descended from the 205 (1962–1964; essentially a fixed-gear version of the 210C). The U-206, produced from 1964 through 1971, was the first stretched-fuselage model. Cessna dropped the 206 designation in 1972, replacing it with Stationair, which continued in production, along with the 207 Skywagon. The airframes are the same, except that the 207 is about 3½ feet longer, making it a seven-place machine. In 1978 the 206 series became the Stationair 6, featuring club seating, and the 207 became the Stationair 7. The 206/Stationair 6 has been available with supercharging since 1966; the 207/Stationair 7 has had a supercharged version since 1969. Engines have been the 285-hp Continental IO-520 or TSIO-520 in both series. Specs are for 1980 Turbo Stationair. The Stationair 8 replaced the Stationair 7 in 1979.

109. **Cessna Models 401, 402, 404** and **411**—1965 / Business twins / 39 ft. 10½ in. / 35 ft. 10 in. / 6,300 lbs. / 3,719 lbs. / 26,180 ft. / 1,454 miles at 236 mph / Two 300-hp Continental TSIO-520-E / 261 mph. The Model 411 was introduced in 1965, a big turbocharged twin for cargo or club seating; the 401, 402, and 404 followed. The 401 and 402 were each known as Utiliner and Businessliner, depending upon configuration, and the 404 was the Titan. The 411 was a pressurized version of the 402, which was discontinued in 1969. The 401 and 402 had 300-hp engines; the 404 had 375-hp engines and no tip tanks with a new wing. In 1978 the Titan was offered, a pure freighter. The 1972 Model 402B specs above are representative.

110. **Piper Cherokee Six, PA-32, Lance,** and **Saratoga**—1966 / Six-place business and utility / 36 ft. 2 in. / 28 ft. 2 in. / 3,600 lbs. / 20,000 ft. / 897 miles at 21½ gph and 190 mph / 294-hp Lycoming TIO-540-S1AD / 209 mph. The Cherokee 6 has a stretched fuselage (4 feet 5 inches longer than the Warrior), seats six, and has a complex fuel system. Offered initially with choice of 260 or 300-hp engines, the Six was produced alongside the new Lance, which was first delivered in 1975 with the same horsepower, same size, and was clearly intended to replace the Six at some point soon. Then Piper put a T-tail on the new Lance to make the Lance II, resulting in flight characteristics analogous to a 6×6 Army truck, and it took a while to reposition the Lance's horizontal tail, while Piper considered giving the Lance III a Warrior-type wing. The result of that was the Saratoga and Turbo Saratoga, known as the Saratoga SP (for "special performance"). Specs are for the PA-32-301T Turbo Saratoga, 1982 model.

111. **deHavilland Twin Otter, DHC-6**—1966 / Twin turboprop, seating up to 20, built in Ontario, Canada / 65 ft. 0 in. / 51 ft. 9 in. / 12,500 lbs. / 7,320 lbs. / 26,700 ft. / 793 miles with 2,550 lbs. payload / Two P&W PT6A-27 of 620 shp / 182 mph.

The Cherokee Turbo Lance II. The T-tail was a mistake; this one flew like a 6×6 truck. That's author Christy, with wife Rene (white suit) and Julia Lee Downie, wife of aviation writer Don Downie.

112. **Bellanca 260, Viking** and **Super Viking**—1967 / Cabin monoplanes / 34 ft. 2 in. / 26 ft. 4 in. / 3,325 lbs. / 2,210 lbs. / 17,000 ft. / 800 miles at 187 mph / Lycoming IO-540-G1E5 of 285 hp (300 hp takeoff) / 195 mph. Pioneer aircraft designer Giuseppe Bellanca produced a limited number of efficient monoplanes during the late 1920s and the '30s. After WWII, he continued his Cruisair series, the last of which was the fabric-covered, four-place, 200-hp Cruismaster. Bellanca had retired when an Alexandria, MN, group bought the design and produced the Bellanca 260. Two additional changes of ownership followed, and the company enjoyed stable management until forced into bankruptcy in 1980. The 260 was fitted with the 285-hp Continental in 1967 to produce the Viking, and the Super Viking was in production (about 100 per year) by 1978. Specs above describe the Super Viking 300, 1974 model.

113. **Cessna 421 Golden Eagle**—1967 / Business twin / 41 ft. 10½ in. / 36 ft. 1 in. / 7,200 lbs. / 4,421 lbs. / 31,100 ft. / 1,542 miles at 30 gph and 265 mph / Two 375-hp GTSIO-520-H / 282 mph. Based on the 401/402 airframe, this pressurized craft received a new wet wing in 1976 as the C model. Popular with passengers, the geared engines have been a source of trouble.

The only modern high-performance retractable with fabric-covered fuselage and an all-wood wing is the Bellanca Viking.

The pressurized Cessna 421 is known as the Golden Eagle. (Cessna photo)

114. **Cessna Cardinal** and **Cardinal RG**—1967 / Four-place sportplanes / 35 ft. 6 in. / 27 ft. 3 in. / 2,800 lbs. / 1,600 lbs. / 17,100 ft. / 945 miles at 171 mph / Lycoming IO-360-A1B6D / 180 mph. The 177/Cardinal (the 177 being the Plain Jane version) entered the market as a fixed-gear four-placer with full cantilever wing and 150 hp as a 1968 model late in 1967. Cessna performed a factory mod on the too-effective stabilators of those in service; the '69 model had 180 hp. The retractable gear Cardinal RG was introduced in 171 with 200 hp; the '72 Cardinals received the Clark Y airfoil prop blades. Specs above are for Cardinal RG, 1973 model.

115. **Piper Cherokee Arrow PA-28R, 180, 200, Arrow II** and **Arrow III, IV**—1967 / Cabin monoplane / 35 ft. 5 in. / 24 ft. 8 in. / 2,750 lbs. / 1,754 lbs. / 16,200 ft. / 1,100 miles at 11½ gph and 165 mph / 200-hp Lycoming IO-360-C1C / 175 mph. The Arrow entered production in 1967 with 180 hp and Piper's automatic landing gear retract system employing the Cherokee 180 airframe. The 200-hp Arrow 200 followed in 1969; the Arrow II, which appeared in '72, is five inches longer than previous models, and has a bigger door, 26 inches more span, and the stabilator from the Cherokee Six. The Arrow III came in '77 with a Warrior-type wing, and the Arrow IV of 1978 was available with turbocharging. Specs are for a 1977 Arrow III.

116. **Boeing 737**—1967 / Short-haul jetliner, 75 to 125 passengers / 93 ft. 0 in. / 100 ft. 0 in. / 114,500 lbs. gross / Range w/max payload of 35,349 lbs., 2,135 miles / Two P&W JT8D-9 turbofans of 14,500 lbs. thrust / 568 mph. Most later orders were for the 200 series, for which specs are given above. An option on late models is the P&W JT8D-15 engine of 15,500 lbs. thrust. On January 1, 1985, a total of 940 were in service worldwide, 391 in the U.S.

117. **Piper Navajo**—1967 / The PA-31 series includes Navajo, Navajo CR (counter-rotating props), PA-31-350 Chieftan, PA-31T Cheyenne II turboprop (with 620 shp), and the Cheyenne PA-31T-1 with 500 shp each engine. Both Cheyennes are pressurized. The stretched Cheyenne III appeared in 1978; the Chieftan was introduced in 1970. The 1979 Chieftan: 40 ft. 8 in. / 34 ft. 7½ in. / 7,000 lbs. / 4,221 lbs. / 27,200 ft. / 1,017 miles at 45½ gph and 254 mph / Two 350-hp Lycoming TIO-540-J2BD and LTIO-540-J2BD, counter-rotating / 254 mph. Pressurization began with the 1971 model. The 1979 Cheyenne II: 42 ft. 8 in. / 34 ft. 8 in. / 9,000 lbs. / 4,976 lbs. / 31,600 ft. / 1,020 miles at 116 gph and 318 mph / Two P&W PT6A-28 turboprops of 620 shp each / 325 mph. The 1979 Navajo CR: 40 ft. 8½ in. / 32 ft. 8 in. / 6,500 lbs. / 4,099 lbs. / 26,400 at 6,500 lbs. / 1,081 miles at 43 gph and 253 mph / Two 325-hp TIO-540-F2BD (one a LTIO) / 253 mph.

118. **Beech, Duke, Model 60**—1968 / Pressurized business twin / 39 ft. 4 in. / 33 ft. 10 in. / 6,775 lbs. / 4,423 lbs. / 30,000 ft. at 6,775 lbs. / 1,279 miles at 47 gph and 259 mph / Two 380-hp Lycoming TIO-541-E1C4 / 275 mph.

119. **Beech A36 Bonanza**—1968 / Low-wing monoplane / 32 ft. 10 in. / 26 ft. 4½ in. / 3,600 lbs. / 1,980 lbs. / 16,000 ft. / 550 miles at 18 gph and 195 mph / 285-hp Continental IO-520-BA; (1984 and onward, 300-hp IO-550-B) / 204 mph. The Model 36, introduced in June 1968, was basically an E33A with 10 inches added to the forward cabin and with the fuselage moved correspondingly forward over the wing, while the aft bulkhead was moved rearward 19 inches to get six cubic feet more cabin volume than was possessed by the Model 35 V-tail. The result was a full six-place airplane. It became the A36 in 1970 when buyers demanded a more civilized interior for an airplane Beech had regarded as a utility craft. It has remained the A36 since with unchanged specs/performance. A turbo version was available by 1980.

The turboprop pressurized Piper Cheyennes were developed from the Navajo PA-31 series, which includes the Chieftan. The stretched Cheyenne III, pictured, was added to the line in 1978. (Piper photo)

120. **Beech 99 Airliner**—1968 / 17-to-19 passenger twin turboprop for commuter airline service: 163 were in service worldwide (85 in the U.S.) in 1985. This machine has a high-speed cruise of 283 mph at 8,000 ft. / Service ceiling is 26,313 ft. / Range is 1,173 miles / Two P&W PT6A-27 turboprops of 680 shp each.

121. **Cessna Model 414** and **Chancellor**—1969 / Cabin-class twin / 44 ft. 1½ in. / 36 ft. 4½ in. / 6,750 lbs. / 4,592 lbs. / 30,800 ft. / 465 miles at 260 lbs. fuel/hr and 252 mph / Two 310-hp Continental TSIO-520-NB / 254 mph. The 414 is a pressurized cabin-class twin with 310-hp engines. Originally five-place, later models are up to eight-place if not club interiors. The 414 became the Chancellor in 1978.

122. **Boeing 747**—1970 / Four-jet airliner / 195 ft. 8 in. / 231 ft. 6 in. / 710,000 lbs. max takeoff weight / 45,000 ft. / 5,790 miles w/177,684 lbs. payload / Four P&W JT9D-3 turbofans of 43,500 lbs. thrust each / 595 mph. A jet airliner seating 374 to 490 passengers eight abreast in a 185-foot cabin, the 747 entered service with Pan Am, New York to London, on January 22, 1970. In 1985, 556 were in service worldwide, 156 in the U.S.

123. **Piper Seneca, Seneca II** and **III, PA-34**—1971 / Six-place owner-flown twin / 38 ft. 11 in. / 28 ft. 6 in. / 4,750 lbs. / 2,875 lbs. / 25,000 ft. / 1,159 miles at 22 gph and 207 mph / Two 220-hp Continental TSIO-360-KB / 225 mph. The Seneca II appeared in 1974 with a turbocharged six-cylinder Continental replacing the original four-jug Lycoming—described by some as a Cherokee Six with two engines. Specs above are for the 1982 Seneca III.

The Beechcraft Duke, a pressurized business twin, has been in the market since 1968. It has a posh interior and lots of performance with a pair of turbo Lycomings of 380 hp each. (Beech photo)

124. **Gulfstream-American Yankee Trainer, AA1, TR-2, Lynx** and **T-Cat**—1971 / Sport monoplane / 31 ft. 6 in. / 22 ft. 0 in. / 2,400 lbs. / 1,285 lbs. / 14,600 ft. / 765 miles at 10.6 gph and 160 mph / 180-hp Lycoming O-360-A4K / 170 mph. Four-placers based on the original Bede-designed Yankee two-placer are the 180-hp Tiger and 150-hp Cheetah. The Tiger appeared in 1975; the Cheetah was announced in '76 and was the former Traveler with the Tiger tail and new paint job. These were based on a single airframe which, as mentioned, began with the two-place Yankee, Trainer, and TR-2, which were powered with the 108-hp O-235-C2 Lycoming. Specs given are for the Tiger version. The Lynx was two-place with 115-hp.

125. **McDonnell Douglas DC-10**—1971 / Three-jet airliner / 155 ft. 4 in. / 181 ft. 5 in. / 430,000 lbs. max takeoff weight / 35,000 ft. / 2,760 miles w/78,000 lbs. payload / Three G.E. CF6-6 turbofans of 40,000 lbs. thrust each / 587 mph. First production models were the series 10 seating 206 to 220 delivered to American and United in July 1971. The first series 20, the intercontinental model, went to Northwest. Sales to overseas airlines began with the DC-10-30, which has engines of 48,100 pounds thrust, compared to the 45,500-pound engines on the

176 SIGNIFICANT U.S. CIVIL AIRCRAFT

Originally the AA1 Yankee, these Bede-designed craft were marketed as Grumman Americans, then as Gulfstream Americans, the same basic airframe serving both two and four-place versions, all of which carried several names. Pictured are the two-place Trainer, also called the TR-2. Engine was the 108-hp Lycoming 0-235.

    first series 20 airplanes. In 1985, there were 346 DC-10s in service worldwide, 174 flown by U.S. airlines.

126. **Cessna 340**—1971 / Cessna's lowest-priced pressurized light twin; follow-on to the discontinued 320 Skyknight; has been described as new fuselage on 310 wings and tail; originally with 285-hp Continentals, went to 310 hp in 1976. The 1984 Model 340: 38 ft. 1.3 in. / 34 ft. 4 in. / 5,990 lbs. / 3,966 lbs. / 29,800 ft. / 480 miles at 24,500 ft. and 258 mph / Two 310-hp Continental TSIO-520-NB / 263 mph.

127. **Rockwell Commander 112A** and **114**—1972 / Four-place monoplane / 32 ft. 9 in. / 24 ft. 10 in. / 2,650 lbs. / 1,688 lbs. / 13,900 ft. / 600 miles at 12.8 gph and 160 mph / 200-hp Lycoming IO-360-C1DN / 171 mph. The 112 is a four-placer directly competitive with the Cherokee Arrow and other 200-hp retractables; the 114 version appeared in 1976 with more power (260-hp IO-540-T4A5D), is 19 mph faster and carries about 400 pounds additional payload. Figures are for the 1976 Commander 112A.

Cessna's lowest-priced pressurized twin, sometimes described as a new fuselage on 310 wings and tail, is the 340. (Cessna photo)

128. **Cessna Citation, I, II, and III**—1972 / Business jet / 53 ft. 6 in. / 55 ft. 6 in. / 20,000 lbs. / 12,280 lbs. / 51,000 ft. (certified) / Range not available / Two Garrett TFE731-3B-100S of 3,650 lbs. thrust each (original Citation had P&W JT15D-1s of 2,200 lbs. thrust / 545 mph. A seven or eight-place twin fanjet business aircraft, the Citation I entered the market in December 1976 ('77 model), with added span and new JT15D-1A engines and performance markedly improved over the original Citation. The Citation II was added in 1978 (operation of the I and II by a single pilot was approved by FAA in 1977). The Citation S/II with improved engine supplanted the II late in 1984, but was not as well received; therefore the II was again available early in 1987. Meanwhile, the Citation III, with supercritical wing and 3,650 pound thrust engines, came along in 1982 and remains top-of-the-line. The Navy flies 15 Citations, a variation of the S/II, designated T-47As. In mid-1986, the Citation fleet became the largest operational bizjet fleet in the world, passing Learjet, which had led for 20 years. There were nearly 1,400 Citations in service. Specs above are for Citation III.

129. **Lockheed L-1011 TriStar**—1972 / Three-jet airliner / 155 ft. 4 in. / 178 ft. 8 in. / Max takeoff weight 409,000 lbs. / 35,000 ft. / 3,285 miles with max payload of 87,811 lbs. / Three RB.211-524 turbofans of 48,000 lbs. thrust each / 562 mph. The TriStar, in its short/medium haul configuration, seats 345 passengers with a crew of 13. Its history was greatly altered by Lockheed's decision to use Rolls Royce engines, and by management problems; R-R went bankrupt and was unable to deliver engines on time, then cash-flow problems at Lockheed resulted when the USAF withheld payment for cost overrun charges on the C-5A, while kickbacks to overseas customers (among other things) contributed to delays (and doubts) affecting the L-1011 program. The company was rescued by government guaranteed loans and new management and is healthy today indeed, but the TriStar had lost too much time and faced too much competition. It is an excellent airplane, however, and 231 were in service worldwide in 1985, 103 of those with U.S. airlines.

SIGNIFICANT U.S. CIVIL AIRCRAFT

One of the best, most efficient, and trouble-free of the modern airliners, Lockheed's L-1011 TriStar entered late into a limited market and forfeited potential sales. (Lockheed California Company)

130. **Piper Aerostar 600 Series**—1973 / Business twin / 36 ft. 8 in. / 34 ft. 9 in. / 6,000 lbs. / 4,259 lbs. / 1,230 miles at 34.3 gph and 255 mph / Two 290-hp Lycoming IO-540-AA1A5 / 301 mph. A Ted Smith design (Douglas A-20, Rockwell Aero Commanders), the Aerostar prototype flew in November 1966 and a few were built by an underfinanced company into the mid-1970s. Then Smith retrieved the design rights and built a few more as the Ted R. Smith & Associates, Inc., in Santa Maria, CA. Three versions were offered, the 600, turbo 601, and the pressurized 601P. Piper bought Aerostar rights in 1978 and built 418 of the three models before closing the California facility in mid-1981. Specs are for the 602P, which was new for 1981.

131. **Cessna Conquest, Model 441**—1978 / Business propjet / 49 ft. 4 in. / 39 ft. 0 in. / 4,243 lbs. / 5,680 lbs. / 35,000 ft. / 2,600 miles at 55.9 gph and 325 mph / Two Garrett AiResearch TPE331-8-404 of 635.5 shp each / 337 mph. A pressurized propjet seating up to 11, the first Conquests had a faulty tail design, resulting in the airplanes being grounded May 25, 1979. It returned to service in 1980 after Cessna replaced tail assemblies at no charge on the first

Another Ted Smith design, the Piper Aerostar is considered the "hot ship" in its class—good performance which you must pay for with a small and noisy cabin. (Piper photo)

173 Conquests. The Conquest II appeared in 1983 with an improved version of the AiResearch turboshaft engine and some detail improvements. Specs are for the Conquest II.

132. **Beech Duchess Model 76**—1978 / Light twin / 38 ft. 0 in. / 29 ft. 0 in. / 3,900 lbs. / 2,466 lbs. / 19,650 ft. / 854 miles at 22 gph and 188 mph / Two 180-hp O-360-A1G6D / Max speed not available. This four-place light twin has been described as the "return of the Travelair"

The Cessna Conquest began service with a faulty trim control, which damaged the reputation of an otherwise sound design. A redesigned tail was the fix Cessna chose. Here is the 1979 model. (Cessna photo)

(Beech's first light twin, spelled as one word; the "Travel Airs" of the late 1920s were spelled as two words. You're welcome) and a "twin-engine Sierra." The latter is closer. Specs describe the 1983 Duchess.

133. **Piper Seminole, Model PA-44-180**—1978 / Four-place light twin with counter-rotating propellers, all-a-same like the Duchess / 38 ft. 6 in. / 27 ft. 7 in. / 3,800 lbs. / 2,406 lbs. / 16,000 ft. / 890 miles at 18 gph and 178 mph / Two 180-hp Lycoming O-360-E1AD / 192 mph.

134. **Beech Skipper, Model 77** and **Piper Tomahawk**—1978 / Two-place trainers; lookalikes with the same engine. How do you tell them apart? The Piper has a nice big rear window, which the Skipper lacks. Performance is nearly the same; the Tomahawk spins nicely, the Beech doesn't want to maintain a stabilized spin. Which one was the first and/or the better machine? The Cessna 150, of course. Anyway, all are out of production now (unless Piper's new owner decides to make more Tomahawks). Following specs are for Skipper: 30 ft. 0 in. / 24 ft. 0 in. / 1,675 lbs. / 1,103 lbs. / 12,900 ft. / 468 miles at 6.5 gph and 105 mph / Lycoming O-235-L2C of 115 hp (112 hp in Tomahawk, which is rated at 100 rpm lower) / 122 mph.

135. **Cessna Cutlass** and **Cutlass RG**—1979 / Four-place sportplane / 36 ft. 0 in. / 26 ft. 11 in. / 2,550 lbs. / 1,513 lbs. / 17,000 ft. / 713 miles at 12.5 gph and 140 mph / 180-hp Lycoming O-360-A4N / 142 mph. Cessna began production of the Cutlass RG in 1979, and it became the best-selling and lowest-priced four-place retractable in the market. The fixed-gear Cutlass was added in 1983, apparently intended as a less-expensive replacement for the 190-hp Hawk XP. Figures are for the fixed-gear 1983 Cutlass.

136. **Cessna Corsair, Model 425**—1980 / Twin propjet / 44 ft. 1 in. / 35 ft. 10 in. / 8,200 lbs. / 4,870 lbs. / 34,700 ft. / 1,020 miles at 92.5 gph and 303 mph / Two P&W PT6A-112

The Piper Seminole, PA-44-180, is a four-place light twin designed to be direct competition for the Beechcraft Duchess. The Seminole has counter-rotating propellers, but its single-engine service ceiling is limited to ground-effect altitudes over much of the American West on warm days.

of 450 shp each / 303 mph. A cabin-class propjet with trailing beam main landing gear (suddenly popular in the 1980s; used on the Beech Musketeers from 1962 and the Ercoupe in 1940) and designed to be directly competitive with the King Air C90 and Piper Cheyenne, the Corsair entered a declining market.

137. **Cessna Crusader, Model 303**—1981 / Business twin / 39 ft. ½ in. / 30 ft. 5 in. / 5,150 lbs. / 3,328 lbs. / 25,000 ft. / 1,029 miles at 32.3 gph and 225 mph / Two Continental counter-rotating TSIO-520-AE (left), LTSIO-520-AE (right) / 248 mph. The six-place turbocharged Crusader entered the market in October 1981 (1982 Model) as the venerable 310 was discontinued. With a large cabin and airstair door, plus trailing beam landing gear, it was one of only five Cessna piston-twins still available in the mid-1980s (the others: 340, 402, 414, and 421).

138. **Piper Malibu**—1982 / Pressurized, six-place single-engine craft, FAA certificated as the PA-46-310, an all-new design / 43 ft. 0 in. / 28 ft. 5 in. / 4,100 lbs. / 2,565 lbs. / 25,000 ft. / 1,656 miles at 18 gph and 247 mph / 310-hp Continental TSIO-520-BE / Max speed not available. In the late 1960s, Piper was briefly owned by a group that included Chris-Craft boats, was later acquired by the Bangor Punta Corporation, then Lear-Siegler, which the company sold to Stuart Millar, pilot/entrepreneur who promised (late '87 as this was written) to revitalize the company.

SIGNIFICANT U.S. CIVIL AIRCRAFT

139. **Cessna Caravan, I and II**—1983 / Utility propjet / 51 ft. 8 in. / 37 ft. 8 in. / 7,000 lbs. / 3,415 lbs. / 30,000 ft. / 1,146 miles at 62.6 gph and 214 mph / P&W PT6A-114 600 shp flat-rated / 214 mph. A no-nonsense single-engine propjet designed to haul things fast and efficiently, simply constructed for ease of maintenance and aerodynamically conceived for ease of operation, this ungainly machine will replace a lot of the older utility aircraft now flying. The Caravan II (Model 208B) appeared in October 1986 and is four feet longer than the original and carries 500 pounds more payload. Federal Express is among the first operators, possessing 39 of the Caravan Is and taking delivery of 70 Caravan IIs at this writing. Specs are for Caravan I.

140. **Beech 1900 Airliner**—1984 / 19-passenger pressurized propjet designed primarily for the regional airline market; also available in executive configuration / 54 ft. 6 in. / 57 ft. 10 in. / 16,600 lbs. / 14,000 lbs. / 25,000 ft. / 977 miles at 132.2 gph and 303 mph / Two P&W PT6A-65B of 1,100 shp each. The 1900 airliner was markedly improved with a "wet wing" for 1987, increasing the fuel capacity to 670 usable gals.

141. **Beechjet**—1986 / Business jet / 43 ft. 6 in. / 48 ft. 5 in. / 15,780 lbs. max takeoff weight / 41,000 ft. / 2,219 miles at 530 mph / Two P&W JT15D-5 turbofans of 2,900 lbs. thrust each / Max speed unavailable. In 1985, Beech acquired the rights to the eight-passenger business jet built by Mitsubishi, the Diamond II, slicked it up a bit, and renamed it the Beechjet.

142. **Beech Starship I**—1988 / All-composite propjet with twin pusher engines and tandem wings / 54 ft. 4½ in. main (rear) wing; forward wing is swept forward to a 23 ft. 11 in. span in takeoff and landing configuration, and is swept back 30 degrees in cruise to 20 ft.

Beech's 1900 Airliner, which entered the market in 1984, is designed primarily for the regional airline operator, but is also available in custom club interiors for corporate use. The small vertical stabilizers on the T-tail are a distinctive feature that makes this one easy to identify.

The new Beechjet, formerly the Mitsubishi Diamond II, seeks a share of the Learjet/Citation/Falcon/Corvette/Westwind market as an eight-passenger bizjet. Engines are P&W JT15D-5 turbofans of 2,900 pounds thrust each. (Beech photo)

10 in. span / 46 ft. 1 in. / 14,000 lbs. / 11,800 lbs. / 41,000 ft. / 2,520 miles at speeds up to 405 mph (at this writing, the two full-size prototypes were still flying certification tests, and all performance figures given are subject to change) / Two P&W PT6A-67 of 1,200 shp each. Starship's cabin is 21 feet in length and 5 feet 4 inches wide, but seating configuration has not been announced at this writing.

U.S. Civil Aircraft Quiz

Number in parentheses refer to aircraft profiles in this section.

1. What was the first "wooden Lockheed"? (5)
2. Which Lockheed did Lindbergh and wife Ann fly extensively in the 1930s? (17)
3. What U.S. airliner was the first on scheduled flights across the North Atlantic? (49)
4. Which came first into the market, the Cessna 150 or 172? (85, 89)
5. What kind of engine powered the Wiley Post Model A? (36)
6. What type of aircraft construction was pioneered in America by Jack Northrop? (20)
7. Who introduced the autogiro in the United States? (25)
8. Which airframe maker designed and built the first Navions? (67)
9. What is a Kachina? (75)
10. The designer of the Piper Aerostar also designed another well-known general aviation twin. It was _____? (130)
11. In what year was the first Learjet delivered, 1964 or 1974? (106)
12. Was the Boeing 80A in service with United Air Lines a monoplane or biplane? (13)
13. The classic Beech Staggerwing was assigned Model Number _____ by Beech. (35)
14. Which was the first to be successfully flown, the autogyro or the helicopter? (25)

The Beech Starship I is a tandem-wing twin propjet of pusher configuration. The degree of sweepback in the forward wing is adjustable in flight for maximum slow or high-speed efficiency and control. Of all-composite construction, this aircraft is aimed at the corporate market and is in the 400-mph class. (Beech photo)

15. In what year was the first Beech King Air delivered, 1964 or 1974? *(105)*
16. What airplane was called the "Wichita Fokker"? Why? *(4)*
17. How many seats in the Fairchild 24 (careful, now)? *(31)*
18. Which came first, the Cessna 180 or the 172? *(80, 85)*
19. What was the first American-built pressurized airliner to enter service? *(52)*
20. Who designed the Culver Cadet, Dart, and the M20, among other aircraft? *(53)*
21. The Sikorsky S-42 flying boat was the vehicle with which Pan Am pioneered scheduled flights over which ocean? *(32)*
22. In what year did the Cessna 152 replace the 150? What was the major reason for the change? *(89)*
23. Which civilian Lockheed was the basis for the famed WWII Hudson? *(44)*
24. How many years was the Beech Model 18 (or a variant) in consecutive production? *(43)*
25. The first U.S. jetliner, the Boeing 707-120, entered service with Pan Am on October 26th of what year? *(90)*

VI

U.S. Manned Space Flights

Mission	Crew	Date	Elapsed Time Hrs/Min/Sec
Mercury-Redstone 3	Shepard	May 5, 1961	00:15:22
Mercury-Redstone 4	Grissom	July 21, 1961	00:15:37
Mercury-Atlas 6	Glenn	Feb. 20, 1962	04:55:23
Mercury-Atlas 7	Carpenter	May 24, 1962	04:56:05
Mercury-Atlas 8	Schirra	Oct. 3, 1962	09:13:11
Mercury-Atlas 9	Cooper	May 15–16, 1963	34:19:49

Total Time, Project Mercury: 53:55:27

Mission	Crew	Date	Elapsed Time Hrs/Min/Sec
Gemini-Titan III	Grissom, Young	Mar. 23, 1965	04:53:00
Gemini-Titan IV	McDivitt, White	June 3–7 1965	97:56:11
Gemini-Titan V	Cooper, Conrad	Aug. 21–29, 1965	190:55:14
Gemini-Titan VII	Borman, Lovell	Dec. 4–18, 1965	330:35:31
Gemini-Titan VI-A	Schirra, Stafford	Dec. 15–16, 1965	25:51:24
Gemini-Titan VIII	Armstrong, Scott	March 16, 1966	10:41:26
Gemini-Titan IX-A	Stafford, Cernan	June 3–6, 1966	72:21:00
Gemini-Titan X	Young, Collins	July 18–21, 1966	70:46:39
Gemini-Titan XI	Conrad, Gordon	Sept. 12–15, 1966	71:17:08
Gemini-Titan XII	Lovell, Aldrin	Nov. 11–15, 1966	94:34:31

Total Time, Gemini Program: 1939:44:08

Mission	Crew	Date	Elapsed Time Hrs/Min/Sec
Apollo-Saturn 7	Schirra, Eisele, Cunningham	Oct. 11–22, 1968	260:09:03
Apollo-Saturn 8	Borman, Lovell, Anders	Dec. 21–27, 1968	147:00:42
Apollo-Saturn 9	McDivitt, Scott, Schweickart	Mar. 3–13, 1969	241:00:54
Apollo-Saturn 10	Stafford, Young, Cernan	May 18–26, 1969	192:03:23
Apollo-Saturn 11	Armstrong, Collins, Aldrin	July 16–24, 1969	195:18:35
Apollo-Saturn 12	Conrad, Gordon, Bean	Nov. 14–24, 1969	244:36:25
Apollo-Saturn 13	Lovell, Swigert, Haise	Apr. 11–17, 1970	142:54:41
Apollo-Saturn 14	Shepard, Roosa, Mitchell	Jan. 31–Feb. 9, 1971	216:01:57
Apollo-Saturn 15	Scott, Worden, Irwin	July 26–Aug. 7, 1971	295:11:53
Apollo-Saturn 16	Young, Mattingly, Duke	Apr. 16–27, 1972	265:51:05
Apollo-Saturn 17	Cernan, Evans, Schmitt	Dec. 7–19, 1972	301:51:59

Total Time, Apollo Program: 7506:01:31

Mission	Crew	Date	Elapsed Time
Skylab SL-2	Conrad, Kerwin, Weitz	May 25–June 22, 1973	672:49:49
Skylab SL-3	Bean, Garriott, Lousma	July 28–Sept. 25, 1973	1427:09:04
Skylab SL-4	Carr, Gibson, Pogue	Nov. 16, 1973–Feb. 8, 1974	2017:15:32

Total Time, Skylab Program: 12351:43:15

Mission	Crew	Date	Elapsed Time
Apollo-Soyuz Test (ASTP)	Stafford, Brand, Slayton	July 15–24, 1975	217:28:23

Total Time, ASTP: 652:25:09

Space Transportation System (Space Shuttle)

Mission	Crew	Date	Elapsed Time
STS-1 (OFT)	Young, Crippen	Apr. 12–14, 1981	54:20:53
STS-2 (OFT)	Engle, Truly	Nov. 12–14, 1981	54:13:12
STS-3 (OFT)	Lousma, Fullerton	Mar. 22–30, 1982	192:04:49
STS-4 (OFT)	Mattingly, Hartsfield	June 27–July 4, 1982	169:11:11
STS-5	Brand, Overmeyer, Allen, Lenoir	Nov. 11–16, 1982	122:14:25
STS-6	Weitz, Bobko, Peterson, Musgrave	Apr. 4–9, 1983	120:23:42
STS-7	Crippen, Hauck, Ride, Fabian, Thagard	June 18–24, 1983	146:23:59
STS-8	Truly, Brandenstein, Bluford, D. Gardner, W. Thornton	Aug. 30–Sept. 5, 1983	145:08:40
STS-9	Young, Shaw, Garriott, Parker, Lichtenberg, Merbold	Nov. 28–Dec. 8, 1983	247:47:24
41-B	Brand, Gibson, McCandless, McNair, Stewart	Feb. 3–11, 1984	191:15:55

U.S. Manned Space Flights 187

Orbiter Flights To Date
25 TOTAL FLIGHTS

No. of Flights	CHALLENGER OV-099	COLUMBIA OV-102	DISCOVERY OV-103	ATLANTIS OV-104
1	STS-6 4/ 4/83 — 4/ 9/83	STS-1 4/12/81 — 4/14/81	41-D 8/30/84 — 9/ 5/84	51-J 10/ 3/85 — 10/ 7/85
2	STS-7 6/18/83 — 6/24/83	STS-2 11/12/81 — 11/14/81	51-A 11/ 8/84 — 11/16/84	61-B 11/26/85 — 12/ 3/85
3	STS-8 8/30/83 — 9/ 5/83	STS-3 3/22/82 — 3/30/82	51-C 1/24/85 — 1/27/85	
4	41-B 2/ 3/84 — 2/11/84	STS-4 6/27/82 — 7/ 4/82	51-D 4/12/85 — 4/19/85	
5	41-C 4/ 6/84 — 4/13/84	STS-5 11/11/82 — 11/16/82	51-G 6/17/85 — 6/24/85	
6	41-G 10/ 5/84 — 10/13/84	STS-9 11/28/83 — 12/ 8/83	51-I 8/27/85 — 9/ 3/85	
7	51-B 4/29/85 — 5/ 6/85	61-C 1/12/86 — 1/18/86		
8	51-F 7/29/85 — 8/ 6/85			
9	61-A 10/30/85 — 11/ 6/85			
10	51-L *1/28/86			

*UNSUCCESSFUL

Space Transportation System (Space Shuttle)

Mission	Crew	Date	Elapsed Time
41-C	Crippen, Scobee, van Hoften, G. Nelson, Hart	Apr. 6–13, 1984	191:40:05
41-D	Hartsfield, Coats, Resnik, Hawley, Mullane, C. Walker	Aug. 30–Sept. 5, 1984	144:57:00
41-G	Crippen, McBride, Sullivan, Ride, Leestma, Scully-Power, Garneau	Oct. 5–13, 1984	197:23:37
51-A	Hauck, D. Walker, Allen, A. Fisher, D. Gardner	Nov. 8–16, 1984	191:44:56
51-C	Mattingly, Shriver, Onizuka, Buchli, Payton	Jan. 24–27, 1985	73:33:27
51-D	Bobko, Williams, Hoffman, Seddon, Griggs, Walker, Garn	April 12–19, 1985	167:55:23
51-B	Overmyer, Gregory, Thagard, Lind, W. Thorton, van den Berg, Wang	Apr. 29–May 6, 1985	168:08:47
51-G	Brandenstein, Creighton, Lucid, Fabian, Nagel, Baudry, Al-Saud	June 17–24, 1985	169:39:00
51-F	Fullerton, Bridges, Musgrave, England, Henize, Acton, Bartoe	July 29–Aug. 6, 1985	190:45:26
51-I	Engle, Covey, van Hoften, Lounge, W. Fisher	Aug. 27–Sept. 3, 1985	170:17:42
51-J	Bobko, Grabe, Hilmers, Stewart, Pailes	Oct. 3–7, 1985	97:46:38
61-A	Hartsfield, Nagel, Buchli, Bluford, Dunbar, Furrer, Messerschmid, Ockels	Oct. 30–Nov. 6, 1985	168:15:51
61-B	Shaw, O'Connor, Cleve, Ross, Spring, Neri-Vela, C. Walker	Nov. 26–Dec. 3, 1985	165:04:49
61-C	Gibson, Bolden, Chang-Diaz, Hawley, G. Nelson, Ccnker, B. Nelson	Jan. 12–18, 1986	146:03:51
51-L	Scobee, Smith, Resnik, Jarvis, Onizuka, McNair, McAuliffe	Jan. 28, 1986	00:01:13

Total Time, STS Program through Jan. 1, 1988: 18,632:47:59

U.S. Man-Hours in Space through January 28, 1986

Program	Mercury	Gemini	Apollo	Skylab	Astp	STS	Cumulative
Man-hours in Space	54	1,940	7,506	12,352	652	18,632	41,136:37:49
Number of manned flights	6	10	11	3	1	25	46
Crewmembers	1	2	3	3	3	2 to 8	

Cumulative U.S. Man-hours in Space: 41,136:37:49

VII

U.S. Aircraft Company Genealogies

Aero Commander (Aero Design & Engineering Company): Founded 1947; acquired by Rockwell Standard Corporation which, on September 22, 1967, was merged with North American Aviation, Incorporated, to become North American Rockwell Corporation (later, Rockwell International Corporation). The first Aero Commander, Model 520, designed by Ted Smith, entered production in August 1951, Bethany, OK.

Allison (originally Indianapolis Speedway Team Company): Founded 1915; in 1919 became the Allison Experimental Company. During 1920s converted surplus Liberty engines to inverted configuration for the Loening amphibian; purchased by Fisher Brothers Investment Corporation in 1929, which in turn sold it to General Motors later that year, where it became the Allison Division of GM. Designed the V-1710, a liquid-cooled V-12 in 1930 for the Navy's *Macon* and *Akron* airships. After both crashed, V-1710 development continued; used in the P-38, P-39, P-40, A-36, and F-82. Gas turbine engine production at Allison began in 1945 with the General Electric J33.

Beech Aircraft Corporation: Founded 1932 by Walter and Olive Ann Beech in Wichita, KS. Walter, Clyde Cessna, and Lloyd Stearman had formed Travel Air Manufacturing Company in 1924, which was sold to Curtiss-Wright in 1929. Beech was an officer in Curtiss-Wright in St. Louis until 1932. First Beech aircraft was the Model 17 Staggerwing. Following Walter's death in 1950, Mrs. O.A. Beech became chief executive officer. The company became a subsidiary of the Raytheon Company in February 1980. Mrs. Beech retained her position as Chairman of Beech Aircraft, and was elected to Raytheon's board of directors and to Raytheon's executive committee. Current Beech president is Max E. Bleck, succeeding Linden Blue, who succeeded Frank Hedrick.

    Raytheon was founded in Cambridge, MA, in 1922 as a maker of radio tubes; became a producer of radar systems during WWII, and later expanded into missile guidance systems and other areas of electronics, including sonars for the U.S. Navy.

Bell Aircraft Corporation: Founded 1935 by Lawrence Dale Bell with Robert J. Woods and Ray Whitman. At age 16, Bell had been employed by Glenn Martin in 1911. By 1925, Bell was Vice President and General Manager at Martin; left Martin in 1928 when Martin moved from Cleveland to Baltimore, and joined Consolidated Aircraft in Buffalo, NY. First Bell airplane was the XFM-1 Airacuda of 1937, followed by the P-39 Airacobra; first U.S. jet, P-59, in 1942; first Bell helicopter flew in 1946; Bell X-1 first to break sound barrier in 1947. Now the Bell Aerosystems Company, an operating company of Textron. Helicopter company is in Ft. Worth, TX.

Bellanca (Columbia Aircraft Corporation): Founded 1926 by Giuseppe Mario Bellanca and Charles Levine. Bellanca, at age 22, had designed and built his first airplane in 1908 in his native Italy. His first design after coming to America was the Bellanca CF monoplane of 1923. His 1939 three-place Cruisair and the post-WWII Model 14–19 Cruisemasters established the configuration for the Model 260 and Vikings of the 1960s and '70s into the '80s. After Bellanca's death in 1960, the production facilities were moved from New Castle, DE, to Alexandria, MN, and successive owners were Northern Aircraft, Downer Aircraft, Bellanca Aircraft Company, and Bellanca Sales, the latter a subsidiary of Miller Flying Service, a Texas oil patch FBO. Bellanca suspended production and filed bankruptcy in 1980. (Bellanca acquired the Champion Aircraft Company of Osceola, WI, in 1960. *See* Champion.)

Boeing (Pacific Aero Products): Founded 1916. The oldest continuously operating airframe manufacturer in the U.S. was formed in Seattle, WA, in July 1916 as a partnership between Seattle lumberman William E. Boeing and Navy officer G. Conrad Westervelt. The name was changed to Boeing Airplane Company in WWI, and to Boeing Aircraft Company in 1934 following the government-decreed break-up of the giant United Aircraft & Transport Corporation, of which the Boeing Airplane Company, with its subsidiary Boeing Air Transport, was by then a part. In 1948, Boeing Airplane Company was readopted, and today it is the Boeing Company, with eight subsidiaries which include the Boeing Commercial Airplane Company, Renton, WA; Boeing Aerospace Company, Kent, WA; Boeing Vertol Company, Philadelphia, PA; and Boeing Wichita Company, Wichita, KS (the latter which grew from Stearman Aircraft Company, which was purchased by Boeing in 1929, along with the first Northrop company). Boeing bought DeHavilland of Canada in 1986.

Cessna Aircraft Company: Founded 1927 by Clyde Cessna following Cessna's departure from Travel Air; briefly known as the Cessna-Roos Company, with Victor Roos, formerly with Bellanca, as a partner. Clyde Vernon Cessna was a 32-year-old farm implement mechanic in Enid, OK, when he built his first airplane in 1911 and taught himself to fly it. He built improved versions and barnstormed until joining Lloyd Stearman and Walter Beech to form Travel Air in 1924. Cessna retired in 1936 (he died in 1954), and nephew Dwane Wallace took charge of the company, which was barely afloat during the Great Depression of the 1930s. As a public corporation registered in Maryland, the Cessna Wichita facilities grew under Wallace's guidance into the world's largest manufacturer of light aircraft. During the 1980s this production was gradually shut down, except for the Citations, Caravan, and Conquest, and General Dynamics, Cessna's new owner, announced in January 1987 that it was writing off $420 million of the purchase price of Cessna. General Dynamics bought Cessna in May 1986.

Champion Aircraft Company: Founded 1955 in Osceola, WI, by WWII pilot Bob Brown to return to production close derivatives of the Aeronca Champion, which went out of production in 1951. Moderately successful, by 1964 Brown introduced the popular Citabria with a choice of engines. In 1970, Bellanca acquired the Champion company. Bellanca was bankrupt in 1980, and the Champion aircraft line (Citabrias, Decathlon, Scout) was purchased by B&B Aviation of Tomball, TX. In

September 1985, Great Lakes Aircraft of Claremont, NH, purchased Champion assets, saying it planned to put these machines back onto the market.

Convair (Convair Division of General Dynamics): Founded 1923 by Seattle native Reuben Fleet, who learned to fly as one of the first Air National Guard officers (1916); he formed the Consolidated Aircraft Corporation in 1923 from the liquidated remains of WWI airplane makers Gallaudet Aircraft and Dayton-Wright. Building with an order for primary training planes from the Army and Navy, along with other military aircraft (including flying boats) during the 1920s, and working in the WWI Curtiss factory at Buffalo, NY, Consolidated slowly grew and absorbed the Thomas-Morse Aircraft Company (Ithaca, NY). In 1934, Fleet moved the company to San Diego (at which time VP and General Manager Lawrence Bell resigned, remained in the vacated Consolidated plant, and opened for business as Bell Aircraft Corporation). In 1940, Fleet bought Hall-Aluminum Aircraft Corporation, and the following year merged with Vultee Aircraft Corporation of Downey, CA. Vultee, controlled by AVCO (which also owned Stinson, among others), owned 440,000 shares of Consolidated, so the Consolidated Vultee Aircraft Corporation that resulted was in the hands of AVCO until 1947, when controlling interest in Consolidated Vultee Aircraft—contracted to ''Convair''—was purchased by Floyd Odlum's Atlas Corporation (by which time founder Reuben Fleet had retired). Early in 1953, General Dynamics, which had been formed by John Jay Hopkins, bought control of Convair from the Atlas Corporation. In recent years, General Dynamics has been the third largest contractor to the U.S. Department of Defense, behind McDonnell-Douglas and Rockwell International. Its main plants are in Ft. Worth and San Diego.

Continental Motors Corporation: Founded 1900. Formed in Detroit at the turn of the century, the company's ''Red Seal'' engines powered cars, trucks, and boats worldwide by the time it entered the aircraft market in 1929 with its A-70 air-cooled radial of seven cylinders and 165 hp (R-545), which was soon fitted to three Waco models and the Kellett autogiro, among others. The R-670 of 210 to 220 hp followed in 1931, along with the opposed-type A-40 rated at 37 hp, and which is generally regarded as the father of all opposed-type air-cooled lightplane piston engines for the following half-century; developed liquid-cooled lightplane engines in the mid-1980s and had under development at least two power ranges of the Wankel rotary for lightplanes. Also produced the propulsion unit for the Navy's Harpoon air-to-surface antisubmarine missile. Reorganized as Teledyne Continental Motors (Aircraft Products Division) in 1969, with manufacturing facility in Mobile, AL. The parent Teledyne Industries, Inc., is a NASA contractor.

Fairchild Airplane Manufacturing Corporation (Division of Fairchild Aviation Corporation): Founded 1926 by Sherman Fairchild, with Graham Grosvenor as president. Both were then on the board of Colonial Air Transport, and both would be directors of the Aviation Corporation (AVCO), formed as a holding company a couple of years later by some heavy financial guns for the purpose of acquiring promising aviation properties (North American Aviation was formed by another group of financiers at about the same time for the same reason). AVCO soon controlled Colonial, Fairchild, American Airways (later American Airlines), and a long list of other aviation companies, including Stinson and Lycoming (the latter two by way of auto magnate E.L. Cord's holdings). Meanwhile, Fairchild worked from the former Lawrence Sperry plant in Farmingdale, Long Island, to produce a series of hefty cabin monoplanes and, in 1929, acquired the Kreider-Reisner Aircraft Company in Hagerstown, MD. Amos Kreider and L.E. Reisner formerly worked for Waco (the Advance Aircraft Company), and their biplanes very much resembled Wacos. In 1931, the Fairchild Airplane Manufacturing Corporation became the American Airplane & Engine Corporation, a reorganization with AVCO director F.G. Coburn as president (he was also president of American Airways), which developed the air-cooled, in-line Rover engine into the six-cylinder inverted Ranger and produced the large Fairchild cabin monoplanes as Pilgrims for the captive American Airways at Farmingdale, while Sherman Fairchild ran the K-R plant at Hagerstown, building the Fairchild 22 and 24 personal airplanes. The Ranger Engines Division became a subsidiary of Fairchild Engine & Airplane Corporation in 1936 after the 1934 Air Mail Act forced AVCO to choose between its airline and manufacturing interests. Fairchild expanded during WWII and after, primarily as a Defense Department contractor. After merger with Hiller, it acquired Republic Aviation Corporation in 1965 and Farmingdale-based Republic became a division of the Fairchild Hiller Corporation, which then had nine divisions in 14 plants in five states. Corporate headquarters remained in Hagerstown, and them Germantown, MD. However, after the A-10 Thunderbolt production ended in 1984, the company's manufacturing activity eroded and the Hagerstown facility was closed. At this writing, Fairchild is evidently out of the airplane business for good.

Garrett Corporation (AiResearch Manufacturing Division): Founded 1936 by John Clifford Garrett as the Aircraft Tool & Supply Company at Glendale, CA, after nine years experience with Lockheed and Northrop (this Northrop Corporation was a division of Douglas and later became the Douglas El Segundo Division; there were/are other Northrop companies which we will discuss later). Within a year the company was renamed Garrett Supply Company. In 1939 the company was incorporated as the Garrett Corporation, the parent of three divisions: Airsupply Division, Garrett Supply Division, and AiResearch Manufacturing Division. The latter embraced, in 1941, the AiResearch Manufacturing Company of Arizona at Phoenix, while the main plant was moved to a site on the Los Angeles International Airport. By 1965, the Garrett Corporation comprised seven divisions and two subsidiaries. In 1981 the AiResearch name was dropped in favor of Garrett Turbine Engine Company (Phoenix), where the highly successful TPE-331 turboprop and TFE-731 turbofan were produced. The Garrett TFE-76 is a small turbofan of 1330 pounds thrust, weighing 400 pounds, designed for the T-46A trainer. Garrett is owned by the Signal Companies.

Gates Learjet Corporation: Founded 1962 by William P. Lear as Learjet Industries to produce a six-passenger corporate jet, a product believed by many to have no market. Lear's formal education had ended with the eighth grade, but obvious courage and unusual talent had driven him to make and lose a couple of fortunes in the fledgling electronics field before settling down with Lear, Incorporated, to gain another fortune (electromechanical products including an advanced autopilot), which he committed to Learjet. By the time the first Learjet flew, October 7, 1963, Bill Lear's personal $10 million investment had been spent, along with an additional $8 million borrowed from Wichita banks, and Lear was forced to go public with an offering of 500,000 shares of Learjet common, Bill Lear retaining 62 percent of the stock. In 1965, Lear added a Stereo Division, Avionics Division, and purchased Brantley Helicopter, all of which proved to be losers, especially the Brantley project. Then, in 1967, Charles C. Gates of Denver-based Gates Rubber Company purchased Bill Lear's interest in Learjet (actually, Bill called the company "Lear Jet" and its products "Learjets"). Gates restructured, with emphasis on product support after the sale through Combs-Gates service centers, posh FBOs, a subsidiary and, with Harry Combs as president, continued production of the Learjet in several models at facilities in Wichita, KS, and Tucson, AZ. On September 9, 1987, Gates announced the sale of his 64.8 percent of Gates Learjet to Integrated Acquisitions, a wholly owned subsidiary of Integrated Resources, Incorporated.

General Dynamics Corporation: *see* Consolidated.

General Electric Company: Founded 1892; established by the merger of Edison General Electric (originally, Edison Electric Light Company) and the Thomas Houston Company. G.E. was an early designer/builder of steam turbines for the generation of electricity, and the company's expertise in that field led to a request from the National Advisory Committee for Aeronautics (NACA, forerunner of NASA, organized in 1915) for help in developing aircraft engine superchargers, which were seen as small gas-driven centrifugal turbines. G.E.'s Dr. Sanford Alexander Moss spent much of the next 15 years (1917–1931) working on turbosuperchargers, mostly at the Army Air Corps' McCook field. As a direct result of Moss' work—he is generally considered the father of the turbo in this country—the Army Air Forces' Gen. Hap Arnold secretly brought one of Britain's new Whittle jet engines to G.E. in 1941 and asked G.E. engineers to copy and improve it. That resulted in the G.E. J33, the first of a long line of successful turbojets. G.E. has far too many other interests to mention here, including contracts with NASA and the Defense Department.

Great Lakes Aircraft Corporation: Founded 1928 by Col. Benjamin F. Castle and Charles F. van Sicklen to take over the balance of a Martin contract (in the Martin plant) for a Navy torpedo bomber as Martin moved from Cleveland to Baltimore. Charles Meyers and Cliff Liesey designed the Great Lakes 2T-1 sport-trainer, the company's most successful product. GLAC closed its doors late in 1933, a victim of the Great Depression and an unsuccessful light amphibian design. The 2T-1 biplane was revived by Doug Champlin in the late 1970s, briefly manufactured in Enid, OK. In September 1985, another Great Lakes Aircraft Company, this one in Claremont, NH, purchased the assets of the defunct Champion line, Citabria, Decathlon, and Scout.

Grumman Aircraft Engineering Corporation: Founded 1930. LeRoy R. Grumman and five associates formed this company to seek Navy contracts for airplanes, starting with a small order for airplane floats. Grumman, born in 1895, was the son of a Huntington, Long Island, carriage builder; he earned a degree in mechanical engineering from Cornell, was a WWI Naval aviator, and worked for Grover Loening building the Loening amphibian during the 1920s. For many years, the Grumman company sold almost exclusively to the Navy—amphibians, fighters, and torpedo bombers. In later years Grumman Aerospace Company built lunar modules and other space hardware. In 1978 American Jet Industries bought Grumman for a reported $52.5 million to form Gulfstream American for the production of civil aircraft. In May 1980, the Tesoro Petroleum Corporation of San Antonio offered $125 million for Gulfstream American, as the manufacturing rights to the Ohio-based Grumman American Aviation Corporation's line of single-engine lightplanes (originally Yankee), the Tiger, Cheetah, etc., were sold to International Transport & Earth Moving Equipment Company, LTD, of Monte Carlo. The original Grumman Company headquarters remained in Bethpage, Long Island, NY, and is a major Department of Defense contractor. Late in 1985, Chrysler Corporation bought Gulfstream.

Hamilton Standard (Division of United Technologies): Founded 1926. United was originally founded by William E. Boeing of Boeing Airplane & Transport Corporation, and Fred B. Rentschler of Pratt & Whitney. In 1928, Boeing organized United Air Lines from Boeing Air Transport, National Air Transport, Varney Air Lines, and Pacific Air Transport. Next, Rentschler entered the combine with P&W to form a holding company known as United Aircraft & Transport Corporation. United, in turn, bought Hamilton Propeller, Standard Steel Propeller, Stearman Aircraft, Sikorsky Aviation, and Northrop. Hamilton and Standard became Hamilton Standard (conflicting patent claims made acquisition of both desirable) at Windsor Locks, CT. Stearman became Boeing Wichita, into which the first Northrop company disappeared; United Aircraft eventually became United Technologies, bereft by law of airline affiliations, its three divisions being P&W, Sikorsky, and Hamilton Standard. In 1984, United Technologies was among the top 10 U.S. contractors to NASA and to the Department of Defense, with Hamilton Standard producing a variety of aircraft and spacecraft components, as well as propellers. United's headquarters remain at Hartford, CT.

Hughes Aircraft Company: Founded 1934. Howard R. Hughes learned to fly in 1928 at age 23. Four years earlier he had gained legal control of his father's estate (possible under Texas law), built upon the rotary oil drilling bit invented by his father. In 1934 Hughes formed Hughes Aircraft to design and build a racer that would capture the world's landplane speed record. Other record-breaking projects followed during the 1930s. During WWII, Hughes Aircraft, with main offices in Culver City, CA, grew as a defense contractor, and after the war moved into guided missiles, advanced weapons systems, and space hardware. In 1964 Howard Hughes set up the Hughes Medical Institute for medical research and funded it by giving it all the stock in Hughes Aircraft. The other companies, including Hughes Helicopter, were wholly owned by Howard Hughes (except for TWA, which he controlled, but was forced by court order to sell his stock). Hughes died April 15, 1976. In 1983, the Hughes Estate offered to sell Hughes Helicopters and McDonnell-Douglas acquired that company.

Lake Aircraft Corporation (Colonial Aircraft Corporation): Founded 1959. Originally produced in Sanford, ME as the Colonial Skimmer, designed by Dave Thurston, a former Grumman engineer, in 1947. Thurston's Colonial company was sold to Lake in 1959, and the amphibian became the Buccaneer as a four-placer. As the Skimmer it was two-place, and not actually FAA-certified until 1955. In 1980, Armand Rivard, a former Lake dealer in Laconia, NH, purchased the assets from Lake Aircraft of Tomball, TX, and announced a number of improvements to the new LA-4 Buccaneer. By 1985 the company operated from the Kissimee (FL) Airport.

Lockheed Aircraft Corporation: Founded 1932 from the bankrupt remnants of the company that gives it its name and a proud, pioneering past. In 1911, 21 year-old race car driver Allen Loughead (pronounced "Lockheed," and changed to that spelling in 1923) learned to fly a Curtiss pusher and, with elder brother Malcolm, built a float-equipped biplane that they flew, on June 15, 1913, from San Francisco Bay. Moving to Santa Barbara, they acquired the help of 21 year-old John K. "Jack" Northrop, an architectural draftsman, and during WWI built a couple of flying boats for the Navy. This tiny company went broke in 1921 when their midget biplane failed to find any customers. The brothers returned in 1926 with a new Northrop design called the Vega and, working from a rented warehouse in Hollywood, built the first of 197 wooden Lockheeds. These seemed almost daily to claim some new air record in the hands of the most famous pilots of that day—the Lindberghs, Wiley Post, Amelia Earhart, etc. Meanwhile, Malcolm had invented a hydraulic brake system for automobiles (Chrysler was his first customer in 1924), and Allen moved Lockheed Aircraft to Burbank. In July 1929, a holding company was put together by Midwest financiers, Detroit Aviation Corporation, which purchased 87 percent of the Lockheed stock (this group, which included Charles Kettering of General Motors; Ryan-Mahoney Aircraft, builder of Lindbergh's *Spirit of St. Louis*; Parks Air College, Detroit's Grosse Isle Airport; and Eastman Aircraft, the builder of an amphibian).

Meanwhile, Northrop left the company and Jerry Vultee took his place. But the Great Depression was upon the land, and Detroit Aviation Corporation slipped into bankruptcy in 1931. The assets were bought for $40,000 in 1932 by the founders of today's Lockheed Corp. They were: investment banker Robert E. Gross (who had earlier backed Stearman in Wichita), Walter T. Varney, Lloyd Carlton Stearman, Mr. & Mrs. Cyril Chappellet, Thomas Fortune Ryan III, and R.C. Walker. Ably managed by Carl B. Squier, a former barnstormer and Army Air Corps pilot, who brought in Hall L. Hibbard to head up engineering, who in turn discovered Clarence "Kelly" Johnson, who would activate Lockheed's famed "Skunk Works" (the secret department that has, since P-38 days, produced the most exotic Lockheeds), this was the foundation of a company that is today Number Four as both space and defense contractor, and which has diversified into many civilian markets as well. Allen Lockheed left the company in 1929. In September 1987, Lockheed Aeronautical Systems Company replaced the company's three aircraft divisions.

U.S. AIRCRAFT COMPANY GENEOLOGIES

LTV Corporation: Founded 1947. James Joseph Ling (the name is Bavarian) was 25 years old in 1947 when, with $2,000 capital, he started an electrical contracting business. Possessing a ninth-grade formal education, plus a hitch in the Navy, Ling would appear to be ill-equipped to serve as a captain of industry, but he put together a conglomerate within 20 years that was 38th on Fortune's fattest corporations list. Included in his acquisitions was Wilson & Company, meat processors, pharmaceuticals, and sporting goods ("meat balls, goof balls, and golf balls"), along with Temco and Vought. He later added Braniff, National Car Rentals, and Jones & Laughlin Steel, although the Justice Department forced him to sell Braniff, National Car, Wilson, and a couple of others in an anti-trust action. By 1970 it was clear that he was overextended and Ling was forced to relinquish much of his control while the bankers on his board tried to sort things out and put the Dallas-based corporation on a firmer footing. By 1984, LTV was 14th in the size of defense contracts it held, and had confounded those who predicted 14 years earlier that it could not survive.

Lycoming (AVCO Lycoming): Founded 1908 in Williamsport, PA, Lycoming grew as a supplier of automobile engines to the early car makers, and the company's association with E.L. Cord, providing power for his Auburns, Dusenbergs, and Cords, led to Cord gaining control of Lycoming in 1929. He also controlled Stinson, and both Stinson—which used Lycomings almost exclusively—and Lycoming were thrust into AVCO's orbit in 1932 as Cord became a major (140,000 shares) stockholder as a result of AVCO's purchase of Cord's two small airlines, Century Air Lines and Century Pacific Airlines. Today, Lycoming remains an important AVCO property. (*See* Convair and Fairchild for other details of AVCO formation and subsequent operations.)

Martin (Glenn L. Martin Company/Martin Marietta): Founded 1909. Glenn Luther Martin designed and built his first airplane—and taught himself to fly it—in 1908. He incorporated as the Glenn L. Martin Company in Santa Ana, CA, in 1911, moved to Los Angeles in 1912, and sold his first airplanes to the Army in 1914. He merged with the Wright Company to form the Wright-Martin Aircraft Corporation in 1917; later that year he left Wright-Martin to form the Glenn L. Martin Company of Cleveland. The Martin plant was moved to Middle River, MD, (Baltimore) in 1929. Glenn Martin remained head of his company until retiring in 1952. The company has not produced a Martin-designed airplane since the 1950s (the SP-5B Marlin flying boat for the Navy). As the parent, Martin Marietta Aerospace Corporation has since directed its efforts to space hardware, and by 1984 was second in value of space contracts (behind Rockwell International) and 12th in value of Defense Department contracts. Meanwhile, on September 17, 1982, Bendix Corporation bought control of Martin Marietta in a hostile take-over.

McDonnell Douglas Corporation (Douglas Aircraft, 1920; **McDonnell Aircraft,** 1939); Merged 1967. Donald Wills Douglas, son of a Brooklyn bank cashier, resigned from the Naval Academy in 1911 after two years as a midshipman to enter MIT and earn a degree in aeronautical engineering. In 1915 he was hired as chief engineer by Glenn Martin, who was then in Los Angeles. Douglas left Martin in 1920 and, with $600 capital, rented office space in the back of a Santa Monica barbershop and went into business for himself. He was 28 years old, with a wife and son to support. The company was briefly known as Davis-Douglas as a concession to the first customer, who had to pay for his airplane in advance. It was a hefty biplane fitted with a WWI surplus Liberty engine. It was known as the Cloudster, and although its unreliable powerplant failed to take it across the U.S. nonstop as Mr. Davis envisioned, the Cloudster did serve as the basis for more than 50 torpedo planes built for the Navy during the next three years, as well as the World Cruisers in which U.S. Air Service pilots made the first round-the-world flight in 1924. Douglas Aircraft Company sold almost exclusively to the Army until 1933, when the first of the fabulous DC series air transports appeared. After WWII, Douglas slipped easily into military aircraft production with some notable successes and, although a bit behind Boeing in entering the jet airliner market, its DC-9 (and MD-80 spinoff) was/is a moneymaker. Its DC-8 and DC-10 were less so. With dwindling military orders, Douglas ended 1966 with a $27,600,000 loss, and it was at that time that Jim McDonnell and Donald Douglas got together to talk merger.

James Smith McDonnell, Jr., born April 8, 1889, grew up in Little Rock, AR, where his father was a successful merchant and cotton buyer. Jim graduated from Princeton in 1921 with honors in physics, then spent two years at MIT studying aeronautical engineering. He entered the Air Service and learned to fly at Brooks and Kelly Fields, and returning to civilian life worked briefly for Huff-Deland Airplanes, Incorporated at Ogdensburg, NY,* then moved on to Consolidated Aircraft at Buffalo. McDonnell left Consolidated in 1925 to work for Bill Stout at Dearborn, MI, whose Stout Metal Plane Company was at first backed, then purchased, by Henry Ford, and from which soon emerged the famed Ford Tri-motor. In 1926, McDonnell was lured to the Hamilton Aero Manufacturing Company in Milwaukee, which was making wooden propellers and aluminum flying boat hulls. Tom Hamilton wanted McDonnell to design an airplane constructed entirely of the new duraluminum alloy used in the Ford-Stout machines. The result was the Hamilton Metalplane, used chiefly by newly-formed Northwest Airways. McDonnell remained at Hamilton until 1930, by which time the success of Hamilton's new steel propeller had resulted in his company being gobbled up by the United Aircraft & Transport combine (*see* Boeing). United closed down the airplane manufacturing department of Hamilton, and McDonnell temporarily took the engineering test pilot's job at Great Lakes recently vacated by Charlie Meyers, after which McDonnell went to the Glenn L. Martin Company in Baltimore, where he remained, as chief engineer, through 1938.

Determined by then to start his own company as the threat of war grew in Europe and America's future WWII allies began ordering warplanes from U.S. factories, McDonnell was able to gather enough capital—$165,000 in cash and pledges from relatives and friends—to form McDonnell Aircraft Company, working from the rented second floor of a small building adjacent to the Lambert-St. Louis (Missouri) Municipal Airport, July 6, 1939. Within a year, McDonnell went public, offering 3,000 shares of stock at $120 per share. The first couple of years held more promise than profits, McDonnell's first significant contract, obtained in 1943 was for what turned out to be the U.S. Navy's first shipboard jet fighter, the Phantom I, developed concurrently with the USAAF Bell P-59. After that, McDonnell enjoyed one success after another, culminating in the 1,600-mph F-4 Phantom, which first flew in 1958, and the Gemini space vehicles just five years later. In 1966, McDonnell acquired a number of electronics and aerospace-related manufacturers, mostly by way of stock swaps.

The following year, after eyeball-to-eyeball talks between Jim McDonnell and Donald Douglas, their respective shareholders voted to henceforth love, honor, and share one another's dividends. The two were officially united April 28, 1967, and the resulting McDonnell Douglas Corporation became the second largest aerospace company in the nation. In 1984, it ranked first in defense contracts, and sixth in space contracts.

Mooney Aircraft Company: Founded 1946. Albert W. Mooney was a brash, lanky redhead of 19 in 1925 when he talked himself into a job as a draftsman for the newly formed Alexander Aircraft

---

*Huff-Daland became Keystone Aircraft in March 1927, when E.N. Gott, former president of Boeing Airplane Company, took over from Thomas Huff and moved the factory to Bristol, PA. Keystone merged with Loening Aeronautical Engineering Corporation in 1929, and Keystone-Loening became a subsidiary of Curtiss-Wright soon after. Loening's general manager was LeRoy Grumman, later to found his own company. An early (1921) Huff-Daland subsidiary, Huff Dusters, Inc., of Monroe, LA, was headed by pioneer duster pilot C.E. Woolman, and this outfit survived independently throughout the 1920s to eventually evolve into Delta Airlines.

Company (the Alexander Film Company produced short advertising film clips for motion picture theaters). Mooney had a high-school education and a deep interest in airplanes that had been apparent since age 12, and he had clearly acquired some sound engineering practices, because he designed the Alexander Eaglerock, a handsome three-place biplane that was successfully marketed by that Denver-based company. Mooney was chief engineer at Alexander when he left that company in 1929 to build airplanes on his own in Wichita. His brother Arthur went along, and was to remain as Al's practical mechanical expert throughout the years that followed. The brothers produced a couple of low-wing, four-place cabin airplanes similar to the Bullet, Mooney's last design at Alexander, but the market was depressed by the beginning of the Great Depression and the company closed its doors in 1931. Mooney then went to the Bellanca Aircraft Corporation, then at New Castle, DE, where he worked on the big military transport Bellancas. He moved on to Monocoupe Aircraft in St. Louis in 1935, then to Culver Aircraft in 1938, where he designed the Cadet, and several wartime version of the Cadet as radio controlled target drones (PQ-8, PQ-14). Mooney's move to Culver coincided with Culver's purchase of the rights to the Mooney-designed Dart from Monocoupe.

In 1946, Al Mooney and Charles G. Yankey formed Mooney Aircraft Company, Incorporated in Wichita to offer the Mooney Mite, a little single-placer with retractable landing gear; plywood-skinned, the first ones were fitted with a 26-hp Crosley automobile engine and priced at $1,995. More than 200 Mites were sold, most of them with 65-hp Lycomings and Continentals, before Mooney was forced to vacate the Wichita facility due to the needs of the military as the war in Korea dragged on. At that point (mid-1953), *Flight* magazine publisher George Haddaway, of Dallas, obtained financial backing to move Mooney to Kerrville, TX, and that was when Al Mooney designed the M-20, the single-engine four-placer that has provided the basis for all Mooneys since. However, the company was broke before the M-20 was produced, and a couple of ex-military pilots who operated a west Texas flying service stepped in to pay off Mooney's $200,000 debts at a reported 10¢ on the dollar, got the new Mk 20 certificated in 1955, and were selling almost 200 per year when Al Mooney left the company in 1959 for a job with Lockheed-Georgia.

Owners Hal Rachel and Norm Hoffman, along with partner Ed Hunnicut, brought in Ralph Harmon in 1960 to give the Mk 20 a metal wing, and although sales grew to 800 units annually by 1968, a premature and underpriced pressurized Mooney Mustang, acquisition of a modernized Ercoupe offered as the Mooney Cadet, and a sales-assembly agreement with Mitsubishi for their MU-2 turboprop conspired to bankrupt the company once again. The company was then bought by American Electronics Laboratories of Pennsylvania, apparently as a tax writeoff, because AEL chose bankruptcy for Mooney.

Then, Butler Aviation International, Inc., purchased Mooney assets for 150,000 shares (par $20) of Butler preferred, and built a few Mooneys as single-engine Aerostars (Butler briefly held manufacturing rights to the twin-engine Aerostar, but built none) before production ended in 1971. In 1973, Republic Steel bought Mooney assets and production resumed in 1974. Ably managed, Mooney has continued to grow since that time. (Piper acquired the Aerostar rights, and Ercoupe rights were bought by Univair in 1975. Based in Aurora, CO, Univair is a major source of parts for most out-of-production lightplanes.) In August 1984, Mooney was sold to a consortium of two French companies.

North American Aviation: Founded 1928. James Howard "Dutch" Kindelberger, born in 1895, left high school prior to graduation in Wheeling, WV, worked as a draftsman and, during WWI, learned to fly in the U.S. Air Service. In 1919, he found a job as a draftsman with Glenn Martin in Cleveland (where Donald Douglas was chief engineer and Lawrence Bell was factory manager). Douglas left Martin in 1920 to form his own company in Los Angeles, and Kindelberger joined Douglas as chief engineer in 1925. Dutch would remain with Douglas until 1934, by which time his reputation was made due to the success of the new Douglas DC series, and he was offered the job of building an airplane manufacturing division for North American. North American had been formed in 1928 strictly as a holding company, which acquired a number of aviation manufacturing companies along with Eastern Air Lines. Its organizers included Bankamerica Blair, Hayden, Stone, & Company, and C.M. Keys, who had controlled Curtiss Aeroplane & Motor Company since 1923 and who engineered its merger with Wright Aeronautical Corporation in 1929 to form Curtiss-Wright. Keys took C-W into the North American orbit with the 29 C-W subsidiaries (among which were Travel Air, Curtiss-Robertson at St. Louis, Curtiss-Caproni, Keystone, Moth, etc.). General Motors also bought into North American, bringing its General Aviation Company (Fokkers), and the Berliner-Joyce Aircraft Company. However, when the Air Mail Act of 1934 decreed that airlines and aviation manufacturers could not have a common parent, GM, which owned a large block of TWA stock as well as Eastern, opted for the airlines, and what remained of North American would have to be a manufacturing operation. Board chairman Ernest Breech picked Dutch Kindelberger to take charge of North American's industrial remnant, offering Kindelberger the old Curtiss-Caproni plant in Baltimore, but Dutch remained in Baltimore only long enough to promote an Air Corps' order for 42 basic trainers and gather a cadre of skilled aircraftsman from the idle Fokker plant.

He moved to Los Angeles, leased a site on the new municipal airport, and raided Douglas for chief engineer Lee Atwood and project engineer Stan Smithson. In February 1936, the first North American BT-9 (which evolved into the AT-6) came off the production line. The 0-47 and B-25 followed, and the legendary P-51 in 1940. North American built 42,683 military airplanes during WWII; after the war Dutch Kindelberger's string of successes continued, starting with North American's first jet, the FJ-1 Fury for the Navy, quickly followed by the F-86 Sabre for the USAF. This company remains number one in space contracts and number two in defense contracts, although it is now Rockwell International. Rockwell Standard Corporation appeared on the aerospace scene in 1964 when it acquired Aero Commander; merger with North American produced North American Rockwell in 1968, and internal reorganization in 1973 changed the name to Rockwell International, with an autonetics and a Los Angeles Division.

Northrop Aircraft Company (Avion Corporation): Founded 1928. John Knudsen "Jack" Northrop was born November 10, 1895, in Newark, NJ. His parents moved to Santa Barbara, CA, when Jack was nine and he graduated from high school there in 1913. When the Loughead brothers started their company in Santa Barbara in 1916 (*see* Lockheed), Northrop joined them as a draftsman. He entered the Army during WWI, but was furloughed to work on the Loughead's flying boat contract with the Navy. In 1919, along with Allen Loughead and Tony Stadlman, Northrop perfected a method for the manufacture of molded shell fuselages, employed in the design of a small, single-space personal biplane for the expected boom in private flying which did not occur. Capital gone, the company was liquidated in 1921 and Northrop went to work for Douglas, who had opened for business in Santa Monica the year before (*see* McDonnell-Douglas). Northrop participated in the design of the Douglas World Cruisers, then, in 1927, joined Allen Lockheed again (by then using the phonetic spelling of his name) to build a five-place monoplane that used the process developed for the earlier sportplane. Financing was found, and a workshop located in Hollywood, from which the Northrop-designed Vega emerged for its first flight on July 4, 1927. A series of highly successful wooden Lockheeds followed, employing the basic Vega fuselage and wing, but Northrop left Lockheed in 1928 to form his own company, Avion Corporation, in Burbank, CA. Where he produced the advanced Northrop Alpha, a fast, six-passenger, low-wing all-metal craft featuring stressed-skin construction. This craft, along with Northrop's ideas for a flying wing design, attracted the attention of William Boeing, and in 1931 United Aircraft & Transport Corporation (which owned Boeing, United Air Lines, Varney, Stearman, etc.) bought Avion, moved it to Wichita, and merged it with

U.S. Aircraft Company Geneologies

Stearman. Much of Avion's stock was held by W. Kenneth Jay, who had also backed Lockheed. Jay was an accountant, a former Air Service pilot, and had profited from an investment in Malcolm Lockheed's hydraulic brake invention for automobiles; Jay again backed Northrop when Northrop refused to go to Wichita, resigned, and returned to Douglas, whereupon the new Northrop Corporation was formed at El Segundo as a division of Douglas in 1932. Donovan R. Berlin, who would later design the P-36/P-40 at Curtiss-Wright, was chief engineer.

Northrop remained at El Segundo until the end of 1938, during which time he designed the A-17 and the prototypes of the Douglas SBD Dauntless and A-20 Havoc. He formed Northrop Aircraft, Incorporated at Hawthorne, CA, in 1939, and during WWII produced the P-61 Black Widow night fighter while continuing experiments with flying wings—a program which, despite great promise, was canceled by the Air Force in 1949 after two huge YB-49 flying wing jet bombers were lost in crashes. Jack Northrop left the company in 1952 for semi-retirement, but the company has continued to prosper, its current aircraft being the F-5 and F-20. The parent is Northrop Corporation, which has more roots than a banyan tree, including a maintenance company with military contracts worldwide. Northrop Services, Inc., is 27th in space contracts, and 26th in defense contracts.

Piper Aircraft (Taylor Brothers Aircraft Corp.): Founded 1929. The Bradford, PA, Board of Commerce financed the move of Taylor Brothers Aircraft from Rochester, NY, after Gordon Taylor was killed in the crash of the Taylor Chummy, a two-place parasol monoplane. A principal investor was William T. Piper, active in the oil business since 1914 developing local oil field holdings, who became a director in the company. C. Gilbert Taylor was president and chief engineer. The Chummy did not sell and the company was bankrupt early in 1931. Piper purchased the assets and reorganized under the name Taylor Aircraft Company with Gilbert Taylor as president and Piper treasurer. Within a few months, the company received a new 37-hp Continental A-40 engine which offered the best combination of economy, reliability, and power for Taylor's E-2 airframe, a two-place tandem-seating high-wing monoplane. From 1931 to 1936, the company sold about 100 Taylor Cubs. Taylor left the company in 1935 to build Taylorcrafts in Alliance, Ohio. In 1937, the company became Piper Aircraft Corporation, moved to new quarters in an empty silk mill in Lock Haven, PA, and offered the Model J-3 the following year with 50 hp (prior to that time it was the Model J-2). In 1938 the J-3 Cub sold for $1,300 and 736 were produced. The 65-hp version was available in 1940, a year in which 3,197 were built. With additional window area, the J-3 served as the L-4 in Army dress and NE-1 in Navy colors during WWII.

After the war, Piper remained strong in the personal plane market and, in 1960, introduced the popular Cherokee series of single-engine craft, pioneered in the light twin market, and the Super Cub remained in production into the early 1980s. A family-run business for many years, Piper president and board chairman was William Thomas Piper; born 1881, Knapps Creek, NY; vice-president, operations, was Thomas Francis Piper, born August 13, 1914, Portsmouth, Ohio; vice-president, research and development was Howard "Pug" Piper, born November 3, 1917, Bradford, PA; and the executive vice-president was William Thomas Piper, Jr., born September 8, 1911, Sharpsburg, PA. But Piper marketing practices and product support was weak, and the company never had a discernible public relations department. In 1969, aware that Piper was having problems, Grumman offered to buy 300,000 shares of Piper common, authorized but unissued, at $65 per share. Chris-Craft (the small boat maker), which already owned 200,500 shares (12.5 percent of the total shares outstanding), made the same offer, but the Piper family, which owned about 35 percent of the 1,640,000 shares outstanding, claimed it wasn't interested. William Piper Sr., died a year later (1970) and in 1978 Bangor Punta Corporation gained control of Piper. Then Lear Siegler, Incorporated, acquired the company from Bangor Punta and, in 1984, closed the Lock Haven facilities.

In 1985, Lear Siegler sold Piper to Forstman, Little & Company, which in turn sold to Stuart Miller in December 1986.

Pratt & Whitney Aircraft: Founded 1925. Frederick Brandt Rentschler founded Pratt & Whitney Aircraft. Born in Fairfield Township, Butler County, Ohio, November 8, 1887, he was a Princeton graduate; he spent eight years in the family oil and steam turbine manufacturing plant, two years as an Air Service airplane engine inspector at Wright-Martin during WWI, and in 1919 organized Wright Aeronautical Corporation from the liquidated remains of Wright-Martin to continue production of Hispano-Suiza aircraft engines (built under license from a French firm). Then, asked by the Navy to develop Charles Lawrence's nine-cylinder, air-cooled radial, Rentschler's enginemen, Mead and Willgoos, adopted a new air-cooled cylinder and sodium-filled exhaust valve perfected at McCook Field by Sam Heron and Edward T. Jones to produce the first of the highly successful Wright Whirlwinds (one of which would power Lindbergh's *Spirit of St. Louis*) in 1927. Rentschler foresaw the impact the Whirlwind would have, left Wright Aeronautical in 1924, founded Pratt & Whitney and, with his two top enginemen from Wright designing what was, essentially, a bigger Whirlwind, came up with the first Wasp, the R-1340, originally rated at 400 to 420 hp. A long line of big air-cooled radials followed; meanwhile, in 1928, Rentschler joined William Boeing to form United Aircraft & Transport Corporation (*see* Boeing). Thus, Pratt & Whitney became a division of United—today, United Technologies—and Rentschler's Pratt & Whitney stock was traded for United stock and, after several stock splits, was valued at $21,000,000 by 1933. His original 1,375 shares of Pratt & Whitney had cost Rentschler $275 in 1925.

Where did Pratt & Whitney come from? Well, before the Civil War, Francis Pratt and Amos Whitney were machinists in Colt's pistol factory. In 1860, they formed a partnership to open their own machine-tool shop in Hartford, CT. In 1925, the Pratt & Whitney Tool Company, by then a division of Niles-Bement-Pond, put up the $250,000 to finance Rentschler's Pratt & Whitney Aircraft. Pratt & Whitney remains a major division of United Technologies, which is eighth in defense contracts and 10th in space contracts. Frederick Rentschler died in 1956.

Rockwell International (Rockwell Standard): *See* North American Aviation.

Ryan Aeronautical Company (Mahoney-Ryan Aircraft Corporation): Founded 1925. Tubal Claude Ryan was born in Parsons, KS, January 3, 1898; he attended Oregon State College, and entered the Army Air Service in 1920, where he learned to fly. Ryan left the Army in 1922 and started Ryan Flying Company at San Diego with a WWI surplus JN-4 Jenny. During the next three years he converted half a dozen WWI surplus Standards to four-place "airliners" and, with friend B. Franklin Mahoney providing capital, established Ryan Airlines, a more or less regularly scheduled service between San Diego and Los Angeles. In 1925, with engineering help from Hawley Bowlus, Ryan built the first Ryan M-1 airplane. Ryan airplanes were famous after Lindbergh flew one to Paris in 1927. The Lindbergh airplane was built by Ryan Airlines, but Ryan sold out to Mahoney late in 1927 and the B.F. Mahoney Aircraft Corporation was in turn sold to a group of St. Louis businessmen (some of whom had financed Lindbergh). The Mahoney name was retained, and subsequent Ryan Broughams were built in St. Louis.

Meanwhile, in 1931, Claude organized the Ryan Aeronautical Company in San Diego and that firm, building airplanes and training pilots, grew in size through WWII and became a Defense Department contractor in 1948 with the Ryan Firebee drone. After that, the company built components for other airframes makers and bought control of Continental Motors in 1965. In 1968, Teledyne, Inc., of Los Angeles bought Ryan for $128 million, and the company became Teledyne Ryan Aeronautical Company. Claude Ryan continued as a director. He died in 1982 at the age of 84, by which time Teledyne Industries was 20th among space contractors.

Scaled Composites, Incorporated: Founded 1982. Elbert L. "Burt" Rutan was 38 years old in 1982 when he formed Scaled Composites to develop proof-of-concept aircraft on the high desert airport at Mojave, CA. An innovative and prize-winning aircraft model builder at age 16, Rutan graduated from California Polytechnic University, learned to fly as a civilian and, in 1965, took a civil service position as a flight test project engineer at Edwards AFB ("the lowest pay and highest risk job available"). Rutan left the flight test job in 1972 to work briefly for Jim Bede, while developing a canard design of his own (the VariViggen), then returned to Mojave in 1974 to found his own company, Rutan Aircraft Factory, to market plans for the VariViggen. Other successful designs for the amateur plane builder followed. Then, after Scaled Composites, a separate company at the same site, fabricated and built a scaled-down prototype of the Beechcraft Starship, Scaled Composites became a subsidiary of Beech Aircraft Corporation, and Rutan continued as president of this firm.

Sikorsky Aircraft (Sikorsky Aero Engineering Corporation): Founded 1923. Igor Ivanovich Sikorsky was born in Kiev, Russia, May 25, 1889; he trained as an engineer and attended the Naval College at Petrograd. In 1909-1910 he built and attempted to fly a couple of helicopters, built fixed-wing aircraft, and from 1912 through 1918 was chief engineer at the Russian Baltic Car Factory at St. Petersburg, where he built the first successful four-engine airplanes. Sikorsky came to the U.S. in 1919 and four years later established Sikorsky Aero Engineering on Long Island, producing a series of successful flying boats and amphibians. The company was purchased in 1929 by United Aircraft & Transport Corporation for "about $2,500,000" (*Time* Magazine, July 29, 1929). In 1939, Sikorsky Aircraft remains an important United Technologies property, continuing in its role of leading helicopter manufacturer at its main plant in Stratford, CT.

Sperry Corporation (Sperry Rand Corporation, Sperry Gyroscope Company): Founded 1910. The Sperry Gyroscope Company was founded by Elmer A. Sperry, a 50-year-old inventor, engineer, and scientist who held a couple hundred patents and had developed many practical electrical and electromechanical devices for automobiles, ships, and industry. Turning his attention to the gyroscope, which until then had been little more than a curiosity, Sperry invented the gyrocompass, the first installation of which went into the Navy's USS *Delaware*. Sperry's three sons worked with him, son Lawrence specializing in aviation-related devices, each of which seemed to beget others. In 1912, Lawrence Sperry demonstrated the first autopilot, and in 1919 had the first gyro-controlled turn indicator. There would be much more, everything from bombsights (Carl Norden was a Sperry employee) to guided missiles. And although Lawrence Sperry died in 1923 at age 30 when his plane went down in the English Channel, the company's aviation products continued to proliferate.

In 1929, Elmer Sperry sold out to the North American Aviation combine (*see* North American), and by 1933 General Motors held controlling interest in Sperry—GM being a big investor in North American—and in 1955 Remington Rand bought Sperry to form Sperry Rand. In 1984, Sperry was 16th in defense contracts and 30th in space contracts. In June 1986, the Burroughs Corporation announced that it had paid $4.8 billion for Sperry.

Taylorcraft Company (Taylor Brothers Aircraft Corporation): Founded 1936. After C. Gilbert Taylor left the Taylor company as William Piper's associate in Bradford, PA (*see* Piper listing for early Taylor operations), he formed another Taylorcraft Company late in 1936 in Alliance, OH as Piper prepared to move to Lock Haven and became the Piper Aircraft Corporation. The first Taylorcraft (commonly called "T-craft") was the 40-hp Model A, essentially a side-by-side version of the E-2 Cub, introduced in 1937. By 1941, this machine had evolved into the 65-hp B12 model, slightly modified versions of which the Army bought as the YO-57 and L-57A (400 of them), and another 1,400 as the L-2. After the war, 2,800 were built as BC-12Ds until production ceased in 1947. Gilbert Taylor purchased the assets of the defunct company in 1949, and produced the BC-12D and a four-place version of it until the late 1950s. Then, in 1973, former T-craft dealer Charles Faris of Chicago purchased the jigs and rights to the design and began producing the BC-12D with modern materials and fitting it with the 100-hp 0-200 Continental. He priced it (much too low, as it turned out) at $9,250 and called it the F-19 Sportsman. The new T-craft, despite repeated price increases, sold surprisingly well. Tragically, however, Feris, at age 63, learned that he had bone cancer and T-craft (F-19) production stopped in the late 1970s. In 1985, George Ruckle of Mackerville, PA bought the dormant company and moved the jigs and tooling to the old Piper facility at Lock Haven. Production is intermittent at this writing.

VIII

Aerobatics

The first inside loop was performed in 1913 by Adolphe Pegoud of France. WWI introduced the Immelmann Turn, the chandelle, and spin-recovery techniques. With more power and stronger airframes, aerobatic pilots could offer a very exciting show by the time the flying machine was 25 years old. Jimmy Doolittle performed the first outside loop in 1927; Len Povey invented the Cuban-Eight in 1936, and "Squeek" Burnett originated the inverted ribbon pickup during the early 1930s. Tex Rankin did 31 consecutive outside loops, and "Fearless Freddie" Lund was trailing colored smoke from his Waco Taperwing as he flew a heart-stopping akro routine during those simpler times before WWII changed the world.

There were a lot of other very able aerobatic pilots (usually called "stunt pilots") in those days, but there was no way to fairly compare them or judge one's degree of precision. That was changed in the later 1950s by the Aresti system of scoring an aerobatic performance. It is the standard method of scoring throughout the world.

Aerocryptographics

The Aresti Aerocryptographic System, or the *Aresti Key*, as it is more often called, was devised by Count Jose L. Aresti, a colonel in the Spanish Air Force and a long-time aerobatic pilot. This system assigns simple symbols to all basic maneuvers such as loops, rolls, turns, etc. Combinations of these are put together to represent the compound maneuvers.

Aresti divided all maneuvers into nine "families:" 1) Lines and lines plus angles; 2) Horizontal turns; 3) Vertical turns; 4) Spins; 5) Wing slides; 6) Tail slides; 7) Loops; 8) Rolls; and 9) Half-loops plus half-rolls; half-rolls plus half-loops (the split-S is an example of a maneuver in this family).

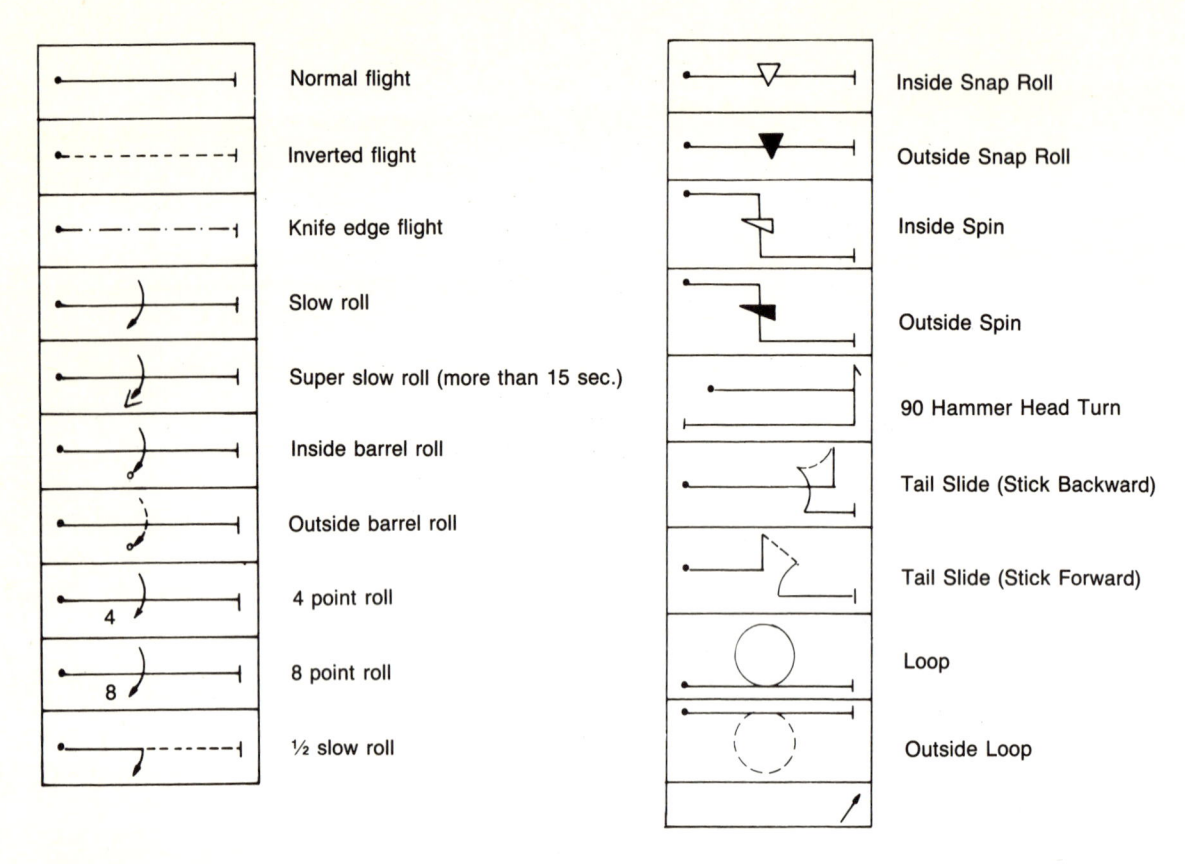

Symbol	Maneuver
•———————┤	Normal flight
•— — — — — —┤	Inverted flight
•—·—·—·—·—┤	Knife edge flight
Slow roll symbol	Slow roll
Super slow roll symbol	Super slow roll (more than 15 sec.)
Inside barrel roll symbol	Inside barrel roll
Outside barrel roll symbol	Outside barrel roll
4 point roll symbol	4 point roll
8 point roll symbol	8 point roll
½ slow roll symbol	½ slow roll

Symbol	Maneuver
▽ symbol	Inside Snap Roll
▼ symbol	Outside Snap Roll
Inside spin symbol	Inside Spin
Outside spin symbol	Outside Spin
Hammer head symbol	90 Hammer Head Turn
Tail slide symbol	Tail Slide (Stick Backward)
Tail slide symbol	Tail Slide (Stick Forward)
Loop (circle)	Loop
Outside loop (dashed circle)	Outside Loop

Aresti's Aerocryptographics allow akro pilots to diagram any aerobatic program with simple symbols. Every aerobatic maneuver is assigned a unique symbol, recognized worldwide. These are representative; there are many more.

Each Aresti figure is numbered for quick identification. For example, a normal inside loop is Fig. 8-1 (1). Also, each figure is assigned a coefficient of difficulty called the K-factor. The inside loop, Fig. 8-1 (2), has a K-value of 12 in competition. Judges award a grade of 1 to 10 for each maneuver, then this grade is multiplied by the maneuver's K-value to determine a contestant's score. Thus, if a contestant was awarded a grade of 8 for his loop, his score from that particular judge would be 8 times 12, or 96 points for the loop.

This doesn't mean that a pilot who performs good loops—or has an airplane that loops well—can do 20 loops in sequence and end up with a good score, because each time a maneuver from the same line of Aresti figures is repeated, its K-value decreases and soon reaches zero. For example, let's say a contestant has performed a normal inside loop, Fig. 8-1 (1), and K equals 12. Later in his performance he makes a downward outside loop, Fig. 8-1 (2), which has a K-value of 24 and is in the same line of figures in the Aresti book. Then he does still another loop, Fig. 8-1 (3), possessing a K-value of 16. In scoring, the judges would figure his first loop with its assigned value of 12, but the second loop would lose half of its coefficient of difficulty and would be scored at 12 instead of 24. For the third loop, normally with a K-value of 16, a three-fourths reduction would leave

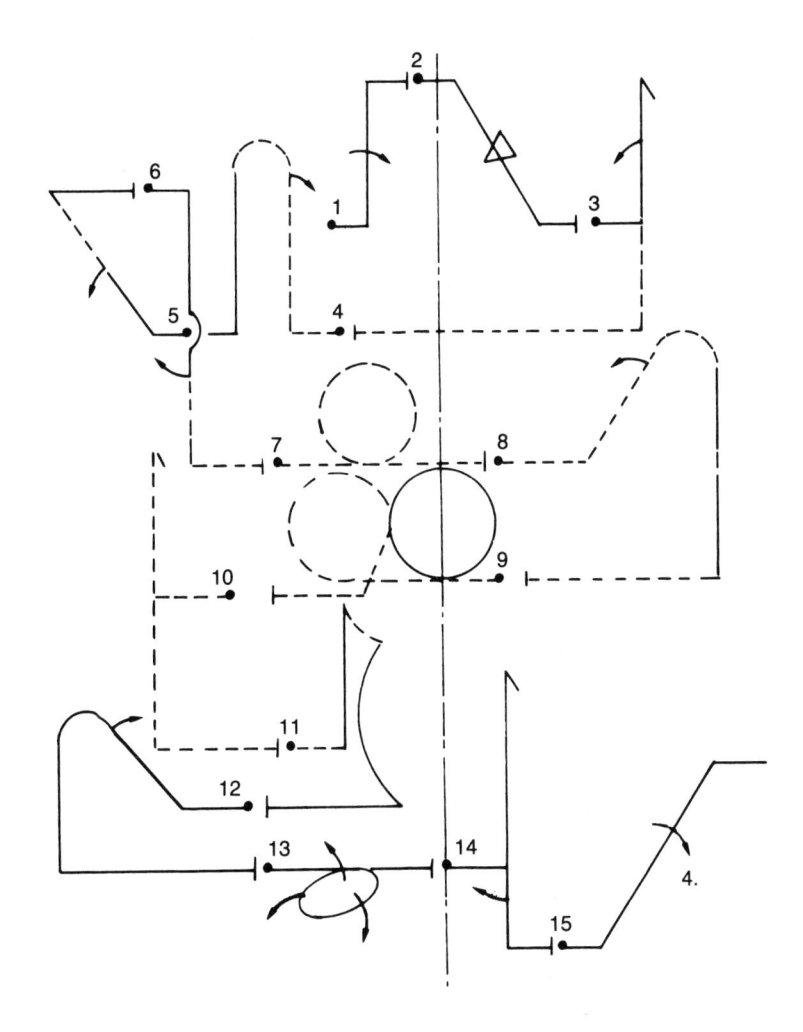

A typical aerobatic program as shown by Aresti figures: 1) From normal flight, a slow roll in a 90-degree climb and finish in normal flight (K=27). 2) From normal flight, do a flick roll in a 45-degree dive and end in normal flight (K=16). 3) From normal flight, perform a 90-degree wing slide and a slow half-roll in a climbing line ending inverted (K=34). 4) From inverted, do a half slow roll in a 90-degree climb and half inverted loop, ending in normal flight (K=32). 5) From normal flight, do a half slow roll in a 45-degree climb and end in normal flight (K=18). 6) From normal flight, do a half slow roll in a 90-degree climb ending in inverted flight (K=27). 7) From inverted, do an outside climbing loop ending inverted (K=28). 8) Beginning inverted, perform a half slow roll in a 45-degree climb and half outside loop, ending inverted (K=30). 9) From inverted flight, do a vertical-eight-lying-down and finish inverted (K=34). 10) Starting from inverted, perform a 90-degree wing slide and end inverted (K=32). 11) Start inverted and do a stick-back tail slide ending in normal flight (K=21). 12) From normal flight, do a half slow roll in a 45-degree climb and a half-loop, finishing in normal flight (K=16). 13) Beginning in normal flight, do three rolls in a horizontal circle to the outside of the turn and end in normal flight (K=36). 14) From normal flight, do a 90-degree wing-slide and half slow roll in a diving line. End in normal flight (K=29). 15) Beginning in normal flight, perform a four-point hesitation roll in a 45-degree climb and end in normal flight (K=17).

it with a K-value of four. If he made yet another loop from the same line of figures, the contestant would get nothing for it.

Additionally, the Aresti System also assigns K-values to the harmony, rhythm, and diversity of an aerobatic sequence, its framing within an ideal zone, and then provides for penalties for violation of time limits.

Proper framing is a critical factor because it carries a K-value of 80. "Framing" is an appropriate term because one must plot and fly an aerobatic program in a balanced manner—that is, space the maneuvers evenly on each side of the flying area's centerline, and equidistant from each end. Normally, reference marks on the ground will aid in framing at official contests. However, the actual size of the aerobatic zone will depend upon the speed of one's aircraft. Eight hundred by 1,200 feet would be enough for a clipped-wing Cub; the clean monoplanes require about 2,000 by 4,000 feet.

The aerobatic zone has a maximum and minimum altitude limit. The upper limit varies between 2,225, 2,600, and 3,250 feet according to which of the three aerobatic programs (Known Obligatory, Unknown Obligatory, and Freestyle) the contestant is flying. The lower limit of the zone is 325 feet above the surface. All planes are equipped with barographs to ensure that these limits are observed.

Because of the maneuver-repeat penalty (there are a couple of exceptions), the turnarounds at each end of the aerobatic zone must be considered when planning a Freestyle program. A simple turn won't add much to one's score, but takes valuable time. So it's necessary to pick maneuvers that will reverse direction—an Immelmann or split-S, for example—and that will also leave one well positioned for the next maneuver. This is, of course, a consideration in selecting all maneuvers; the K-value for rhythm is 40.

As suggested above, in national and international competitions one normally flies three programs: 1) The Known Obligatory, usually made up of about 15 maneuvers, an Aresti diagram of which is published months before the competition; 2) The Unknown Obligatory, which is agreed upon by the team captains at the meet and is unknown to the contestants until 24 hours before it is to be flown. It may not be practiced; and 3) The Freestyle, which each contestant plans for himself/herself, an Aresti diagram of which must be furnished to the judges before it is flown. There is a 10-minute time limit on the Freestyle program and its total K-value may not exceed 700 points. The two obligatory programs have time limits of six and eight minutes, respectively.

At the completion of these performances, the champion team is determined by picking the country possessing the most total points among its top three scorers. To determine the international individual champion, the top 16 scorers refly the Unknown Obligatory maneuvers and their Freestyle programs. Beginning in 1960, the international competition has been sanctioned by the *Federation Aeronautique Internationale*, and is held every two years. The FAI also recognizes the national competitions. The U.S. representative of the FAI is the National Aeronautic Association, 1400 Eye Street, NW, Suite 550, Washington, D.C. 20005

U.S. World Aerobatic Teams

The World's Aerobatic Championships, officially begun in 1960, are scheduled every two years with the host country changing with each contest. Except for the 1976 contest held in the Soviet Union, judging has been reasonably fair—well, sort of fair. Following blatant bias by the Soviet officials in 1976, the Tarasov-Bauer System for computer analysis of the scoring was adopted and the scoring markedly improved.

Beginning in 1964, the participants are listed here in the order each finished in the preceding U.S. National Aerobatic Championships (unlimited class). The highest U.S. place in the world contest is given in parenthesis.

1960 Czechoslovakia

Frank Price (24th)

1962 Hungary

U.S. Team Score: 4th
Duane Cole, Lindsey Parsons (5th), Rodney Jocelyn

1964 Spain

U.S. Team Score: 8th
Frank Price (35), Harold Krier, Robert Nance

1966 USSR

U.S. Team Score: 6th
Harold Krier, Charlie Hillard, Bob Herendeen (26), Art Scholl

1968 East Germany

U.S. Team Score: 3rd (Contest shortened by weather)
Charlie Hillard, Harold Krier, Art Scholl, Bob Herendeen (3rd), Marion Cole, Mary Gaffaney (5th in womens' division)

1970 Great Britain

U.S. Team Score: 1st
Bob Herendeen (2nd), Art Scholl, Charlie Hillard, Bob Schnuerle, Gene Soucy, Mary Gaffaney (3rd in womens' division)

1972 France

U.S. Team Score: 1st
Gene Soucy, Charlie Hillard (1st), Art Scholl, Tom Poberezny, Bill Thomas, Mary Gaffaney (1st in womens' division), Carolyn Salisbury

1974 No contest held

Tom Poberezny, Bill Thomas, Art Scholl, Clint McHenry, Gene Soucy, Henry Haigh

Soviet aerobatic team flew the YAK-18 in the mid-1960s, later switched to the YAK-50, a slightly scaled-down version of the Model 18. (photo courtesy V. Polikashin)

The American aerobatic team in the Soviet Union, 1966. Left to right, Team Captain Bob Hoover, Charlie Hillard, Art Scholl, Harold Krier, and Bob Herendeen. (photo courtesy V. Polikashin)

1976 USSR

U.S. Team Score: 4th
   Leo Loudenslager, Henry Haigh (13th), Clint McHenry, Bill Thomas, Bob Davis, Betty Everest (6th in womens' division)

1978 Czechoslovakia

U.S. Team Score: 2nd
   Leo Loudenslager, Kermit Weeks (2nd), Henry Haigh, Randall Melton, Bob Carmichael

1980 United States

U.S. Team Score: 1st
   Henry Haigh, Kermit Weeks, Leo Loudenslager (1st), Randall Melton, Tom Collier, Betty Stewart (1st in womens' division), Patti Johnson, Paula Moore

1982 Austria

U.S. Team Score: 2nd
   Leo Loudenslager, Henry Haigh (2nd), Kermit Weeks, Jim Roberts, Bill Witt, Betty Stewart (1st in womens' division), Brigitte de St. Phalle, Linda Meyers, Patti Johnson Nelson

1984 Hungary

U.S. Team Score: 1st
   Kermit Weeks (2nd), Henry Haigh, Harold Chappell, Alan Bush, Gene Beggs, Bob Davis, Julie Pfile, Linda Meyers, Debbie Rihn (3rd in womens' division), Brigitte de St. Phalle

1986 Great Britain

U.S. Team Score: 2nd
   Kermit Weeks (2nd), Henry Haigh, Harold Chappell, Clint McHenry, Gene Beggs, Julie Pfile (2nd in womens' division), Linda Meyers, Debbie Rihn, Ellen Dean, Debbie Wagstaff

Soviet Women's aerobatic team, 1966. Governments of Eastern Bloc nations finance their teams. Free World teams pay their own expenses, aided by contributions from industry and individuals. (photo courtesy V. Polikashin)

United States Aerobatic Champions, Unlimited Class

Year	Men's Champion	Women's Champion
1960	Harold Krier	Joyce Case
1961	Harold Krier	Joyce Case
1962	Duane Cole	
1963	Frank Price	
1964*	Duane Cole	Mary Aikens
1965	Harold Krier	Joyce Case
1966	Bob Herendeen	Margaret Ritchie
1967	Charlie Hillard	Mary Gaffaney
1968	Harold Krier	Mary Gaffaney
1969	Bob Herendeen	Mary Gaffaney
1970	Gene Soucy	Mary Gaffaney
1971	Gene Soucy	Mary Gaffaney
1972	Gene Soucy	Mary Gaffaney
1973	Tom Poberezny	Mary Gaffaney
1974	Art Scholl	Mary Gaffaney
1975	Leo Loudenslager	Betty Stewart
1976	Leo Loudenslager	Betty Everest
1977	Leo Loudenslager	
1978	Leo Loudenslager	
1979	Henry Haigh	Betty Stewart
1980	Leo Loudenslager	Betty Stewart
1981	Leo Loudenslager	
1982	Leo Loudenslager	Patti Johnson Nelson
1983	Kermit Weeks	
1984	Kermit Weeks	Julie Pfile
1985	Kermit Weeks	Julie Pfile
1986	Clint McHenry	Julie Pfile
1987	Clint McHenry	Julie Pfile

*Official recognition by the National Aeronautic Association began in 1964.

IX

American Aces

Prior to the U.S. entry into WWI, a number of Americans fought with Britain's Royal Flying Corps, Royal Navy, the French Flying Corps, and in a French equipped and commanded squadron, the *Lafayette Escadrille*, composed entirely of American volunteers. Most were later discharged to join U.S. air units after America entered the war. A few chose to remain with their British and French comrades in arms. Therefore, it seems useful to identify the service with which the leading American aces achieved all or most of their air victories:

- LE: *Lafayette Escadrille*
- RN: Royal Navy
- RFC: Royal Flying Corps (became the Royal Air Force in 1918)
- FAS: French Aviation Service (*Service d'Aeronautique*) or French Flying Corps
- USAS: U.S. Air Service (Actually, the Air Service was not officially so designated until 1920, but it was called little else in 1917-1918)

Top Scoring American Aces of World War I (10 or More Victories)

Rickenbacker, Capt. Edward V. (USAS)	26
Lambert, Capt. William C. (RFC)	22[1]
Luke, 2nd Lt. Frank, Jr. (USAS)	21[2]
Gillette, Capt. Frederick W. (RFC)	20

---

1. For years, Capt. S.C. Rosevear (RFC), 23 victories, was listed as the second ranking U.S. ace of WWI. There is recent proof that Rosevear was a Canadian.

2. Luke's record is given as 18, 19, or 21, depending upon where one looks in official records. His total score on his last flight has long been a source of controversy among air historians. Luke was the only airman in U.S. military history to be awarded the Medal of Honor for a deed done while under military arrest.

Malone, Capt. John (RN)	20
Wilkenson, Maj. Alan M. (RFC)	19
Hale, Capt. Frank L. (RFC)	18
Iaccaci, Capt. Paul T. (RFC)	18
Lufbery, Maj. Raoul G. (FAS/LE)	17
Kullberg, Lt. Harold A. (RFC)	16
Rose, Capt. Oren J. (RFC)	16
Warman, Lt. C.T. (RFC)	15
Libby, Capt. Frederick (RFC)	14
Vaughn, 1st Lt. George A. (USAS)	13
Baylies, Lt. Frank L. (FAS/LE)	12
Bennett, 1st Lt. Louis B. (RFC)	12
Kindley, Capt. Field E. (USAS)	12
Springs, Capt. Elliot W. (USAS)	12
Iaccaci, Lt. Thayer A. (RFC)	11
Landis, Capt. Reed G. (USAS)	10
Putnam, 1st Lt. David E. (LE/USAS)	10
Swaab, Capt. Jacques M. (USAS)	10
Ingalls, Lt. David S. (U.S. Navy)	5[3]

Top Scoring Army Air Forces Aces of World War II (15 or More Victories)

Bong, Maj. Richard T.	40
McGuire, Maj. Thomas B.	38
Gabreski, Col. Francis N.	31[4]
Johnson, Lt. Col. Robert S.	28
MacDonald, Col. Charles H.	27
Preddy, Maj. George E.	25.83
Meyer, Col. John C.	24[4]
Wetmore, Capt. Ray S.	22.59
Schilling, Col. David C.	22.5
Johnson, Lt. Col. Gerald R.	22
Kearby, Col. Neel E.	22

---

3. Ingalls was the only Navy ace in WWI. In U.S. Navy uniform, he flew with RAF Squadron 213 to achieve ace status. U.S. Navy pilots had little chance at air combat in WWI. Ingalls was later an assistant secretary of the Navy and director of Pan American Airways.

4. Additional victories in the Korean War.

Mahurin, Lt. Col. Walker M.	22[4]
Robbins, Col. Jay T.	22
Christensen, Capt. Fred J.	21.5
Voll, Maj. John J.	21
Lynch, Lt. Col. Thomas J.	20
Westbrook, Lt. Col. Robert B.	20
Gentile, Capt. Donald S.	19.84
Beeson, Maj. Duane W.	19.33
Duncan, Col. Glenn E.	19
Carson, Maj. Leonard K.	18.5
Eagleston, Lt. Col. Glenn T.	18.5[4]
Older, Lt. Col. Charles H. (AVG/USAAF)	18.25
Beckham, Col. Walter C.	18
Green, Col. Herschel H.	18
Zemke, Col. Hubert	17.75
England, Lt. Col. John B.	17.5
Reed, Maj. William N. (AVG/USAAF)	17.5
Hill, Maj. David L. (AVG/USAAF)	17.25
Thornell, Maj. John F., Jr.	17.25
Brown, Maj. Henry W.	17.2
Foy, Maj. Robert W.	17
Hampshire, Capt. John (AVG/USAAF)	17
Johnson, Col. Gerald W.	17
Varnell, Capt. James S., Jr.	17
Hofer, 1st Lt. Ralph K.	16.5
Godfrey, Capt. John T.	16.33
Anderson, Lt. Col. Clarence E., Jr.	16.25
Dunham, Col. William D.	16
Harris, Lt. Col. Bill	16
Welch, Maj. George S.	16
Beerbower, Capt. Donald M.	15.5
Peterson, Maj. Richard A.	15.5
Whisner, Maj. William T., Jr.	15.5[4]
Blakeslee, Col. Donald J.M. (Eagle Sqdn/USAAF)	15
Bradley, Col. Jack T.	15
Brown, Capt. Samuel J.	15
Cragg, Maj. Edward	15
Goodson, Lt. Col. James A.	15

Herbst, Col. John C. 15
Homer, Maj. Cyril F. 15

The AVG was the American Volunteer Group, commonly called the "Flying Tigers," American civilians flying for China. Most returned to U.S. military units when the Tigers were disbanded, July 4, 1942.

The Eagle Squadron was a British unit made up of American volunteers, formed prior to U.S. entry into WWII.

Top Scoring U.S. Navy and Marine Aces of World War II (15 or More Victories)

McCampbell, Capt. David (USN)	34
Boyington, Maj. Gregory (USMC)	28[5]
Foss, Capt. Joseph J. (USMC)	26
Hanson, Lt. Robert M. (USMC)	25
Harris, Lt. Cecil E. (USN)	24
Valencia, Lt. Cmdr. Eugene (USN)	23
Walsh, Capt. Kenneth A. (USMC)	21
Aldrich, Capt. Donald N. (USMC)	20
Fleming, Lt. Patrick D. (USN)	19
Smith, Col. John L. (USMC)	19
Vraciu, Lt. Alexander (USN)	19
Thomas, Capt. Wilbur J. (USMC)	18.5
Nooy, Lt. Cornelius N. (USN)	18
Kepford, Lt. Ira C. (USN)	17
Stimpson, Lt. Charles R. (USN)	17
Baker, Lt. Douglas (USN)	16.5
Swett, Capt. James E. (USMC)	16
Byrnes, Lt. Matthew S., Jr. (USN)	15
Spears, Capt. Harold L. (USMC)	15

United States Air Force Aces of the Korean War

McConnell, Capt. Joseph, Jr.	16[6]
Jabara, Lt. Col. James	15[6]
Fernandez, Capt. Manuel J., Jr.	14.5
Davis, Maj. George A., Jr.	14[6]
Baker, Col. Royal N.	13[6]
Blesse, Maj. Frederick C.	10
Fischer, Capt. Harold E.	10
Garrison, Lt. Col. Vermont	10[6]
Johnson, Col. James K.	10[6]

---

5. Includes 6 victories with the Flying Tigers (AVG).

Moore, Capt. Lonnie R.	10
Parr, Capt. Ralph S., Jr.	10
Foster, Capt. Cecil G.	9
Low, 1st Lt. James F.	9
Hagerstrom, Maj. James P.	8.5[6]
Risner, Maj. Robinson	8
Ruddell, Lt. Col. George I.	8[6]
Buttlemann, 1st Lt. Henry	7
Jolley, Capt. Clifford D.	7
Lilley, Capt. Leonard W.	7
Adams, Maj. Donald E.	6.5[6]
Gabreski, Col. Francis S.	6.5[6]
Jones, Lt. Col. George L.	6.5
Marshall, Maj. Winton W.	6.5
Kasler, 1st Lt. James H.	6
Love, Capt. Robert J.	6
Whisner, Maj. William T., Jr.	5.5[6]
Baldwin, Col. Robert P.	5
Becker, Capt. Richard S.	5
Bettinger, Maj. Stephen L.	5
Creighton, Maj. Richard D.	5[6]
Curtin, Capt. Clyde A.	5
Gibson, Capt. Ralph D.	5
Kincheloe, Capt. Ivan C., Jr.	5
Latshaw, Capt. Robert T., Jr.	5
Moore, Capt. Robert H.	5
Overton, Capt. Dolphin D., III	5
Thyng, Col. Harrison R.	5[6]
Westcott, Maj. William H.	5

USAF and U.S. Navy Aces of the Vietnam War

DeBellevue, Capt. Charles D. (USAF)	6
Cunningham, Lt. Randy (USN)	5
Driscoll, Lt. William (USN)	5
Feinstein, Capt. Jeffrey S. (USAF)	5
Ritchie, Capt. Richard S. (USAF)	5

---

6. Indicates victories over Korea in addition to victories scored in WWII, e.g., Col. Gabreski's 6.5 victories over Korea, added to his 31 victories in WWII, give him a total score of 37.5 confirmed air-to-air combat victories.

X

Medal of Honor Recipients

United States Air Force

World War I	Rank at Time	Date of Action	Place of Action
Bleckley, Erwin R.	2nd Lt.	10/6/1918	Binarville, France
Goettler, Harold E.	2nd Lt.	10/6/1918	Binarville, France
Luke, Frank, Jr.	2nd Lt.	9/29/1918	Murvaux, France
Rickenbacker, Edward V.	Capt.	9/25/1918	Billy, France
World War II			
Baker, Addison E.	Lt. Col.	8/1/1943	Ploesti, Romania
Bong, Richard I.	Maj.	10/10-11/15/1944	Southwest Pacific
Carswell, Horace S., Jr.	Maj.	10/26/1944	South China Sea
Castle, Frederick W.	Brig. Gen.	12/24/1944	Liege, Belgium
Cheli, Ralph	Maj.	8/18/1943	Wewak, New Guinea
Craw, Demas T.	Col.	11/8/1942	Port Lyautey, Morocco
Doolittle, James H.	Lt. Col.	5/18/1942	Tokyo, Japan
Erwin, Henry E.	SSgt.	5/12/1945	Koriyama, Japan
Femoyer, Robert E.	2nd Lt.	11/2/1944	Merseburg, Germany
Gott, Donald J.	1st Lt.	11/9/1944	Saarbrucken, Germany
Hamilton, Pierpont M.	Maj.	11/8/1942	Port Lyautey, Morocco
Howard, James H.	Maj.	1/11/1944	Oschersleben, Germany

	Rank at Time	Date of Action	Place of Action
Hughes, Lloyd H.	2nd Lt.	8/1/1943	Ploesti, Romania
Jerstad, John L.	Maj.	8/1/1943	Ploesti, Romania
Johnson, Leon W.	Col.	8/1/1943	Ploesti, Romania
Kane, John R.	Col.	8/1/1943	Ploesti, Romania
Kearby, Neel E.	Col.	10/11/1943	Wewak, New Guinea
Kingsley, David R.	2nd Lt.	6/23/1944	Ploesti, Romania

World War II

	Rank at Time	Date of Action	Place of Action
Knight, Raymond L.	1st Lt.	5/25/1945	Po Valley, Italy
Lawley, William R., Jr.	1st Lt.	2/20/1944	Leipzig, Germany
Lindsey, Darrell R.	Capt.	8/9/1944	Pontoise, France
Mathies, Archibald	SSgt.	2/20/1944	Leipzig, Germany
Mathis, Jack W.	1st Lt.	3/18/1943	Vegesack, Germany
McGuire, Thomas B., Jr.	Maj.	12/25-26/1944	Luzon, P.I.
Metzger, William E., Jr.	2nd Lt.	11/9/1944	Saarbrucken, Germany
Michael, Edward S.	1st Lt.	5/11/1944	Brunswick, Germany
Morgan, John C.	F/O	7/28/1943	Kiel, Germany
Pease, Harl, Jr.	Capt.	8/7/1942	Rabaul, New Britain
Pucket, Donald D.	1st Lt.	7/9/1944	Ploesti, Romania
Sarnoski, Joseph R.	2nd Lt.	6/16/1943	Buka, Solomon Islands
Shomo, William A.	Capt.	1/11/1945	Luzon, P.I.
Smith, Maynard H.	SSgt.	5/1/1943	St. Nazaire, France
Truemper, Walter E.	2nd Lt.	2/20/1944	Leipzig, Germany
Vance, Leon R., Jr.	Lt. Col.	6/5/1944	Wimereaux, France
Vosler, Forrest L.	TSgt.	12/20/1943	Bremen, Germany
Walker, Kenneth N.	Brig. Gen.	1/5/1943	Rabaul, New Britain
Wilkins, Raymond H.	Maj.	11/2/1943	Rabaul, New Britain
Zeamer, Jay, Jr.	Capt.	6/16/1943	Buka, Solomon Islands

Korea

Davis, George A., Jr.	Lt. Col.	2/10/1952	Sinuiju, North Korea
Loring, Charles J., Jr.	Maj.	11/22/1952	Sniper Ridge, N. Korea
Sebille, Louis J.	Maj.	8/5/1952	Hamch'ang, South Korea
Walmsley, John S., Jr.	Capt.	9/14/1951	Yangdok, North Korea

Vietnam

Bennett, Steven L.	Capt.	6/29/1972	Quang Tri, S. Vietnam
Dethlefsen, Merlyn H.	Maj.	3/10/1967	Thai Nguyen, N. Vietnam

MEDAL OF HONOR RECIPIENTS

Fisher, Bernard F.	Maj.	3/10/1966	A Shau Valley, S. Vietnam
Fleming, James P.	1st Lt.	11/26/1968	Duc Co, S. Vietnam

Vietnam	**Rank at Time**	**Date of Action**	**Place of Action**
Jackson, Joe M.	Lt. Col.	5/12/1968	Kham Duc, S. Vietnam
Jones, William A. III	Lt. Col.	9/1/1968	Dong Hoi, N. Vietnam
Levitow, John L.	A1C	2/24/1969	Long Binh, S. Vietnam
Thorsness, Leo K.	Lt. Col.	4/19/1967	North Vietnam
Wilbanks, Hilliard A.	Capt.	2/24/1967	Dalat, S. Vietnam
Young, Gerald O.	Capt.	11/9/1967	Da Nang, S. Vietnam

United States Navy and United States Marine Corps

World War I and Prior

Hamman, Charles H.	Ens. (USN)	8/21/1918	Pola, Austria
McDonnell, Edward O.	Ens. (USN)	4/21-22/1914	Vera Cruz, Mexico
McGunigal, Patrick	Fitter 1st Class (USN)	9/17/1917	Atlantic
Moffett, William A.	Cmdr. (USN)	4/21-22/1914	Vera Cruz, Mexico
Ormsbee, Francis E., Jr.	CMM (USN)	9/25/1918	Pensacola Bay
Robinson, Robert G.	GSgt. (USMC)	10/8-14/1918	Europe
Talbot, Ralph	2nd Lt. (USMC)	10/8-14/1918	Europe

1920 through 1938 Actions

Bennett, Floyd	CWO (USN)	5/29/1926	North Pole
Byrd, Richard E.	Lt. Cmdr. (USN)	5/29/1926	North Pole
Corry, William M.	Lt. Cmdr. (USN)	10/2/1920	Pensacola
Hutchins, Carlton, B.	Lt. (USN)	2/2/1938	Pensacola
Schilt, Christian F.	1st Lt. (USMC)	1/6-8/1928	Nicaragua

World War II

Bauer, Harold W.	Lt. Col. (USMC)	9/28-10/3/1942	South Pacific
Boyington, Gregory	Maj. (USMC)	9/12/1943-1/3/1944	Solomon Islands
DeBlanc, Jefferson J.	Capt. (USMC)	1/31/1943	Kolombangara Is., Pacific
Elrod, Henry T.	Capt. (USMC)	12/8-23/1941	Wake Island
Fleming, Richard E.	Capt. (USMC)	6/4-6/1942	Battle of Midway
Foss, Joseph J.	Capt. (USMC)	10/9-11/19/1942	Guadalcanal

Galer, Robert E.	Maj. (USMC)	Aug-Sept/1942	South Pacific
Gordon, Nathan G.	Lt. (USN)	2/15/1944	Kavieng Harbor
Hall, William E.	Lt. (jg) (USN)	5/7-8/1942	Battle of the Coral Sea
Hanson, Robert M.	1st Lt. (USMC)	11/1/1943, 6/24/1944	South Pacific
McCampbell, David	Cmdr. (USN)	June, October 1944	Philippine Sea and Leyte Gulf
O'Hare, Edward H.	Lt. (USN)	2/20/1942	Rabaul
Powers, John J.	Lt. (USN)	5/4-8/1942	Battle of the Coral Sea
Smith, John L.	Maj. (USMC)	8/21-9/15/1942	Guadalcanal
Swett, James E.	1st Lt. (USMC)	4/7/1943	Solomon Islands
Van Voorhis, Bruce A.	Lt. Cmdr. (USN)	7/6/1943	Solomon Islands
Walsh, Kenneth A.	1st Lt. (USMC)	8/15 & 8/30/1943	Vella LaVella
Antrim, Richard N.	Lt. (USN)	April, 1942	POW
Edson, Merritt A.	Col. (USMC)	9/13-14/1942	Guadalcanal
Finn, John W.	Chief (USN)	12/7/41	Pearl Harbor
Gary, Donald A.	Lt. (jg) (USN)	3/19/1945	aboard USS *Franklin*
O'Callahan, Joseph T.	Lt. Cmdr. (USN)	3/19/1945	aboard USS *Franklin*
Ricketts, Milton E.	Lt. (USN)	5/8/1942	aboard USS *Yorktown*